FINDING WORK
WORK
A HANDBOOK

FINDING WORK

WORK

A HANDBOOK

James D. Bramlett

PYRANEE
BOOKS

Zondervan Publishing House
Grand Rapids, Michigan

FINDING WORK: A HANDBOOK

Copyright © 1986 by James D. Bramlett

This is a Pyranee Book
Published by the Zondervan Publishing House
1415 Lake Drive, S.E., Grand Rapids, Michigan 49506

Library of Congress Cataloging in Publication Data

Bramlett, James D.
  Finding work: a handbook.

    "Pyranee Books."
    Includes bibliographies.
    1. Job hunting—United States. 2. Vocational guidance—United
States. 3. Work (Theology) 4. Christian life—1960– . I. Title.
HF5382.75.U6B73   1986   650.1'4   86-15903
ISBN 0-310-39031-1

Unless otherwise indicated, the Scripture text used is the New American Standard Bible, copyright © 1960, 1962, 1963, 1968, 1971, 1972, 1973, 1975 by the Lockman Foundation, La Habra, California.

Scripture quotations marked KJV are taken from the King James Version of the Bible. Quotations marked RSV are from the Revised Standard Version.

Edited by David Hazard

Printed in the United States of America

87 88 89 90 91 92 / AH / 10 9 8 7 6 5 4 3

Contents _____

APPENDIXES

Acknowledgments

Appreciation is expressed to the National Association of Evangelicals for allowing us to use their directory of Christian organizations. May the NAE be blessed for this service.

Special appreciation is extended to my dear wife Mary Ann for her constant encouragement. "Many daughters have done nobly, but you excel them all" (Prov. 31:29).

*Dedicated to
my three sons:
Jim, Steve, and Scott.*

Introduction

You need this book if you are a Christian and are going to be looking for any kind of job.

You especially need this book if you are a Christian and are considering a Christian vocation or if you are planning on going to college.

This book is unique for Christians, covering the subject of vocational guidance and job hunting from A to Z—from discerning God's calling and will for your life, to preparing resumes and interviewing, to knowing how to act on the job once you get it.

I saw the need for such a volume several years ago. As a personnel director and vice president of human resources in one of the nation's largest Christian organizations, I screened tens of thousands of applicants for thousands of jobs over a period of years. I saw applicants do it the wrong way; I saw them do it the right way. Many times I thought how nice it would be if everyone hoping to enter a Christian vocation could have a handbook to guide them.

Well, this is it. You will find hundreds of suggestions. Any one of them may be the difference in getting the position you desire. But more importantly, I have included some valuable spiritual guidance that I have learned over the years, some from other people and some the hard way via my own experience. You will discover how the Lord fits into your vocational planning and job-hunting process.

There are many stages in the vocational decision-making process, and you may be at any one of them. Maybe, you are right out of school and have never held a job before. Perhaps, you are an old hand but are starting to feel a restless nudge to do something else with your life. No matter where you are, there is something here for you.

I have included many real-life situations, using the experiences of real people to illustrate some of the principles. Appendix I is a collection of some especially interesting real-life employment situations. In most cases throughout the book, fictitious names have been used.

While the book was being written, I had the opportunity to share my vision for it with some longtime friends, a pastor and his wife. Wilma immediately saw the potential and exclaimed, "This is really needed. I've known so many people, especially in the Christian college I attended, who needed something like this. Because of a lack of guidance or family pressures, many of them were planning to enter ministry work for which they weren't called or talented. This could really be a help to so many people."

That is my prayer.

James Bramlett

PART I

Finding God's Will

Chapter 1 —————————————
HOW TO DETERMINE
A CALLING

Most of us have heard the term "calling." Perhaps you've heard it used in referring to your pastor's being called to your church. Or perhaps you may have heard about dear old brother so-and-so who felt a "call" to preach and headed off to Bible college or seminary on his way to the pulpit.

Maybe you have asked yourself, "Will I ever hear 'the call'?" And maybe, "What will it sound like if I hear it? Will I hear a voice? See handwriting on the wall?" You may even be a little scared: You may see yourself some day at a good, fulfilling job when suddenly you hear a call to go to Africa and live a life of total deprivation.

Usually when you think of receiving a call, your mental image is preaching from the pulpit of a nice, neat church or going to the bush country of Africa. After all, is there really anything in between?

That's what happened to me. I felt a call when I was a teenager. I envisioned myself either in a pulpit or in Africa. Somehow by God's grace, I pursued neither as God's will for me. Sometimes I had pangs of guilt when I thought about not being a preacher or a missionary. These feelings were caused by misunderstanding the incredibly wide scope and variety of God's many kinds of callings. For years, the call was clear but not the *calling,* a concept to be pursued in a moment.

My guilt feelings were caused also by the Holy Spirit's

promptings that He wanted a deeper commitment and a closer walk with me at that time, although I didn't interpret it that way. Surely I had many areas of needed improvement, but either because of my hard-headedness or improper teaching, I did not perceive how to have a closer walk. I have since learned to trust God's sovereignty in these matters; He has a timing and a progression for each of us.

God was molding me, just as He is molding you. With His power, He has absolutely no problem communicating with us whenever He wants. Saul's dramatic encounter on the road to Damascus is a prime example. God had a *priority* message for Saul that came with such speed and force, Saul had to pick himself up from the ground and say, "Who are you, Lord?" Of course, God doesn't speak to us exactly the same way He spoke to Saul, later Paul. The point is, God can penetrate our thick skulls any time He chooses. More often than not, His messages are softer and gentler. Later, I will discuss some of the ways He gets His messages to us.

The vital thing to know is this: *Every believer has a calling of some kind.* God has a special and unique plan for each of you. Your own calling, whatever it is, is every bit as important as any other. It may include employment in a Christian or secular organization; a Christian or secular vocation, or both; spare-time activities or your role as full-time homemaker—really any area worthy of endeavor.

On the one hand, there are many who are called to full-time Christian work. On the other hand, I know people who, in God's perfect will and calling for their lives, are in secular employment and whose church responsibilities are an avocation. You probably know many of them too. Nevertheless, God has called everyone to be salt and light in the world, and if all believers were encapsulated in Christian organizations, what would happen? It's scary to think what government or business would be like if there were no Christians there.

So, if you are asking yourself, "Do I have a calling?" the answer is yes! Instead of comparing yourselves with others or trying to follow their paths, you have to discover where God wants *you* to be.

Though God's callings are varied, I would never minimize a call to full-time Christian work. It is true that a Christian vocation is a place of special service, where no one should be just for the income but for God's plan and also for the ministry in which he serves. On occasion, I have known people who have worked for Christian organizations for the wrong reasons, such as prestige or power, with awful results. John was one of those men.

John supposedly had superior skills in his vocation and was hired in spite of problems with his references and one manager's discernment that he was not right for the organization. John was later promoted and given wide-ranging responsibilities and authority.

It soon became apparent that John's motives were selfish, not to serve God, and he exhibited signs of neurotic behavior. Now the organization had a problem. Havoc broke out in the departments: Those oppressed under John's management were resigning en masse; those who remained were crying for help. Marriages were straining, and two cases of immorality emerged. The entire organization was being hurt operationally by the strife.

Not long thereafter, John and the manager who hired him were discharged. Although their departure brought a rapid return to tranquility, employee stability, and increased operational effectiveness, it was too late to stop the damage to many lives or prevent wounds that left scars for many years.

This is an extreme example, a vivid example, of how things do not go right when you miss God's calling and enter into a Christian vocation without spiritual commitment.

On the other hand and more typically, there is the case of Robert.

Robert was called by the Lord to fill a professional position in a Christian organization. His inner sense of calling prompted him to apply. During the screening, it became obvious to everyone that Robert was God's man for the job. Robert too felt he was led to leave his business and enter full-time Christian service in this particular organization, even though his previous annual income was nearly $100,000, and this organization could not come close to that salary.

Nonetheless, Robert and his family calculated their needs to determine the very least he could make and still survive. He had a postgraduate degree and several years of top professional experience, but to Robert, that was not important. He prayerfully concluded that he and his family could sacrifice and get by on $15,000 a year at the very least. Even so, he felt a little selfish by establishing even that low figure, so he did not mention it during follow-up interviews. He was determined that money would not stand in the way of God's calling for him.

During the final meeting, in which a job offer was made, Robert was still praying that his figure of $15,000 was not too much. Of course, the company officials did not know about that figure and the depth of his commitment. They offered him an annual salary of $30,000—high for that company, but low compared with what Robert's skill and experience would demand elsewhere.

Surprised, Robert wept tears of joy at God's goodness. He perceived it as a great blessing, even though it was only about 30 percent of what he was making before. He was sure God had seen his heart and honored his commitment.

Furthermore, both Robert and the ministry have been rewarded. His efforts have resulted in much unity, efficiency, and peace. He was later promoted and his salary raised. Robert was called, and he responded in meekness and humility.

Someone has said that the Lord really desires a radical

commitment. The world is full of radicals—many of whom are radically committed to destroying God's kingdom and His people. In response, God's people need to have radical faith and love, as well as a radical commitment to serve Him. And that raises a very important question: How can you really tell whether you have a calling into a full-time Christian vocation? Through my own past struggles with this question, the following simple truths emerged:

God will begin to reveal it deep in your spirit.

It will become a longing and a desire, put there by God Himself.

It will be somewhat like the pull of a magnet: You can resist it but you really do not want to.

It will be like an itch, needing relief via fulfillment.

It will not be coercive: The Holy Spirit is gentle; your will must still come into play.

The end result of the direction of these feelings will be to glorify the Father and the Son rather than yourself.

During one of my early struggles to determine God's will for my life, I decided to seek the counsel of my pastor, a learned and impressive servant of God, several years my senior. A few days later, seated in his office, I was sure I was going to hear God speak through this wise man. After a minimum of small talk, I asked, "Dr. Martin, how can a person know if he has a calling from God?"

I fully expected a long and scholarly dissertation from this educated gentleman. He might even pull down one or two of the thick books that lined his shelves and go over some theological points with me; he replied, however,

"You know you have a calling when it is something you just have to do or else you will be miserable."

That's it! That's really all the advice I received, but I learned something else that has been confirmed many times since: *Spiritual truth is typically succinct and to the point.*

God does not need to waste words and apparently is not interested in impressing us with His vocabulary. He gave us only one Book; he could have given us a library (libraries have been filled with man trying to improve on what He said). Jesus too, you remember, was very much to the point.

Truth is simple; people complicate things. I knew I had my answer. Maybe you do too.

Chapter 2 _____

HOW TO FIND
GOD'S WILL

Some people seek and labor for years to find God's will, but they don't have to. It's really easy. The secret is in acknowledging that God *is* God, recognizing His lordship in your life while, at the same time, not trusting in your own understanding. Does that sound familiar? It's the wisdom of Solomon.

> Trust in the Lord with all your heart, and do not lean on your own understanding. In all your ways acknowledge Him, and He will make your paths straight (Prov. 3:5–6).

Some people argue that God gave us reason and understanding, so shouldn't we "lean" on it just a little bit? Admittedly, there is an argument for that. According to your faith, be it unto you. Frankly, I recommend you read on.

THAT FIRST CRUCIAL STEP

The very first and crucial step in finding God's will is to *make a decision in your heart that His will is what you really want*. That may sound simple, but it's critical. You have to decide if you really want His will and are willing to trust Him for your future. What better deal could you have than to be in the will of One who is total love, total caring, and total concern for your good? There really is no reasonable alternative.

If you agree, He already sees your heart. Still, it would be good to say a simple prayer because He likes to hear from you, something like this one:

"Lord, as of this moment, I want Your will to be done in my life. Amen."

As soon as you sincerely do this, something astounding happens. Suddenly, you have released the reins of your life to Him, and He has taken them. You can relax, knowing that He has it all under control: You are exactly where He wants you *today* and you will be where He wants you *tomorrow*. You no longer have to worry or be anxious if, say, two years ago you "blew it," made a bad decision and feel you are not in the right place today. Your prayer has just made where you are the right place to be. He will redeem the past to optimize the future for you because your God is sovereign in all things.

Do you really want God's will? Did you pray that prayer? Well, you asked for it, and for all practical purposes, you've got it!

WAYS IN WHICH HE SPEAKS TO US

Isn't it nice to have the One who created and rules the whole universe interested in your individual lives so much that He guides your every step and direction? His purposes are always good; thus, all His direction is for your ultimate benefit, and the benefit of others, and for His glory. What a deal!

But many Christians have trouble finding God's guidance on specific matters and day-to-day decisions, such as what to study in school, where to apply for a job, or which job to pursue. It is easy to discern God's will in general terms but sometimes more difficult to translate it into specific applications. Let's discuss several ways in which God speaks to us, generally as well as specifically.

HE SPEAKS THROUGH HIS WORD

When facing a decision, pray and then do some Bible reading. Expect a possible answer. Sometimes, the answer to a specific need comes from a particular passage; other times, from the context in a place where you never thought possible. It happens, and when it does, it is an awesome feeling to realize the sheer power of the Word and how God uses it.

One day at work, I was facing a tough decision. I really was struggling, still carrying the burden at quitting time, as I walked to my car to drive home.

The incredible happened the moment I turned on the ignition. I had left the radio switch on, and the tuner was set at a secular station. At that precise second, words from the Bible came blaring through my speakers—the Word of God from a secular station and through a secular song. And it directly addressed my situation, giving me a very precise answer to a difficult matter. I have rarely been so awed at God's concern for me and at His power. He is truly the God of the incredible. Instances such as this have clearly shown me that God can be with each of us in everyday situations. He doesn't reveal Himself only when we are in our prayer closets and when we are reading the Bible. But I do not recommend that you wait to hear God's voice come spontaneously from your radio. I suspect that normally He prefers you to open and use the Bible. It is important to know that God uses His Word to give us specific guidance.

No matter how God communicates a message of guidance to us, He *will not* violate His Word, even though He may stir our spirits in other ways.

HE SPEAKS IN YOUR SPIRIT

It is impossible to describe methodically how a transcendent God communicates to our inner person, but He does.

Sometimes, you just have a "knowing." It may be a "still, small voice" or a booming voice within you. Some call it an "inner witness."

This inner steering mechanism that you have is one of the least understood and appreciated of God's methods but probably the most important. It is important because it is basic to the New Covenant, where God has chosen to make His own dwelling place within us, the mystery that Paul talks about as "Christ in you" (Col. 1:27). It may be easily accepted with the mind but too profound and mysterious for the heart. Nonetheless, it is true.

The human tendency is to look to outside sources, but Jesus came to replace external religion and form with internal reality. Under the New Covenant, He communicates with us, " . . . not with ink, but with the Spirit of the living God, not on tablets of stone, but on tablets of human hearts" (2 Cor. 3:3).

He lives within you! The Captain of your soul is at the steering wheel. Is He capable of steering this unwieldy and awkward vessel? You bet He is, more than you could ever imagine.

In my experience, God's message in my spirit is the key to His guidance, but it is usually combined with one or more of some other methods.

HE SPEAKS THROUGH OTHERS

Interaction with the corporate body of Christ is very important to God. That's just the way He likes it, undoubtedly because it involves relationships, which are at the top of His priority list. He often chooses to speak through others to get a message to us.

His guidance may come through the counsel of a pastor, elder, or a Christian friend. In fact, it would be wise to seek counsel and prayer support from these people on important decisions, such as vocational direction. "In the multitude of counselors there is safety'' (Prov. 11:14 KJV). This is certainly a biblical approach.

God may also speak through others in a most unexpected way, and often in the unexpectedness, the timing and relevance of a message will carry its own authentication, causing your spirit to leap. This may come in a meeting of believers as someone delivers a general message, and suddenly you know it is intended for you. Or it may come directly from a person who knows he has a "word" for you, and when he speaks, you sense that you have just heard from the throne of God. Remember too that the Lord once spoke through the jaws of an ass, another reminder that He is not limited. Tune into the divine wavelength and always be expectant.

If you are married, discussion and unity with your spouse are desirable. God will often use a spouse to guide us. Similarly, He may choose to speak through parents, who often have keen insight. Respect for their God-given wisdom and role is important.

I must add a word of caution: Always be careful with seeking advice from others. For some, it's a cop-out for seeking God Himself. Many are always looking for advice about what to do and will leap at the first suggestion. There are times when one may have to act courageously and go contrary to the advice of others to do God's will. This is difficult, but sometimes necessary, to do.

Never use this means alone for guidance. Check it carefully against the others.

HE SPEAKS THROUGH CIRCUMSTANCES

God is the God of circumstances; circumstances are not there by accident. They may include opportunity or removed opportunity, perhaps a new geographical location, increased or limited finances.

Weigh everything carefully. Ask yourself, *Which of*

these circumstances may God have established to direct my steps? Some? All? God has determined those circumstances for a purpose.

For some of you, God may want you to burst out of your circumstances by faith in His power, defying the natural and seemingly impossible to create a new set of circumstances. This may be true in your vocation if you believe you are locked into a situation for which there appears no escape. There is an escape. If you feel oppressed by your circumstances, ask for and expect a miracle. Then by faith, do something bold. The results will glorify Him.

HE SPEAKS THROUGH YOUR DESIRES

Some believe that surely God's will must be undesirable and that unless you are careful, He will probably figure out some way to make you miserable. One day a pastor's wife said to me, "God sure knows how to hurt us!" I was amazed at her lack of understanding of His ways. Such a thought dishonors our Father, who delights in blessing us. We hurt ourselves. Others may hurt us; Satan may try to hurt us. But our Father? Never! His loving-kindness is better than life (Ps. 63:3).

Your heart's desire, once you are oriented toward pleasing God, may be your best indicator of what God's will for your life may be, whether it is in Christian employment per se or in secular employment.

The Lord Himself plants desires within everyone to sense and act upon. Any strong vocational desires, which you have, may be from Him. With only one condition, He will satisfy them.

Delight yourself in the Lord; And he will give you the desires of your heart (Ps. 37:4).

FINAL KEY

There is one more important key to finding God's will for your vocational life. Use it and you will be launched into an exciting and adventurous future; ignore it and you may be shipwrecked on the shoals of fear, disappointment, and missed opportunity.

I was struggling years ago with questions about direction when I discovered the key that sets all else in motion: Regardless of how much guidance you get, no matter how much or how little, *you have to step out in faith with it.* That's just the way it is. You walk by faith, not by sight, and the Bible says that faith pleases God. When you think you've got it and you know the direction, "go for it."

Divine guidance is like the rudder of a boat. When the boat is in motion, the rudder can affect the boat's movements right or left. If the boat is still, the rudder has no effect at all.

It is important to be still as you pray, to seek God's voice within, to read His Word, and wait upon Him. But there is a point when you have to get up and start moving. Jesus told His disciples to wait but He also told them to "go." Waiting is scriptural, but if you are waiting for lightning to strike, an audible voice, or the appearance of an angel, you may be waiting forever. Pray through all the aforementioned steps, and you will probably have enough to go on.

The apostle Paul was a man-on-the-move, who did not always know God's entire plan in advance. Once when he started out in one direction to proclaim the gospel, the Holy Spirit let him go so far before saying, in effect, "Hey, Paul. Stop. Turn. I want you to go that way instead." Paul's rudder was working because Paul was in motion. So, take what you believe to be God's leading and step out with it.

Here is another important point: Once you have sought the Lord's wisdom in the matter, you've received what you believe is the answer and stepped out with it—*do not doubt*.

> But let him ask in faith without any doubting, for the one who doubts is like the surf of the sea driven and tossed by the wind (James 1:6).

Full speed ahead! Doubting thoughts *will* enter your mind but reject them and press on. Remember, however, that as you are moving forward, like the apostle Paul, the Holy Spirit may divert you and alter your course. That does not mean you started in the wrong direction but that you need to get moving. You see through a glass darkly and cannot always see very far ahead. The Word is a lamp unto our feet, not a spotlight shining two hundred yards ahead. God undoubtedly has a purpose in these seemingly circuitous routes.

Someday you will look back and say, "He guided me every step along the way."

PART II
Finding Yourself

Chapter 3
HOW TO FIND YOUR GIFTS AND TALENTS

You are a unique creature. There are things about your specific make-up and life experiences that give you an insight and an ability in certain ways that cannot be duplicated by anyone. Your gifts and talents have come from your heavenly Father, and what's more, He has a special plan for your life. He is going to use you in a way that He cannot use anyone else.

I am using the terms "gifts" and "talents" interchangeably and primarily in a vocational sense, though many gifts and talents may go beyond vocation and are manifested in different areas. Both mean abilities that have been given to you. You *are able* to do certain things better than you can do other things; you *enjoy* doing certain things better than you do other things—a distinction that is important.

There is obviously a correlation between what you are *able* to do and what you *enjoy* doing. But there may be some things that you are able to do well but you do not enjoy. Even though you have multiple talents and gifts, you probably should pursue vocationally only that one (or those very few) where both ability and enjoyment coincide.

The things that you are able to do best usually become apparent early in life. Rarely do these gifts result in excellence of performance without the cultivation of training, practice, and experience. You may be highly gifted as a musician, but many hours of study and practice will be necessary to develop this gift. Until the gift is cultivated, it is only a potential.

When you think of gifts, you usually think first of the artistic gifts, such as music and painting, but gifts really include every form of human endeavor. Giftedness includes *what* you can do, *how* you do it, and *how* you relate it to other people. Even your personality can be one of your gifts.

Have you ever noticed a really good salesperson? The amazing thing about a *good* salesman is that he can sell you something you hadn't planned on buying and make you glad you did. He might even make you think it was your idea and that he's selling it to you as a favor! A gifted salesperson comfortably flows in his interactions with people. Many tend to think of the supersales type as loud, extroverted, and gregarious, and that's often the case. Still, there are highly successful people who are not outgoing. In both is a common personality ingredient that enables them to *inspire trust* and to *persuade*. Both make it happen, that is, they make the sale.

Let's take a look at an unusual and multitalented person in the Bible, the wife described in Proverbs 31. Note that among other things she is a salesperson, even making what she sells. She selects wool and flax and works "with hands in delight." She purchases real estate, plants, and trades. In addition to her obvious talents, she also has some admirable personal characteristics that help make her successful. She gets up while it is still dark; she opens her mouth in wisdom; she does not eat the bread of idleness.

This lady is a superwoman, someone diligently exercising her God-given gifts and talents. She is in the place of God's will, doing what she is supposed to do.

What is the result? Well, she is obviously well adjusted and happy. She is described as having strength and dignity and "she laughs" when contemplating the future.

Strength and dignity do come from being in the right place that God has for you. You sense His favor, which brings inner confidence and strength. You know that demands on you may be difficult but you have this indescribable assurance that He will see you through and that He has equipped you for the job. Plus, you can even "laugh at the future" because life and even the unknown have a dimension of merriment brought about by trusting God and knowing that you are in His will. This is joy, a fruit of the Holy Spirit.

Conversely, if you are not exercising your gifts and not in the right place, there can be a dread about work, an uneasiness and apprehension brought about by the requirement for you to do things for which you are ill equipped. You can lose your joy, and your life can become unhappy even though you may not know why.

SPIRITUAL VERSUS VOCATIONAL GIFTS

Can you really differentiate between spiritual and vocational gifts? Not really, since all gifts come from the Father and are in that sense spiritual. But there are certain gifts that are primarily for ministry and may or may not be vocationally related, such as those described in Romans 12:6–8, which include prophesying, serving, teaching, encouraging, contributing, leading, and showing mercy. Other gifts, mentioned in 1 Corinthians 12:8–10, are called manifestations of the Spirit, usually thought to be supernatural endowments used when believers are assembled. First Corinthians 12:28 adds some more gifts, or "appointments," and Ephesians 4 adds others that are usually considered ministry offices in the church.

Some of these gifts and appointments can obviously involve a full-time vocational pursuit in a church or church-related occupation. Typically, but not exclusively, this might include serving, teaching, administrating, and evangelizing or pastoring.

Is there anything wrong with earning a livelihood from a spiritual gift in a church-related job? Definitely not. The New Testament is clear on this point. (See 1 Cor. 9:3–12.)

Vocational gifts can include much more. God has placed us in a complex society, where there are thousands of types of jobs and needs for varying skills. Someone has estimated that there are about twenty thousand different types of jobs in this country, and I suspect that's conservative. The point is, you can probably *do* a lot of them. But which are best suited for you? Which can you do best? Which will make you the happiest?

FINDING YOUR GIFTS

There are two principal ways of finding your own gifts: Do it yourself through self-analysis, sometimes called self-assessment. And get outside help with vocational testing and counseling.

You can, of course, combine the two, checking one against the other. Since both methods are imperfect, this would be the surest way to achieve accurate results. (A later chapter is devoted fully to professional testing.)

Right now, let's take a look at some self-assessment techniques. Systematic methods are available commercially to help you do this, and I recommend you give them a try. Here are some of the most popular books: *Self-Assessment and Career Development* by John P. Kotter, Victor A. Faux, Charles C. McArthur (Prentice-Hall, Inc., 1978); *What Color Is Your Parachute?* by Richard Nelson Bolles (Ten Speed Press, 1984); *The Truth About You,* written from a Christian perspective, by Arthur F. Miller and Ralph T. Mattson (Fleming H. Revell Company, 1977) and, by the same authors, *Finding a Job You Can Love* (Thomas Nelson Publishers, 1982). A fun method of self-assessment can be found in the *Quick Job Hunting Map*, a booklet by Richard N. Bolles and Victoria B. Zenoff (Ten Speed Press).

Self-assessment basically means taking inventory of yourself to measure what gifts and talents you really have. You are encouraged to survey your entire life as far back as you can remember to recall activities in which you excelled and/or enjoyed. It sounds simple and in a way it is. Yet it can be very time consuming if you are to achieve truly accurate results.

I am going to give you a taste of the self-assessment method. If you do it correctly and conscientiously, it may give you what you want to know or at least prick your interest enough to pursue this further. I believe it will help you, not only in demonstrating the principle of self-assessment, but in actually perceiving a talent that you may have otherwise taken for granted and thus overlooked.

Start with a prayer, since you will really need the Lord's wisdom. You are going to be looking backward at your entire life and you need the Holy Spirit to assist you.

Then get a paper and pencil or pen. You can do this alone, although it may help to get input from people who have known you a long time.

STEPS

1. At the top of your paper, write *List 1—Activities At Which I Have Excelled.*

2. Systematically go back in your memory as far back as you can, to preschool if possible. Try to recall every activity or everything you ever did. It will be easier if you try to do it year-by-year, using school years to help you recall. For example, slowly walk through grammar school, then high school. It will help you to recall different residences, schools, friends, neighbors,

relatives, or anything that can form an association. During these years, try to recall these areas:

hobbies
school subjects of special interest
extracurricular activities
favorite books
favorite games
heroes or heroines
special travels
pastime activities
favorite movies
special awards or recognition
church activities and friends
jobs held, including summer

3. On your paper, write, no matter how seemingly small or insignificant, *anything you ever did well, you ever did better than most other things,* or *you ever did better than most of your other friends.* For each item, include the year or your age as a later reminder.

   Don't rush. This may take days. Ponder it; sleep on it. It's worth the time. Let your thoughts flow freely. If in doubt, write it down and judge it later. Prejudging can inhibit thought.

4. On a second sheet of paper, write *List 2—Activities I Have Enjoyed the Most.*

5. Repeat Step 2.

6. On your second piece of paper, write down anything you ever did, no matter how seemingly small or insignificant, *that you seemed to enjoy more than other things, that gave you the most satisfaction,* and *that you were inclined to want to do again because of the*

enjoyment. Then review Step 3. The same rules apply to this step. Take your time.

7. On a third sheet of paper, write *List 3—Personal Characteristics.* Write the following categories and rate yourself on a scale of 1 to 5 according to the definitions below:

Analytical. Discovering what, how, why.
Numerical. Good at numbers.
Mechanical. Good with hands, tools, equipment.
Technical. Scientifically oriented.
Organizational. Teamwork, decision making, leadership.
Interpersonal. Good with people.
Artistic. Good at one or more of the fine arts.
Competitive. Likes to win, excel.
Working independently. Prefers to work alone.
Outdoors. Prefers to work outdoors.

Rating Scale

    5. Applies to a very large degree— highly applicable.

    4. Applies to an above-average degree.

    3. Applies to an average degree.

    2. Applies to a below-average degree.

    1. Applies to little or no degree.

8. Now take all three lists and lay them out before you. Study them individually and collectively, looking for themes, for commonality, for patterns that are like threads weaving through your life.

    If you have done this exercise carefully, you have painted a picture of yourself. It may be a little rough,

but even the most sophisticated methods often produce only a rough picture. Your efforts can be
amazingly accurate.

*See what items on List 1 also appear on List 2.
Circle them.*

Check the items you have circled against List 3 and
the categories in which you have rated yourself a 3 or
higher. A 4 or a 5 rating is especially significant.

What you now have are activities where you have
demonstrated ability *and* enjoyment that also conform
to a general category or categories you consider to be
descriptive of yourself.

9. All you have to do now is to convert these activities
into an occupational category. After you have completed the last steps, such an occupational category or
categories will probably become obvious.

If you are still having trouble making occupational
associations, go to your library and peruse the two
hundred and fifty occupations listed in the *Occupational Outlook Handbook,* published by the Department of Labor.

10. The final step is eliminating any occupational category
that is not feasible due to your circumstances. For
example, the above exercise may have shown that you
have a special talent in athletics, but you are now sixty
years old. It is unlikely that athletic competition would
be a viable vocational alternative for you at this time,
but you might consider a sports-related job.

Now, determine which final categories cause your
spirit to leap and say, "Yes, this is it!"

Do not be discouraged if you lack refinement in any
of these areas, such as training or experience. Take
one step at a time. All you have been looking for is
latent talent or ability, so all of these need develop-

ment.

Nevertheless, refined or not, the talent is yours. God gave it, and with His help, it will be brought to fruition.

NOW WHAT?

You have made progress toward deciding upon your specific gifts and talents. You may have even completed the task. If you are still not satisfied, rethink the previous ten steps. Maybe, you did it too hastily. I've given you an outline—a blueprint. You have to fill in the blanks.

You should also consider having some testing done as discussed in the next chapter. You can compare the results of this with what you already have accomplished.

In any case, assessment is foundational to all other steps in the vocational planning process and can affect your whole life. Give it the time and attention it deserves.

Chapter 4

HOW TO USE VOCATIONAL TESTING

Does the term "vocational testing" scare you? It scares some people and can especially rattle you when you are being interviewed for a job and the interviewer says, "Oh, by the way, we have a few questionnaires we would like for you to fill out." Then, he puts you in a private room, gives you some instructions, winds up a timer and starts to close the door. You object, and he says, "Oh, we just want to know a little more about you, and this is a good way to do it. Besides, everybody takes these, so don't feel bad."

You then stare at the strange-looking form with what seems like a million short questions on it. You have only 20 minutes to finish.

After it's all over, you decide it wasn't that bad. In fact, it was all pretty interesting. You wonder how you came out. The company may tell you or they may not; they may tell you part of the results but not all, depending on their policy. Some consulting psychologists prefer that their test results not be divulged, except possibly in general terms; others are not restrictive.

The company, by using psychological tests, is really trying to look inside your head. They want to find out some things about you that may not otherwise be apparent. When you stop to think about it, it's a little scary. How often does somebody look inside your head?

Well, relax. It's really not all that bad. There is more of a positive than negative side to this. My intent is to remove the mystery for you by explaining what these tests try to do, how they may succeed or fail, and how you can use them to your advantage.

You can initiate the testing process for your own purposes and use it in vocational planning. Do consider this for yourself. Later, you will find suggestions on how to pursue it.

There are many psychological tests available that relate to vocational planning. Many are so-called standard tests that are marketed by their owners or copyright holders, and used by counselors and psychologists for their private use. Many others are developed by psychologists for use in their practices. Most tests go through a statistical validation process using large numbers of testees to establish a data base, referred to as the statistical "population." From this data, the test designer calculates important information, such as the test's *reliability* and *validity*—meaning how accurate the test is in describing or predicting whatever it is intended for. Some tests have not been subjected to such statistical rigor. If you ever decide to use psychological testing in your vocational planning, always inquire about this, especially if you are going to pay for it. A reputable counselor will respect your inquiry and be glad to share such data. Frankly, you will probably not be able to understand it, but at least you will have the comfort of knowing it is a professional test.

There are four particular categories of tests that may be of interest to you in vocational planning. They may also be the most likely used by a potential employer.

Tests that help you determine your vocational interests.

Tests that determine your ability to reason.

Tests that determine your personality characteristics.

Tests that determine your aptitude for certain kinds of work.

VOCATIONAL INTEREST TESTS

These tests offer a systematic way of getting you to describe the kinds of work you like and the kinds you do not like. A typical test will give you a large number of questions, each with several choices of jobs. Then, you select the one you "like most" and the one you "like least." The test evaluation correlates all the questions and answers, giving a collective picture of what you have said about your likes and dislikes.

The test results can be amazingly accurate. You are systematically forced to make choices, and interests may emerge that you were never fully aware of.

For example, I took one of these tests several years ago, and the test revealed, among other things, that outdoor activities were high on my preference list. At first, I thought the test was inaccurate because I had never desired or had an outdoor job. I really am not an outdoor person and don't camp, hunt, or fish. I read the interpretive material that went with the test and discovered that an item with a high score represents a "need" that tends to find fulfillment, if not vocationally then in some other way. I read further that those scoring high on "outdoor activities" often had their need met by reading "outdoor magazines," or "building a cottage on a lake."

I was amazed. At that time, I *was* building a cottage on a nearby lake! But that's not all. Months earlier, I responded to a strange urge and subscribed to both *Organic Gardening* and another outdoor magazine, though I did not even have a garden, nor was I planning one. When the magazines arrived, I perused them, carefully read the good articles, then laid them aside. Yet, somewhere down inside my cranium was a need for the outdoors that was expressing itself. I believe this is related to a later decision to leave the eight-to-five office scene for a different routine that keeps me from being indoors so consistently.

I would never have thought that that particular test result would have had vocational significance in my life, but it did.

Who knows what similar need lies inside your cranium? Would you like to know? I strongly recommend the vocational interest test to help you determine your interests and preferences and to help you find your way into the marketplace. Since there is a correlation between what you are *able* to do and what you *prefer* to do, as previously discussed, these tests can help you uncover your gifts and talents too.

The test that I took was developed and administered by Birkman and Associates, P.O. Box 27528, Houston, TX 77027. Two other standard tests are the Strong-Campbell Interest Inventory and the Kuder Occupational Interest Survey, both of which should be available to professional counselors and consultants. You can also obtain occupational-interest and other evaluations through the mail by writing IDAK Group, Inc., 7931 N.E. Halsey, Banfield Plaza Building, Portland, Oregon 97213-6755. Their occupational coding system is referred to and used in appendix IV.

TESTS THAT MEASURE REASONING ABILITY

I do not like the term "intelligence" test, sometimes called mental alertness tests or measures of verbal and numerical comprehension. Whatever they are called, these tests attempt to measure your ability to read, understand, and reason.

Typically, the tests are timed and are usually a mix of questions that emphasize verbal abilities (the use of words) and numerical abilities (the use of numbers). Most questions are pretty simple but a little tricky, requiring you to think. There may be more questions than the average person can answer during the time limit, so your score will be based on the number of correct answers.

As with virtually all tests, your score is only significant as compared with the population. Your score, then, will indicate how you did relative to everyone else.

Your raw score, the actual number right, is meaningless. It must be converted to a relative score, usually a percentile. A percentile score is a number from 0–100 that tells you how you did relative to everyone else who has taken the test. If your score is 80, that means you did better than about 80 percent of the others, and about 20 percent did better than you. A 99 means only 1 percent did better than you; a 50 is average.

Some of these test scores can be converted into that sometimes dreaded and ambiguous reference, an I.Q. (Intelligence Quotient) score. But whether you call it an I.Q. or something else, it is the relative score as compared with others that makes the difference.

Many books have been written about whether these types of scores have any meaningful accuracy. I will not attempt to enter that debate here, but I will give you some principles that you can use to assess your own such test results, so you won't get too conceited if you did very well or too discouraged if you did not do well.

If you scored well, it means you are probably a good reader and probably very good at verbal and/or numerical skills, depending on how high your score was.

If you did not score well, it *may not* mean the opposite of the above. It *may* mean any of the following:

You tightened up for some reason on this particular test and you might do well on a retake.

You are mentally very sharp but you are a slow reader, for many possible reasons. You can improve this.

You did poorly on either the verbal or the numerical part, not both, meaning you may be very strong on one and weak on the other. If possible, ask the Test Monitor for a breakdown.

Please remember that these tests measure only a very narrow definition of mental alertness. You may have exceptional reasoning ability but did not score well because the reading is so important to taking the test. Do not let a low score cause you to have low self-esteem. You may be unusually bright and your mental abilities will manifest themselves in other ways.

Nevertheless, it is important to remember that reading, verbal, and numerical skills are usually important in most, if not all, administratively oriented jobs. If you scored low, this may tell you that such work is not for you and that you are being guided in a different direction.

But again, make any such judgment cautiously, not just based on a single test score. I know one gentleman who scored horribly on one of the mental alertness tests and has been performing admirably for several years as a top executive of a large corporation.

Test-taking ability can strongly affect these scores. I have taken so many tests in my life that I can add many points to my score by technique alone. It does not mean that I am smarter than someone who has not had similar experience.

Your inner tempo can have an effect, since these tests are usually timed, and you are under pressure to answer as many questions as possible. Some folks just move with a slow but deliberate speed, getting superior results when given the time. People seem to live in different time dimensions.

We *are* "fearfully and wonderfully made," as the Bible says, and each is unique. Human attempts to classify and categorize so often miss the mark.

PERSONALITY TESTS

This is one of the most controversial forms of psychological and vocational testing. These tests attempt to analyze your personality and then predict whether you would be successful in certain vocations. Many of them have various categories of personality traits, and you are rated in each of these categories. These categories vary markedly from test to test with surprisingly little similarity. They may include such traits as sociability, intuitiveness, perceptiveness, extroversion, introversion, persuasiveness, energy, structure, flexibility, adaptability, and so on. There is also much variance in results. You may look at three different results for the same person and you would think there were three different people!

A psychologist making the same observation explained this aptly. Our personalities are multifaceted, like prisms. One particular test will reflect our natures from one angle, another at a different angle. It is all the same person but viewed in different lights. A wise observation, but there is one other factor: Sometimes personality tests are wrong.

I have personally struggled with this type of test more than any other. I have seen them amazingly right; I have seen them amazingly wrong. I have seen them used and misused.

Statistical data would suggest that some of these tests may be as high as 80 percent accurate, which is outstanding. But remember, this is a "statistical average." You are not an average but a specific. If it is accurate for you, then it is 100 percent accurate as far as you are concerned. If it is not right for you, then it is 0 percent accurate. Accuracy of 80 percent means it will be right for eight in ten of the people tested and wrong for two. Will you be one of the eight or one of the unfortunate two? How will you know?

That's the $64,000 question. As a manager, I have wrestled with it for a long time. But I think I finally have the answer, thanks to one of the sensitive counselors at Birkman and Associates. I took her thoughts on the subject and combined them with some of my own to come up with the Bramlett Theory.

If you are trying to decide whether a particular personality test result really describes you, *here is the key:*

> Pray. Agree with the Lord to approach this honestly. Ask for His help. Study the test results. Do not jump to conclusions, either to agree or disagree. Meditate on it. It may take a few hours, maybe days. Gradually, the truth will emerge. *You will bear witness to what is you and what is not you.* What appears as truth, hold onto; what appears not to be you, reject.

Isn't this the way God's guidance works? Let external devices and circumstances confirm or disavow your inner conviction. Where confirmed, be strengthened in your resolve to be what God wants you to be.

There are many different personality tests. One of the popular ones is the Worthington-Hurst, which requires the testee to complete a battery of sentences. Another popular one is the Myers-Briggs, which can help you determine which of many different types and combinations of types best describe your personality and which can be used for vocational counseling and guidance.

APTITUDE AND SKILLS TESTING

Some tests attempt to show whether you have potential skills or aptitude to do various jobs, such as manual, mechanical, or clerical work. Others measure your actual skills, such as your typing speed, although that is not considered a psychological test.

You may have a strong aptitude or potential in an area you do not realize. If you are in contact with a counselor or vocational guidance office, inquire as to what they can offer you in aptitude testing. It is well worth your while.

WHERE TO GET
VOCATIONAL TESTING

If you are in school, try your guidance office. Some state employment agencies and Job Service Centers also offer vocational testing. You can also look in the Yellow Pages under Vocational Guidance or Psychologists.

RECOMMENDED READING

Test Your Vocational Aptitude by Patricia Asta and Linda Bernbach, Arco Publishing, Inc., NY, 1976.

How to Pass Employment Tests, Arco Editorial Board, Arco Publishing, Inc., NY, 1983.

Essentials of Psychological Testing, Third Edition, by Lee J. Cronbach, Harper and Row Publishers, NY, 1970.

PART III

Preparing Yourself

Chapter 5

HOW TO SET VOCATIONAL GOALS

Someone once made the profound observation, "If you don't know where you are going, any road will get you there."

That was the story of my life. After my freshman year at college, I made a drastic change in my major and even then felt unsure. It just seemed like a more interesting subject than the last one. I had not the foggiest idea what I would ever do with the liberal-arts education I was getting. Upon graduation, I accepted a U.S. Air Force ROTC commission as a second lieutenant and decided to give it a try.

My misdirection continued. I reported to the processing base in San Antonio, Texas. Based on my college major, I tried to get into the personnel or intelligence fields, but both were closed at the time. So, I made a profound decision, based on a well-planned and rational strategy for using my gifts and maximizing job satisfaction. I said to my superiors, "Okay, then, since my wife is pregnant, give me the occupation with the longest school available, so we will be settled when the baby arrives."

If you think you've got vocational problems, forget it! That strategy sent me to a forty-three week school in telecommunications and electronics and dictated my occupational efforts, home locations, birthplaces of my children, and their education for years after.

This is an example of the most haphazard kind of planning. Still, a great principle can be learned: In spite of my carelessness, the Lord was in it all. Were those intervening years wasted? No, but only because the Lord is the Great Economist. He redeems all things.

You see, we were "chosen in Him before the foundation of the world" (Eph. 1:4). He knows the end from the beginning (Isa. 46:10). Sometimes you do not know where you are headed, but He does. When planning and goal setting, always remember:

> Commit your works to the Lord, and your plans will be established (Prov. 16:3).

Have you only recently accepted the Lord, asking Him to take control of your life? Are you concerned about those seemingly wasted years? Well, I have good news. One of the Lord's most amazing and endearing traits is to redeem the past and shape it for His glory. If you have received Him, you are now on course. If you have committed your life and works to Him, your plans will be established.

Keeping in mind our earlier thoughts about divine guidance, let's look at some of the practical ways God can help you determine the new course you're about to take.

PLANNING

First, you can set goals and accomplish short-, medium-, and long-range planning. What are the differences and why these three categories?

A long-range goal is where you ultimately want to be in your vocation, a place where, after an appropriate period of training and experience, you would be most fully using the talents that God has given you. A medium-range goal is the intermediate step or steps needed to get you there. Short-range planning is what you have to do now to eat.

Let's discuss each of these.

LONG-RANGE PLANNING

Long-range planning cannot be defined in terms of a certain number of years. One person's long-range goals may be achievable in five years and those of another in twenty. I'm not talking about a place of rest or retirement (postvocational) or necessarily a place of perfect tranquility or even financial security. It is a place where your gifts and talents are honed and refined by preparation, training, and experience, where you have reached a point of optimal fruitfulness in your calling.

The trouble Christians often have is in confusing this with worldly rewards of ever-increasing personal status, title, recognition, and material possessions. Your long-range place may *result* in some or all of these things. They are not evil in themselves, and our Father is generous to His children. But your long-range place may *not* result in these things. Consequently, they should not be the object of your affections and efforts but the incidental side effects of maximizing your God-given potential.

My thoughts turn again to the apostle Paul who, before his dramatic conversion, was held in great esteem by the prevailing value system and was probably peaking in his vocational pursuits. But later after he had really entered into God's ultimate plan for his life, he testified:

> Whatever gain I had, I counted as loss for the sake of Christ . . . I have suffered the loss of all things, and count them as refuse, in order that I may gain Christ (Phil. 3:7–8 RSV).

Paul went upward and onward in a different way than people usually think of. But look at the lasting fruit of his life. Had he remained seeking the world's recognition and status, you would have never heard of him.

My point is that planning for the Christian is different than for others. The result may be the same; the motivation is different.

Goal setting is easy for some and difficult for others. If you simply cannot do it after prayer and consideration, set it aside for a while and don't worry about it. You might be surprised how your mind will clear on the matter after you lay it to rest for a few nights.

For some, there is within a mysterious, compelling desire to "be" a certain thing someday. Those people are like a hound dog after a scent. They go after it relentlessly and usually make it.

If you are one of these, your long-range goal setting is relatively easy. Sometimes, the Father will plant such strong guidance within a person, for whatever reason, and they seem to "know" that they want to be a nurse, doctor, lawyer, domestic engineer (housewife), what have you. Your goal may be drawing you like a magnet.

If not, let's look at some steps that can help establish your long-range goals.

1. Review the gifts and talents that God has given you.

2. Prayerfully take a fresh look within yourself for what may be a God-given desire. Consider an occupational area, a type of work, or a specific job. As thoughts come to your mind, be uninhibited, let them flow freely and write them down. Judge them later.

3. Compare Steps 1 and 2 for compatibility. Give special attention to compatible items. For example, in Step 1, you may have listed a real talent for comprehending and using numbers. In Step 2, you may have found that a career as an accountant has always held a fascination for you. This indicates a probable direction.

4. From the results of Step 3, list as many possible occupational responsibilities as you can where that talent and interest can be used. Scan the appendixes to

this book for help. A trip to your nearest library and a little research is also worth the effort.

5. Look at your list and see if you can picture yourself at any of these positions in the long-range future, say in ten or twenty years. Would any satisfy your heart's desire? If so, put a big circle around it.

6. If you emerged with only one item in Step 5, let that be your long-range goal. If you had two or more items, you should prayerfully choose one as a primary goal and then prioritize any remaining as secondary goals or backups.

MEDIUM-RANGE PLANNING

You now have a long-range vocational goal. Your medium-range goals should include whatever steps, in terms of training and experience, that are necessary to achieve that end. For example, if your long-range goal is to become a general accountant and be in business for yourself, there are certain prerequisites to meeting this goal, such as these:

Earning a bachelor's or master's degree in accounting.

Taking and passing your Certified Public Accountant (CPA) examination.

Getting in a certain number of years of experience in a public accounting firm.

These, then, would be specific medium-range goals. Multiple steps obviously must involve some sequence, so arranging them on a projected time line is also desirable. In the above example, if you are just starting your accounting education, the above steps alone could carry you ten or more years into the future.

Specific medium-range goals, such as the above, should be further analyzed and expanded. For example, for item number 1, decide when and where you want to get your college education. Where are the good schools for this subject? Do you want to stay close to home or are you free to go elsewhere? You are now ready to do some detailed planning.

Appendix II may help you determine the prerequisites for selecting vocational goals and jobs. If the type of job you are looking for is not contained in this selected list, you are encouraged to refer to the *Occupational Outlook Handbook,* published by the U.S. Department of Labor, Bureau of Labor Statistics, available in your local public library or from the Superintendent of Documents, U.S. Government Printing Office, Washington, DC 20402.

SHORT-RANGE PLANNING

This is normally associated with meeting today's needs. Sometimes you have to "take what you can get" for the moment to buy time as you get on track with medium-range goals en route to long-range goals.

At first glance, there would seem not to be very much planning required for the short range, and to some extent that is true. It is best, however, that even short range decisions be made with one eye on the future.

For instance, it is often possible to find immediate employment in a position related to your medium-and long-range goals. If you are hoping to become an accountant but presently lack the formal education, you might find your short-range employment in an accounting-related area. Consider anything that would put you around the accounting function of a company or an accounting firm itself, so you can begin to hear and learn the language. Every occupation, no matter what it is, has an esoteric language spoken only by the people in it. Some say that most specialized education is, in a sense, devoted to learning the vocabulary. Concepts themselves are often relatively simple; it's the language they are couched in that has to be learned.

In the above example, getting a job as a clerk or a helper in an accounting office would be a great way to begin to learn. I know one young man who had just graduated with a liberal arts degree and had entered the job market. For the lack of anything better, he took a job in an accounting office as a clerk typist. They hired him because he did happen to have had one accounting course while in college, plus he was a fair typist because of a high school typing course and practice doing term papers.

The young man started taking accounting courses at night at a nearby university. He soon had completed several night courses and was promoted to an accounting position. He continued taking accounting courses at night and within about two years had worked his way up to the position of budget manager of the corporation. I also happen to know that his work days often ran twelve to sixteen hours. Two years later, he applied and was accepted at Harvard Business School and is now a successful management consultant in Boston with one of the most prestigious firms in the nation.

This is an interesting case because not all goals were clear at the outset. Initially, the goal of his first job was survival, but it was soon transformed into job improvement. A graduate education then became his intermediate goal. The longer-range but still intermediate goal was to contribute in the area of business management, which is what he is now doing. I do not know what his long-range goals are now, but next time I see him I plan to ask. I am particularly interested in this case; he is my oldest son.

This case demonstrates that goal setting is dynamic and that not all goals can always be clear-cut. You do the best you can with the sanctified intelligence that you have, but trust the Lord for the results and the necessary course corrections.

If you believe you have a calling to full-time Christian work in your vocation, give first priority to Christian organizations as you proceed in your short-range planning and even temporary summer jobs, if available. It is worth a try. There are just about as many occupational specialties used in Christian organizations as there are in secular work. It takes many people in many specialties to keep a ministry going. You will find that there are positions in administration, data processing and computers, technical and engineering as well as accounting and financial areas, public relations, media, marketing, and art.

COURSE CORRECTIONS

Now that you have made your plans, be prepared to discard it all. Do not be rigidly locked into any direction. Be prepared for course corrections along the way. Some, at least, will be inevitable. It has been said that a wise man has the right to change his mind, and probably an unwise man never changes his mind.

Be prepared for change and the necessity of altering your course—maybe frequently. But every time you alter it, go full speed until you reach your goal or are redirected. One mark of the flow of God's Spirit is *change*. He is dynamic, always creating, always moving forward. You want to stay in tune and flow with Him.

Commit your works to Him, and your plans will be established, knowing that all things, planned or unplanned, will work together for your good because you love Him and are "called according to His purpose" (Rom. 8:28).

Chapter 6 _____

HOW TO PREPARE YOURSELF EDUCATIONALLY

By now, you have spent time analyzing your gifts and talents, and you have spent some time establishing your vocational goals. The next thing to consider is preparing to accomplish these goals.

It may be that you are already sufficiently prepared, at least for your short- and maybe medium-range goals. If so, you are that much ahead of the game. You may fall into one of the many categories: in high school thinking about the future, just out of high school, just out of college, or maybe you have been in the job market for a long time and you are reassessing your situation and contemplating a new direction. Whatever your category, further preparation for the future is important.

Let's face it, sometimes opportunity or achievement may just happen—but very rarely. Achievement usually comes only after hard work and preparation. To the old saying that genius is as much perspiration as inspiration, I would add a third ingredient: preparation.

WHETHER TO GO TO COLLEGE

You may be debating whether to go to college, to take night courses, or to study for a higher educational degree. It may be for you or it may not.

Consider this: Only about 20 percent of all jobs require a

college education. The rest of them, about 80 percent, are skilled jobs that can be learned in other ways, such as technical or on-the-job training.

One might argue that to rise in management in these positions a college degree would be necessary, but that is not always true. It might help, it certainly will not hurt, but it is not always necessary. One can usually rise to first-line management and beyond without a degree. More important are your *technical* and *interpersonal* skills. Supervisory skills can be acquired through practice, self-study, and company-offered courses and seminars. Some employers stress the need for a degree, but many are just interested in results and performance.

On the other hand, a college degree is sometimes desirable or even mandatory, especially in certain professional areas. And it may be that you function well in an academic environment. You *want* more formal education, much for the sake of it and what it does for you. College offers much more than learning a trade or preparation for a vocation. With it comes improved communications ability, increased knowledge of your culture, government, business environment, and physical environment.

More important is this question: Do you *need* a college education for where you are headed?

My sons represent the gamut. My oldest, Jim, loved school. He got a bachelor's degree, worked for four years, then went back for a master's degree. He is now in his niche. My next son, Steve, is just as bright but technically oriented and wanted to get into a skilled profession. All of his training has been on the job, and he has progressed rapidly in electronics. College would have been a waste of his time and my money. My youngest son, Scott, has set vocational goals that will be enhanced by a degree, which he has obtained.

All three analyzed their situations, aspirations, and goals; all three are comfortable with their decisions.

I'm sure you will do the same.

CHRISTIAN VERSUS SECULAR EDUCATION

If you decide to go to college, should you go to a Christian or a secular school? Let's look at the pros and cons.

Few people know that fully 104 of the first 119 colleges founded in the United States were Christian, dedicated to the idea that God is the basis of all knowledge. Harvard, founded by the Puritans, had in its college laws that each student should consider " . . . the main end of his life and studies to know God and Jesus Christ . . . and therefore to lay Christ in the bottom as the only foundation for all sound knowledge and learning." Yale, Columbia, and Princeton had similar Christian roots; that has changed radically, however.

Charles Malik, past president of the United Nations General Assembly, once asked Cyrus Vance, then Secretary of State, "Do you know what is wrong with your country?" The secretary responded in the negative. "I'll tell you," said Malik. "You have taken Jesus Christ out of your universities."

The chief disadvantage, then, of a secular institution is that you will spend several years being fed knowledge without God or the Bible as a presupposition. Sometimes, biblical truths about origins, human nature, morality, and God are even ridiculed as superstition. There is no conflict with God and the Truth, but there is often conflict between God and man's contemporary perceptions of the Truth.

You are warned to "See to it that no one takes you captive through philosophy and empty deceit, according to the tradition of men . . . rather than according to Christ" (Col. 2:8).

Often, though, secular institutions do offer distinct advantages, including better facilities, better research opportunities, more qualified staffs, and a broader curriculum. Not unimportant is the prestige of holding a degree from a particular institution, possibly enhancing opportunities for you in the future and also your effectiveness for the Lord.

In this question of Christian vs. secular education, there are opposing arguments: One says that Christians should be trained only in Christian environments and with a Bible oriented, or at least respected, curriculum. The graduate should then go and take the world for Christ.

The other argument says that graduates of Christian schools sometimes have difficulty getting high posts in the world's systems. Their chances of exerting meaningful influence are reduced; therefore, it is best to get your education in the top secular universities after or concurrent with a firm grounding in the Word of God.

I believe there is a place for both. I am convinced that God, who is bigger than we often conceive Him to be, does it both ways. One of these directions will be right for you. The Lord will show you the way.

CHRISTIAN COLLEGES AND UNIVERSITIES

For information on Christian colleges, contact one of the following: Christian College Coalition, 1776 Massachusetts Ave. N.W., Ste. 700, Washington, D.C. 20036; Christian College Coordinating Council, P.O. Box 254, Glen Ellyn, IL 60137; American Association of Bible Colleges, P.O. Box 1523, Fayetteville, AR 72701. Then contact the specific college directly and ask them to send you a catalog. Compare their offerings with your vocational goals, financial situation, geographical preferences, and other factors of interest to you. Also check with your church for additional colleges or graduate schools that may be funded by your denomination.

If you are looking for a truly Christian educational institution, the key is whether the school's posture is to honor Jesus Christ as Lord and the Bible as His Word. You will have to discern this in your selection process.

Be cautious on this point with any school you consider. There are some schools that have a loose denominational affiliation and are subsidized by church member donations, but in the name of academic freedom have drifted from the precepts on which they were founded. Academic freedom is often a guise for teaching antibiblical material.

OTHER TYPES OF SCHOOLING

Colleges and universities are not the only way to obtain formal education and, in some instances, are not necessarily the best way. In some cases, preparation can best be met with shorter and more specialized or technical training.

Technical and specialized schools operate in most larger communities. The range of subjects is wide in scope. One way to find them in your community is to look in the Yellow Pages of your telephone directory or you may wish to contact the National Association of Trade and Technical Schools (NATTS). Single copies of two of their publications, *Handbook of Trade and Technical Careers and Training* and *How to Choose a Career and a Career School,* can be obtained from NATTS at 2021 K Street, N.W., Washington, DC 20006.

The National Home Study Council also supplies information about home-study programs. They distribute the

Directory of Accredited Home Study Schools (free) and *There's a School in Your Mailbox* (a slight charge). You can request these from the National Home Study Council, 1601 18th Street, N.W., Washington, DC 20009.

PART IV
Finding a Job

Chapter 7

HOW TO ANALYZE THE JOB MARKET

As a Christian job seeker, there are certain things about the potential job market that you should consider. An important marketing principle is that whenever you have a product to sell, you analyze the potential market. Determine through research what you can about your potential customers: who they are, where they are, how they think, what they want.

It is no less true for the Christian job seeker. The product is you. Your potential customers are your potential employers. You must market yourself; a job search is a selling campaign. All of your efforts, telephone calls, letters, resumes, and interviews are part of your marketing campaign.

Still, there is a special consideration and dimension for the Christian that does not apply to anyone else. Beyond a cold, market analysis, ask yourself if you feel drawn toward a particular ministry or organization. This is what happened to me when I first entered full-time Christian service. I felt almost a magnetism toward a certain organization. I proceeded in that direction, and it was later confirmed clearly that that is where I was supposed to be.

Such an inner witness takes priority over all techniques, even though you may not have any such leadings now. Until or unless you do hear a strong inner voice, proceed with your marketing strategy.

DEFINE YOUR PRODUCT

Review what we covered in previous chapters about your gifts and talents. Which one or ones do you want to market, to use in pursuing a vocation?

In industry, market research helps a company to determine what the characteristics of a product should be, such as shape, size, color.

Just so, you should review your present product. Review your gifts and talents, your interest, your training and experience, and any particular calling you may have discerned, your perception of what God's will for your life may be. If you have not already done so, *write it all down.* Take tablet and pencil and put these down in vertical lists, so you can look at them, add to them, or change them. This will also help you to meditate on them.

The sum total of what you have just done from this exercise is *you,* your product.

Now let's take a look at the market.

JOB-MARKET CONSIDERATIONS

Your potential job market is going to depend, of course, on the specific product you are offering. If your talents are very specialized, your potential market will be narrow. If your talents are general, your market will be wide and will include a large number of potential employers.

For example, if your specific talent is in aviation, your potential Christian market is relatively small because not too many ministries have an airplane. Still, some do because it is either necessary for their work, such as resupplying missionaries in isolated areas or, in some cases, it is a cost-effective alternative to commercial travel. If your talent is in electronics, your market is much larger because there are scores of ministries that use electronics in their work, especially the radio and television ministries. If your gifts are administrative, your market is almost unlimited because that is a skill needed virtually everywhere.

So, as you analyze your potential market—what types of ministries or companies can use your talent—it will narrow the list of possibilities for you.

GEOGRAPHICAL CONSIDERATIONS

Do you prefer a state or specific region of the country? Do you feel a definite calling to work overseas? Let this help you narrow your market further. Of course, the less you are concerned with geographical considerations, the wider your potential market.

TYPE OF MINISTRY

Can you focus on a particular type of ministry that fits your talent and heart's desire? If so, that will narrow your market even further.

There are all kinds of Christian organizations and ministries. Do you lean toward the purely one-on-one evangelical ministry? A social service ministry that helps needy people? A publications or broadcasting ministry? Maybe a ministry devoted to youth is your calling? Maybe to the elderly? The world is full of needs, and there is probably a ministry that focuses on just about each one of them. This is the wonderful characteristic of the body of Christ, being wherever believers are, ministering, caring, loving, sharing the Good News. That is why Jesus said, "Greater works . . . shall he do; because I go to the Father" (John 14:12).

DOCTRINAL CONSIDERATIONS

I normally do not like to mention doctrine because it is sometimes divisive. But it is a reality Christians have to deal with, and it can be a factor in your job search.

Hopefully, you have learned how to be comfortable with believers everywhere, regardless of some points of disagreement on biblical interpretation. It is really liberating just to love and appreciate all other believers. Our fellowship is in Him, not in doctrine.

Yet, Christians are diverse for traditional, historical, or sociological reasons. No one seems to have a corner on all the truth, though most think they do at times. On some points of doctrine, there can be no compromise: the deity of Jesus Christ, the efficacy of His blood, and salvation by grace through faith. But there are other points on which Christians perennially disagree, and if any of these are critically important to you, it will help narrow your job market. For example, if you believe strongly that the supernatural gifts of the Holy Spirit ended when the last apostle died and that anyone manifesting them today is crazy, deceived, or demon-possessed, then you would be most out of place and unhappy in a ministry that believes otherwise.

Do not seek employment anywhere unless you can, in your heart and with the light the Lord has given you, accept that ministry or company as it is, without a critical, judgmental, or superior attitude.

PROFIT VERSUS NONPROFIT

It may surprise you to learn that some organizations that are deeply involved in the work of the Lord are actually commercial, profit-making enterprises. This does not make them any less spiritual or less fruitful for the kingdom. Making a profit is not a sin; operating on donations is not necessarily saintly. It's what you do with both that counts.

If it is important for your own definition of spirituality to work in a nonprofit ministry, best be true to yourself and narrow your potential job market accordingly. If not, your market is obviously wider. For example, many commercial enterprises are purely Christian endeavors, including broadcast stations, publishers, and film producers.

The key is to examine the fruit. Do not harshly judge a company that is concerned with profit performance, which is necessary for survival in a tough, economic world. Consider that investors deserve a return on their capital; what they do with the return is between the Lord and them.

SALARY VERSUS RAISING YOUR OWN SUPPORT

What you can expect in terms of remuneration in the Christian marketplace varies widely, both in *philosophy* of remuneration and an organization's *ability* to pay.

Some ministries believe that a Christian vocation should be a sacrifice in every respect and that if the Lord did not have a place to lay his head, then why should we? Therefore, wages are minimal, at or near subsistence level. A major advantage of this type of philosophy is that commitment is virtually assured from those who embark upon such a ministry.

Others believe that "a laborer is worthy of his hire" and are concerned about not "oppressing" or putting a "yoke" (see Isa. 58) on their employees, and they offer wages that are more competitive with the commercial job market.

Some believe in and would like to offer competitive wages but do not have the financial ability to do so. This also may be a matter of prioritizing. A new project may be deemed more important than a needed salary increase.

Then, there are hybrids of the above, paying top salaries for hard-to-get skilled people but keeping a tight lid on the lesser skilled. This is more of a truly commercial philosophy of paying "what the traffic will bear."

Still, another approach is to require the committed employee to raise his own support from church, friends, or sponsoring organizations. This is a valid form of missionary endeavor and gives sponsors the opportunity of sharing both the responsibilities and the spiritual rewards of the mission outreach.

My purpose in reviewing these approaches is not to judge or evaluate. Moreover, I'd like to caution you about your evaluation: Do not let money make the decision for you. You obviously should not let your calling and service to the Lord be mercenary, opting for the highest salary. On the other hand, don't let it be masochistic, seeking a low wage because that's the most spiritual thing to do.

The goal is to be where the Lord wants you. It may be a place of high or low financial reward, but wherever, it will be the place of greatest happiness and fruit.

To give you a feel for average salaries for selected jobs in the United States, listings from the Department of Labor, Bureau of Labor Statistics, are included in appendixes II and III. A listing of many Christian organizations and ministries is included as appendix IV.

OTHER DIRECTIONS

If you do not feel led into Christian employment and are seeking a position in the general job market, there are many sources of information that will help.

Government agencies, professional societies, trade associations, labor unions, corporations, and educational institutions put out a great deal of free or low-cost career information. One of the best sources for such information is the *Encyclopedia of Associations* (Detroit: Gale Research Company, 1980), a multivolume publication that lists thousands of trade associations, professional societies, labor unions, and fraternal and patriotic organizations.

A publication that identifies pamphlets, brochures, monographs, and other career-guidance publications prepared by federal agencies is *A Counselor's Guide to Occupational Information,* published in 1980 by the United States Department of Labor. This can be purchased for a small charge from the Superintendent of Documents, U.S. Government Printing Office, Washington, DC 20402. Include the GPO stock number 029-001-02490-8.

Vocational counseling is available from the following:

* Career planning and placement offices in colleges.

* Placement offices in vocational schools.

* Vocational rehabilitation agencies.

* Counseling services offered by community organizations, commercial firms, and professional consultants.

* Job Service offices affiliated with the U.S. Employment Service.

SPECIFIC CAREER INFORMATION

Appendix II is especially included to give you a broad cross-section of selected jobs that might be applicable to both Christian and secular organizations and helpful information about these jobs, including these: nature of the work, working conditions, training and other qualifications needed, possible earnings, and sources of additional information.

Chapter 8

HOW TO USE PLACEMENT ORGANIZATIONS

Few Christians seeking full-time work with a Christian organization consider using a placement organization. Yet, these organizations can be helpful, believe it or not.

Some Christian organizations *do* seek help through placement services. This is especially true for certain positions that are difficult to fill, including entry-level positions and executive positions. For example, as a personnel director, I occasionally had need for clerical people and, even though the organization received several hundred applications per month, I could not always find help with all the skills needed. I had to go to a private placement organization.

Keep in mind that a Christian organization that is *less* visible to the public generally has fewer applicants and is *more* likely to use placement organizations. For example, a Christian broadcasting organization is very visible and may get hundreds of unsolicited resumes each month. The mass media attract attention and are less likely to have to search for employees. Conversely, ministries that operate out of the public eye, accomplishing one-on-one ministry, do not attract as much attention.

There is nothing wrong with using a placement organization, but if you are already drawn to a particular ministry or type of work, why not just communicate directly? Still, each situation is different, and there may be good reasons why you feel the need of using a placement firm. Let's look at how these organizations can help you.

TYPES OF PLACEMENT ORGANIZATIONS

There are both government and private organizations that specialize in helping people find jobs.

GOVERNMENT AGENCIES

This is sometimes called public employment service or Job Service. These offices, about twenty-five hundred nationwide, are operated by state employment agencies under direction of the Department of Labor's U.S. Employment Service. They list many available openings within your geographical area, and there is no charge for their services. Though not a good source of jobs with Christian organizations, they have a good handle on the market, especially clerical and blue-collar jobs, even first-line management positions. Their motto is to "bring people to jobs and jobs to people."

To find your local office, look in your telephone directory under the state listing, then look for a heading of Employment Office, Employment Commission, or Job Service.

PRIVATE PLACEMENT FIRMS

There are several different types of private agencies: Some only handle clerical and blue-collar jobs; some specialize in middle management and professional areas; others handle only executive and upper management. They differ greatly as to who pays the bill for their services— you or the employer—and how much.

Traditional Employment Agencies. The employment agency with which most people are familiar deals mostly with clerical and blue-collar positions. There is much competition between the various agencies, and they usually do not offer exclusive listings. Some require payment by the job seeker in the form of a significant percentage of your initial salary. This can really hurt if you are just starting out to work. Some are paid by the employer. There are some hybrid arrangements with pay coming from both. Some of these agencies only get paid when there is a hire, so the pressure on them is intense to get interviews, often resulting in a waste of your time. Placement is often not as selective as it should be.

You might benefit from using this type of agency, and sometimes they handle positions for Christian organizations; however, try to avoid a fee being imposed on you rather than the employer. For that high fee, you would probably be better off without their help, doing your own job hunting. Also, try to avoid any exclusive arrangement that would restrict your own continued searching or the use of other agencies.

Contingency Agencies. Contingency-type agencies generally deal with the next higher level on the job ladder, for example, professional positions in accounting, engineering, data processing, sales, and the like, with annual incomes from approximately $20,000 to $50,000. The fee for this service is usually paid by the employer and may be as much as 30 percent of the first-year salary. Many are plugged into a national network of job openings, so you might want to use one of these as long as it does not cost you anything.

Executive Search Firms. These agencies deal only with the very high executive and upper management positions, the top of the job ladder. Fees for this type of recruiting may be as high as 40 percent of the annual salary for the position plus expenses, whether or not their search is successful. And the expenses, such as travel, can be enormous. Many companies place a high value on their services for filling certain executive positions because a right or wrong decision about a high-level employee can save, make, or cost a large company millions of dollars.

If this is your league, you might find these listed in the Yellow Pages in very large cities. Also, try the *Wall Street Journal* or write the Association of Executive Recruiting Consultants, Inc., 30 Rockefeller Plaza, New York, NY 10020.

CHRISTIAN PLACEMENT SERVICES

One very fine organization you should consider is Intercristo, a nonprofit, Christian organization dedicated to providing placement services for Christians on a worldwide basis.

Intercristo uses a computer matching approach. They have a very large data bank of jobs available with Christian ministries and with companies that are headed by Christians and who only want Christian employees.

They only charge you a small administrative fee to enter your personal data into the computer and do a search for you. The computer will try to match your interests and skills with those of many potential employers.

You simply fill out a form, disclosing essential information about yourself, such as your interests, education, and experience; the computer searches for a position to match. You will be given a print-out of jobs available for which you qualify, along with the names, addresses, and telephone numbers of the potential employers—all you need for further inquiry. Your information will also be sent to the potential employer for his information.

You can contact Intercristo by calling (800) 426-1342 (recording), or (800) 426-1343. Their address is P.O. Box 33487, Seattle, WA 98133.

If you are interested in volunteering for the mission field, another organization is the Christ Corps, a Christ-centered, nondenominational movement that recruits and trains Christian laypeople and places them in assignments in foreign countries, and administers and supports them while there. According to their criteria, you may qualify if you are a committed Christian with basic skills you can use in the life and witness of the church. You may be single or married. One's own support must be raised, but Christ Corps will assist. If interested, contact them at P.O. Box 60707, Washington, D.C. 20039-0707.

Chapter 9 _____
HOW TO PRESENT YOURSELF

This chapter is partly concerned with your mental attitude and your self-image. This is important before we go into the subject of resume preparation. How you see yourself will largely determine what you project when you present yourself to a potential employer. Some very practical tips about your initial contact with a potential employer will also be discussed. But first, we need a proper frame of mind.

You are a product and you are marketing or selling yourself. As with all marketplaces, there are competing products. Your potential customers are going to say, "Should I buy him or that other person I'm considering?" The employer will be greatly influenced by how the applicants are wrapped or packaged, that is, how they present themselves and how they appear during the critical stages of consideration. I want you to consider this marketing principle of packaging as it pertains to you and your efforts. Product packaging is a very important subject and, where tangible goods are concerned, is one that commands much time and attention from the marketing experts. Packaging is designed for attractiveness and shelf appeal, so the product almost shouts, "Take me."

Your wrapping—how you appear to a potential employer—is very important, and I do not mean just your physical appearance. I'm also referring to the inner you— the real you—that part that you want to be most appealing to a prospective employer.

YOUR SELF-IMAGE

What *do* you think about yourself? I have known people whose self-image has defeated them before they ever started looking for a job. It is very important to cover this subject, especially within a Christian context.

My concern here is not with those who are overflowing with self-confidence, although I would suggest that you substitute "His-confidence." My concern is with any reader who may be suffering from a poor self-image, low self-esteem, a lack of confidence, or an inferiority complex. Many things can cause this, such as how you were treated as a child, unhappy experiences in school, or maybe some hard times you have had later in life.

Through prayer, the Lord may allow the root cause, whatever it is, to come to the surface, so it can be recognized. Recognition is a major step toward healing. When you get these things out of the recesses of your mind, they are usually much smaller than you thought and you see them in a new perspective.

Once you gain this perspective, the second step is possible. You can have assurance that you are accepted by God because of Jesus, the Savior, and what He has done for you. In this light, you discover your only possible identity: Without Him, you are truly nothing; with Him, you are truly everything. If you have given yourself to Him, He accepts you.

> Therefore having been justified [acquitted, found not guilty, a legal term] by faith, you have peace with God through our Lord Jesus Christ (Rom. 5:1).

Peace with God. When the Father looks at you, He sees you clothed in the righteousness of His son. You no longer have to feel guilty, because you are one of His and you were bought with a price. He approves of you.

Once you get this revelation in your heart, you can be set

free to be the happy, peaceful, and confident creature that your Father wants you to be. It will enhance your love and affection toward the Lord because of a greater appreciation of what He has done for you, which will affect your whole being. *It will affect you vocationally,* as an outworking of a new inner reality.

Once you are rooted in the knowledge of "the love of Christ which surpasses all knowledge," you can be "filled with all the fullness of God" (Eph. 3:17–19 RSV). This knowledge is vital to your vocational aspirations, for this power at work within us makes us "able to do far more abundantly than all you ask or think" (v. 20).

In summary, let your heart's image of yourself be molded by a clear understanding of your special place in the Savior and by a knowledge of His power working in you. *As you think in your heart about these things, so will you be.* And so will you appear.

Now with some spiritual preliminaries out of the way, let's look at some practical tips on how to present yourself to a potential employer.

IN PERSON, BY TELEPHONE, OR BY MAIL?

Let's say you have picked out one or more organizations that appeal to you. Further, you believe you have talents that could be used. How do you do it? Do you drop by in person first? Do you call first? Or do you mail them a resume? Maybe there is another alternative.

Geography is a major consideration. If the potential employer is a thousand miles away, it isn't practical to travel that far at this stage. Surprisingly, however, some people do. As a former personnel director, I saw many instances when people came from long distances unannounced and with no appointment. Some had spent their last cent to get there, and when they arrived, they had no money for food and shelter. Often, they would say "the Lord told me to come and you would have a job for me." Unfortunately in every case I can think of but one, there was never such an opening. Naturally, we were gracious and loving, though to do so was a burden to the ministry.

What I'm saying is this, if God truly has a place for you with a given ministry, it will be easier—and less taxing on everyone—if you write or call first. Just showing up does not necessarily demonstrate your faith to a potential employer.

Some people are critical of Christian organizations that have standard personnel procedures, decrying them as too bureaucratic, rigid, or legalistic. Yet good, sound (and flexible) personnel practices are wise. More often than not, I have seen their violation result in disaster, and adherence to them can save an organization from many problems. Keep this in mind as you are dealing with organizations and faced with their procedures.

Remember, your ability to hear from God is only half of the equation. I once had dramatic spiritual insight that the Lord had prepared a job for me in a certain place; but I withheld the information during the interview, not wanting to use it as spiritual leverage. If it were truly of God, I reasoned, they would hire me. Besides, I wanted to test it further, to see if it was really of God. I was hired.

I recommend you use the same principles. I must admit that whenever I feel someone using his divine guidance as leverage, I am automatically defensive. Instead of applying this sort of pressure, simply believe that God is big enough to bring the right applicant to the right job at the right time. When you walk in for a scheduled interview, you may be that right person.

Several years ago when my personnel assistant decided to go to seminary, I was forced to find a replacement for him. I checked the files of resumes that had been received over the previous couple of years. One resume looked good to me. The fellow had over twenty years of personnel experience. He seemed to be spiritually motivated. But his resume had been on file for about six months, and chances were that he had found a job. But I decided to call him and check if he were still available and interested.

Sam was astounded at my call. He had just voluntarily resigned from his previous position that very week as an act of obedience to what he thought the Lord was saying. He had no other job offer or possibility. He was just trusting the Lord would provide something. He had even felt led to put his house up for sale, even though he had no idea he would be leaving the area.

The timing of my telephone call was an incredible and dramatic confirmation of God's faithfulness. After going through our rigorous screening procedures, Sam joined the ministry shortly thereafter and became one of the most dedicated and faithful employees. The Lord was surely working on both sides of that arrangement—the need and also the provision.

APPLYING BY MAIL

If you are applying to an organization some distance from you, such as in another city or state, this is what I recommend:

Prepare a good resume.

Telephone in advance, just to let them know that you are sending them your resume. This will put you in their minds and on the alert for your correspondence. It might help; it cannot hurt. Of course, if they are immediately excited and invite you for an interview, then go. This is not likely, however, and they will probably be polite and encourage you to go ahead and send your resume.

Mail your resume with a warm, friendly, but professional cover letter. (See the next chapter about this subject.)

I recommend you follow the above procedure whenever you are a significant distance from the potential employer. An in-person visit is always best but rarely worth the cost from a long distance.

APPLYING IN PERSON

When would you apply in person? Whenever the distance is reasonable, such as within a fifty-mile radius.

Even when you apply in person, do not expect an immediate interview. Be prepared, but you may not get it. They will probably want to have time to review your resume and get back with you, if they see a possibility.

But by applying in person, at least you have established a *presence* and an *impression*. Then whenever they see your resume, they will think of that charming, friendly, impressive, and well-groomed person who brought it in. That is you, isn't it?

Whenever you make any kind of contact with a potential employer, do not make the fatal mistake of thinking he is just a good old, regular guy (or gal) who won't mind if you look or act a little sloppy. After all, the main thing is your spiritual commitment. No need to bother with worldly appearances. Right?

Wrong! Your physical appearance is critically important. Believe it or not, your external appearance almost always reflects an inward attitude that even correlates with work performance and habits. With everyone, neatness makes an impression, as does the lack of it.

SPECIAL CONSIDERATIONS

APPLYING TO A NON-CHRISTIAN COMPANY

Your calling may not be to a Christian organization but to a secular profession and company. This is no less worthy, a point that cannot be emphasized too strongly. As mentioned earlier, what is truly spiritual is to be where the Lord wants you, and a secular career can be as much a calling as working in a Christian ministry or company. God wants His people to be salt and light throughout the world.

I assume you have a commitment to the Lord, or you would probably not be reading this book. But with this commitment, what should your approach be when applying to a secular organization? First, I strongly suggest that you don't apply carrying a big black Bible and wearing a six-inch cross dangling at your neck. And don't greet the personnel director with, "Praise the Lord, brother!" You just might scare them to death. In your contacts with the world, you need to be as wise as a serpent and as harmless as a dove. You share your faith as the Spirit gives opportunity, but it is sometimes counterproductive to wear it on your sleeve.

If asked, never be reluctant to mention your faith and commitment, but let the Spirit be in control. If not asked, or unless the Spirit really gives an opening, save it. Do not be unwise and jeopardize a job opportunity and thereby maybe miss God's best for you.

If during recruiting or later on the job, you detect a conflict of principle—something that the company does or wants you to do that you believe to be ungodly and wrong—pray about how to approach the matter and ask for wisdom. The incident may shatter your relationship with the company; but it is also possible that if handled with *love* and *wisdom,* you might be an agent of change and have a vital influence on individual lives. Isn't that what it's all about? "We are ambassadors for Christ, God making His appeal through us" (2 Cor. 5:20 RSV).

APPLYING TO A CHRISTIAN ORGANIZATION

Although discussed previously, now you need to consider your approach to the specific Christian organization to which you are presenting yourself. God's people come in lots of flavors, with varieties of opinion about behavior, appearance. Do some checking, maybe with a telephone call or two, and find out what peculiarities there may be that you should know. Some companies have rules against smoking; others have rules about weight, dress, and appearance, or strong feelings on some fine points of doctrine.

None of these may ever be a factor for you; yet it is always best to be prepared and not to be surprised, either for you or for your prospective employer.

In conclusion, here are some practical pointers as you proceed further with your job hunting whether Christian or secular:

DO proceed with a firm conviction that God loves you, is with you, and is helping you.

DO let that conviction give you a strong confidence.

DO exhibit to potential employers a commitment and enthusiasm to serve unselfishly and be effective in whatever God has for you.

DO proceed with your resume and letter writing, painting a positive and professional image of yourself.

DO have a resume that will be noteworthy in content, style, format, and accuracy.

DO appear at interviews with your "best foot forward," properly dressed and well-groomed.

DO be positive and confident at all times.

DO find out what you can about any ministry or organization to which you apply, so you will be (and will appear to be) well-informed.

DO NOT approach your job hunting with a complacent or lackadaisical attitude. *It deserves your best effort.*

Chapter 10

HOW TO PREPARE
A RESUME

Your resume is truly a self-portrait. You prepare it, and the subject is you. You are saying, loud and clear, "This is me!" Your resume is your advertisement.

I am amazed at how some people portray themselves. Some people are just careless. Be careful when preparing your resume because it is one of the most important things you will do in your job-hunting process. Extra time in preparation will pay later.

Technically, you do not need a resume. Every company has application forms you can use to paint your portrait, and some companies require you to fill out an application form whether or not you have a resume. But using an application form without a resume lacks *class*. It's like painting your portrait using paint-by-numbers instead of with the skilled hand of a creative artist. You deserve a resume.

If you don't take time to prepare it correctly, however, you would be better without it because your resume is often the first and most critical impression given to a potential employer. Look at your resume from the employer's viewpoint. If your resume is sloppy, you are sloppy. If it is too verbose, you are probably too verbose. If it is too short, you probably have little to offer. If it is full of mistakes, you are probably a mistake. If it is not well organized, you are probably not well organized. If it is full of baloney, well, guess what?

Really, what else can he think? After all, he only has your resume, maybe one or two sheets of paper, and he has to form a judgment, usually a quick one because of other pressing matters. And remember, he has never had the pleasure of meeting you and knowing what a charming, bright, and impressive person you are. He doesn't know that you were just too busy to do a really super job on your resume and you assumed that he would understand. He doesn't understand because he is much busier.

When you give or send your resume, it is assumed that you are saying, "Hey, this is my best shot." Before you make that shot, let's look at three ways you can communicate in the most effective manner.

First, let's size up your audience. Your resume will probably go to a very busy personnel administrator. He needs to fill a job with the best person, with the least amount of effort because there are a million other things that are waiting to be done. Your resume is one of scores of papers to reach his desk that day. Some of them are other resumes. (I have personally reviewed as many as eight hundred resumes in a single month, one hundred at one sitting.)

Your resume comes to the top of the stack. You are actually there by proxy. Now is your big chance. You finally have his attention. Via your resume, you say to him, "Look at me!"

If your resume is poorly done, his immediate reaction will be, "Ugh. Anyone who does such a poor job here will have poor work habits." He will hasten to dispose of it, giving it a quick glance, then assigning a brief code, so his secretary will know to send a nice rejection letter.

On the other hand, if you have taken the time and done good work, his reaction will be, "Hmm. Anyone who would do a nice job like this must be worth considering. I'll look at it closely."

That first glance at your communication is critical, and it

probably takes only five to ten seconds. This is where you really want to attract attention.

THE ATTENTION GETTER

Your best attention getter is not the resume but a cover letter. A good cover letter is absolutely essential. In fact, I consider this as important as the resume attached, and it baffles me that so many people do not use them. No matter how good a resume is, receiving it in the mail without a cover letter is like receiving a cold fish wrapped in a newspaper.

The cover letter adds a little warmth and personality to the necessarily formal resume and is simply a brief introduction and statement of interest and availability. In Christian employment, it is also the perfect place to let them know immediately that you are a Christian and share the organization's values and goals. A good cover letter can actually be magnetizing, drawing the reader to give attention to your resume. Therefore, do not use a form letter. A personalized letter has a much greater effect. Two to four short paragraphs are usually best, never more than a page.

To whom do you address it? Normally, address it to the personnel director. If it is a small ministry or company, address it to the president or whatever title the leader may have and use his name with the title. If you do not already know this information, call and ask.

The cover letter, as well as the resume, should be typed clearly and with no obvious mistakes, even if you have to pay for it and especially if you are seeking a management-level job.

A sample letter is included. Use words such as these if they apply to you; otherwise, use your own words. Be real, be positive, and be upbeat.

A final suggestion. There must be a book somewhere that tells letter and resume writers to exude so much confidence that they come across as egomaniacs. I've read too many of their resumes. Confidence is good, but extreme self-exaltation is not good. Don't succumb to the temptation and say something like this:

"I am confident that my talents can solve your problems in no time." (Reader's reaction: *He doesn't even know what our problems are! It sounds like he would be another problem.*)

A little humility is healthy. Also, be careful what type of person you describe yourself to be.

"I am a strong manager, able to get optimal results from people with minimal costs." (Reaction: *Sounds like an unpopular slave driver. He would probably cause people problems.*)

"I am people-oriented and have unusual skills at relating with fellow employees and subordinates." (Reaction: *Sounds like a goof-off, who wastes time talking all day.*)

"I can help the organization reassess its goals and direction to make a larger impact, and I have some great new ideas." (Reaction: *Sounds like a know-it-all, who would give the boss a hard time. Who needs it?*)

Let your resume, experience, references, and interview include most of these features.

Sample Cover Letter:
Your street number
City, State, Zip
Date, Area code, and telephone number

Mr. Hiram Firum
Personnel Director
Especially Anointed Christian Ministries, Inc.
Anytown, USA

Dear Mr. Firum:

I have always loved Especially Anointed Christian Ministries and have wanted to be a part of it. I want to thank all of you for being such a blessing to me.

Since I am graduating soon, I have been seeking the Lord's will for my life. I definitely feel a call to be in full-time Christian work. It would be a great privilege and blessing if this could be with your ministry.

Enclosed is a copy of my resume. The Lord has gifted me in (your talent), and I know that with His help I could be an asset to your organization. I want to be a part of what you are doing and use my gifts to help further your wonderful work.

I am anxious to meet you and look forward to hearing from you at your earliest convenience.

Sincerely,

Nita Job

THE RESUME

The resume should be a brief summary of yourself, not an autobiography. It should have a certain structure, allowing for some variance, but not too much. There are two main types of resumes, the chronological and the functional. See samples included.

THE CHRONOLOGICAL RESUME

This is the most popularly used resume, so personnel people are very familiar with it. In this resume, employment experience is listed in reverse chronological order, with most recent work listed first. It is a concise, orderly record of work experience; a disadvantage is that it will reveal shortcomings in experience and gaps in employment. I recommend this for your primary consideration, however, because a sharp interviewer will be suspicious and see your attempts to use format to hide lack of experience.

THE FUNCTIONAL RESUME

This format does not contain employment dates but instead emphasizes qualifications, skills, and accomplishments. It stresses a specific ability you are trying to market. This is not a bad format for a student just graduating who has had no work experience. But for anyone else, the interviewer will ask himself, *What has he done, when and where? And why is he trying to hide it?*

You can combine the above two types of resumes, giving both a chronological work history and also functional emphases, but length may be a problem. Again, if you have only a student background and a little work history, a combination might be best for you. The functional part can emphasize some of the strengths you have exhibited in school activities, such as school or campus organizations; your work history can include summer or part-time jobs you have had.

PARTS OF A RESUME

There are several categories of information that are essential to every resume, but do not necessarily have to be in the order given below.

Personal Identification. Your name, address, and telephone number should appear at the top of the first page in the center or at the margin, the former preferred.

Objective. Write your employment objective in one brief sentence. If applicable, use the position, title, or type of responsibility of the job being sought. But do not make this more specific than you really want it to be, or it will box you out of other position possibilities. Also, consider wording your objective differently for resumes sent to different companies.

Education. List degrees earned, when and where. If you have a college degree, do not show high school information; if you have no degree, do show it. Show school honors, awards, and (if superior) your grade point average. Also, show significant additional schooling, such as non-degree work, technical training, special seminars, and structured self-study.

Employment Experience. Show employment experience in reverse chronological order (latest one first). Show company and job titles held, with a brief description of responsibilities and major accomplishments. Also, consider these points, if significant:

Show to whom you reported, if impressive, such as to the president or top executive.

How many people were you responsible for?

How big a budget were you responsible for?

Show significant promotions.

Military Experience. If applicable, show military service time, branch of service, specialty, and highest rank held. Also, show any present reserve activity or obligations.

Personal. There are some things you are not legally required to divulge, and some would urge you not to do so. I recommend, however, that you be totally open. I would tell age, marital and family status, and the condition of your health. If any of these are not important to an employer, such as your age, it will not hurt. If it is important, he is going to find out anyway. The government may say it is not necessary, but the government is not hiring you.

Community/Civic Involvements. List any organizations, offices held, dates, and achievements.

Professional Affiliations. List membership in professional organizations.

Special Skills. List any special skills, such as foreign languages or licenses held.

Interests and Activities. List hobbies and avocations (or combine under *Personal*).

References. At this point, just say the standard, "Available upon request."

All this and brief too? Yes. It may take some practice and a few rewrites, but you can do it. To say a lot in a few words is an art, and your prospective employer may recognize your talent here.

STEPS IN PREPARING A RESUME

It is best to start by doing a thorough self-analysis, using the major points of a resume. Take full inventory of yourself in rough form before you start writing your resume. List everything point-by-point with dates at every relevant point, which will be the raw material for your resume. Next, decide upon a resume format that suits you best.

WRITING YOUR FIRST DRAFT

Brief, action-oriented wording is essential, not long, drawn-out phrases, full sentences, or the pronoun "I." Use past tense *action verbs* and short phrases in describing your experience. For example, say, "Operated computer terminals," instead of saying, "I was responsible for the operation of computer terminals."

Avoid the use of abbreviations where possible. Be consistent in your format, order of information, tense of verbs and style.

Do the best you can on your first draft but remember, it is *only* a draft. Type it or have it typed, so it can be properly critiqued.

CRITIQUE YOUR FIRST DRAFT

It would be wise to get some help from others to review what you have done, especially if they are familiar with the type of work you are applying for or if they are accustomed to reviewing resumes. The impression of others is very important. You may not use all their suggestions but you need their reactions to these questions:

Does it appear neat?

Does it appear orderly?

Is it easy to read?

Does it convey the message you want?

Is the format efficient and attractive?

THE FINAL DRAFT

Incorporate all relevant feedback and begin writing your final draft. Continually try to improve the wording, making every word meaningful. Attractively use all space on each page.

Here are some additional tips for your final product:

Keep length to one or two pages.

Use only one side of the page.

Don't use language from official job descriptions.

Don't normally state details of employment more than ten years past.

Don't include salary history, picture of yourself, or attachments of official documents.

Don't include a covering sheet (this does not mean cover letter, which is recommended).

Always have it typed on a professional typewriter in good condition. I suggest a professional service, but ask for a sample of their work for inspection first.

If you really want to go first class, have it typeset and printed.

Use only high-quality paper. The greatest resume on cheap paper loses its effect. Consider tinted paper.

Have it reproduced only by a high-quality, offset method. This is not expensive, and it will look much better.

(CHRONOLOGICAL FORMAT FOR RESUME OF RECENT GRADUATE)

Name
Address
Telephone Number

OBJECTIVE

Position as programmer, with opportunities for growth and increased responsibility.

EDUCATION

B.S. in Computer Science, June 1983, Colonial State University, Tidewater, Virginia.

Highlights: GPA 3.4/4.0, Deans List; Chairman, Computer Club; Omicron Delta Kappa, leadership fraternity; Cadet Major, Air Force ROTC; Earned expenses through part-time employment

Computer languages learned: FORTRAN, COBOL, BASIC, AND APL.

EMPLOYMENT
EXPERIENCE

Computer Consultant, Colonial State University, 1981–1983. Consultant for the university while attending as full-time student. Aided students in hardware and software applications.

Assistant Manager, Pizza Den, Inc., Tidewater, Va., 1980–1983. Assisted in the management of restaurant. Hired, trained, scheduled, and supervised evening shift. Responsible for four people. Reported to manager. Part-time, approximately 20 hours per week.

MILITARY
STATUS

Second lieutenant, U.S. Air Force Reserve. No active duty commitment.

PERSONAL

Birthdate: November 19, 1960. Single. Health excellent. Special interests: sports, music. Church basketball team. Study guitar. Participate in Bible study group.

COMMUNITY
ACTIVITY

Member, Jaycees; Assistant Scoutmaster, Boy Scouts of America

PROFESSIONAL
AFFILIATIONS

Member, Computer Software Association

SPECIAL
SKILLS

French language, fluent. FAA Private Pilot's License.

REFERENCES

Available upon request.

(FUNCTIONAL RESUME FORMAT FOR SAME PERSON)

Name
Address
Telephone Number

OBJECTIVE

Position as programmer, with opportunities for growth and increased responsibilities.

EXPERIENCE

Programming
Extensive experience in academic environment of programming using languages of FORTRAN, COBOL, BASIC, and APL.

Teaching
Classroom experience for two years teaching students various hardware and software applications.

Management
Responsible for personnel selection, hiring, training, scheduling, and insuring operational effectiveness under high pressure environment.

Public Relations
Maintained outstanding relations with public in difficult retail marketing situation. Improved customer satisfaction, resulting in increased gross revenue and profit for corporation.

EDUCATION

B.S. in Computer Science, Colonial State University, 1983. GPA 3.4/4.0, Deans List. Chairman, Computer Club. Omicron Delta Kappa, leadership fraternity. Cadet Major, Air Force ROTC.

MILITARY
STATUS

Second lieutenant, U. S. Air Force Reserve. No active duty commitment.

PERSONAL

Birthdate: November 19, 1960. Single. Health excellent. Special interests: sports, music. Church basketball team. Study guitar. Participate in Bible study group. Fluent French. FAA Private Pilot's License.

COMMUNITY
ACTIVITY

Member, Jaycees; Assistant Scoutmaster, Boy Scouts of America

PROFESSIONAL
AFFILIATIONS

Member, Computer Software Association

REFERENCES

Available upon request.

(COMBINED FUNCTIONAL-CHRONOLOGICAL FORMAT)

Name
Address
Telephone Number

OBJECTIVE

Position as a programmer, with opportunities for growth and increased responsibilities.

EDUCATION

B. S. in Computer Science, June 1983, Colonial State University, Tidewater, Virginia. Highlights: GPA 3.4/4.0, Dean's List. Chairman, Computer Club. Omicron Delta Kappa. Cadet Major, Air Force ROTC.

AREAS OF EXPERIENCE

Programming and Teaching.

Extensive experience in academic environment of programming with FORTRAN, COBOL, BASIC, and APL. Two years of classroom experience teaching hardware and software applications.

Management and Public Relations.
Have managed people, hired, scheduled and insured operational effectiveness of a high pressure business. Maintained outstanding relations with public in difficult retail marketing situation. Helped improve company profitability while improving customer satisfaction.

EMPLOYMENT HISTORY

Computer Consultant, Colonial State University, 1981–1983. Consultant for the university while attending as a full-time student. Aided students in hardware and software applications.

Assistant Manager, Pizza Den, Inc., 1980–1981 (part-time). Assisted in management of restaurant. Hired, scheduled, supervised evening shift. Responsible for four people.

PROFESSIONAL AFFILIATIONS

Member, Computer Software Association

COMMUNITY ACTIVITY

Member, Jaycees. Assistant Scoutmaster, Boy Scouts of America.

PERSONAL

Birthdate: November 19, 1960. Single. Health excellent. Special interests: sports, music, Bible study. Fluent French.

MILITARY STATUS

Second Lieutenant, USAF Reserve. No duty commitment.

REFERENCES

Available upon request.

AT LAST, YOU ARE FINISHED!

Put your cover letter on top of your resume and mail or take it to your prospective employers.

Folding is acceptable, but it is better if you do not fold. Buy a large envelope for mailing to avoid folding. It will appear neater when reviewed.

Congratulations on finishing your resume. You put a lot of hard work in on it but it was worth it. You will be glad you did.

In job hunting, you need to stand out to an employer every chance you get. The resume is the best place to start.

You can expect an interview soon. Let's get into that subject so you can be well-prepared.

Chapter 11 _____

HOW TO BE
INTERVIEWED

You have done such a magnificent job on your resume, an interview is inevitable. You've probably imagined what it's going to be like when you meet the interviewer. Maybe you've gone so far as to pick out the clothes you'll wear. You've had them cleaned, and now they are hanging in your closet, ready to wear.

It will probably surprise you to learn that for your first interview, you may not need your clothes at all. In fact, your pajamas will do just fine. How's that? The reason is that your first interview may be by telephone.

THE TELEPHONE INTERVIEW

When you speak of an interview, usually your first thoughts are of a face-to-face encounter in the office of someone, such as the personnel director. This is usually correct, but you may first encounter the telephone interview.

To save time and as part of the screening process, an employer may telephone you before inviting you for a personal visit, especially if you do not live in the same city. With a telephone interview, the employer lessens the risk of spending money to bring you there, only to find you do not fit the position. Even if you *are* in the same city, you may first receive a telephone interview before the employer moves to the next step. You may or may not face it. Be prepared.

You should keep in mind that an employer wants to accomplish one or more of the following objectives over the telephone:

He wants to see if you are still available, especially if there has been a significant time lapse since your previous contact.

He wants to get a feel for your personality, to discern if you sound pleasant and rational. In all due respect, one never knows.

He wants to get clarification or elaboration on questions he may have had regarding your resume or application.

A Christian employer may want to find out where you stand spiritually and sometimes doctrinally. For example, an evangelical employer will usually prefer, even require, that you have been born again by faith in the Lord Jesus Christ and that you believe the Bible to be the Word of God. To some, various points of doctrine may be important. In case you may be wondering, it is proper and not illegal for religious organizations to discriminate on religious grounds; therefore, there are no problems with this type of questioning. One exception is FCC licensed radio and television stations where, according to one notable court case, religious criteria can only apply to certain job positions, those that influence program content.

He may ask if you can come for a personal visit and want to set up an appointment.

He may want to obtain references and check them before he spends additional time and money, especially if you live out of town.

The best way to handle the telephone interview, as with all communications, is with courtesy and honesty. In explanations, try not to say too little and cause him to be suspect or too much and sound overly talkative.

THE WALK-IN APPLICANT

Some people are termed "walk-in" applicants, referring to those who "pop in" with no previous communications or appointment. You may choose to hand-deliver your resume rather than sending it through the mail, which is not a bad idea. If you do, you will be a walk-in.

Walk-in applicants may or may not be interviewed at the time. It depends on the organization, how busy they are, how well they are staffed, and how needy they are for a new employee. They may need you so badly that they interview you when you come—don't expect it. Chances are that a walk-in candidate will not be interviewed. The typical organization, especially if it is very visible, receives so many applications that it is just impossible to interview everyone. They have to be selective, based on sheer volume alone.

You will probably be treated very courteously and told something like, "Thank you very much for coming. After this is reviewed if we see any possible openings for you, we'll be in touch with you right away."

Sometimes, an alert receptionist or secretary may be trained to make a cursory review and assessment of the applicant and spot that occasional pearl who has unusually impressive credentials or experience that can fill a need. In such cases, the receptionist may check to see if someone is available to meet you. If someone is available and agrees with the receptionist's judgment, you have an interview.

Present yourself to the receptionist as friendly and eager

and with courtesy, but not too familiar. Mix friendliness with a certain air of professionalism. Be *cautiously* assertive, pointing out how much it means for you to get an interview. Most of the Christians in this business are just old softies anyhow and do not like to disappoint people. You might get your interview.

If you are visiting from out of town, make sure the receptionist knows this. You should not make an appearance from out of town and demand an appointment. It is presumptuous and discourteous to expect people to drop what they're doing to accommodate your poor planning. Still, they may do it for you because of their compassion and to take advantage of your availability.

Be respectful of the receptionist's time but do not be like this applicant:

> *Extreme Applicant Number One* walks in, tersely asks for an application, sits down, fills it out, drops it on the appropriate table or desk, and then walks out without saying a word. (Reaction: *What's wrong with this one? Mad about something?*)

Be friendly but not as friendly as this applicant:

> *Extreme Applicant Number Two* is excessively chatty and wastes an hour of the receptionist's time, acting like a long-lost friend. (Reaction: *Doesn't he know I have work to do? This is probably what he would do on the job!*)

PREPARATION FOR THE INTERVIEW

No matter how you arrive at an interview, you should be prepared. It is critically important that you know the exact time and place of the interview, the interviewer's full name (the correct pronunciation), and his title.

You should also find out some specific facts about the company or ministry, such as what it does, where its major offices are, a little about its history and future plans. If you cannot find this out anywhere else, telephone the company and ask someone beforehand, preferably someone in the public relations department. If applying to a secular firm, you may be able to get information in your local library in reference books such as these: *Dunn and Bradstreet Reference Book, Standard and Poor's Corporation Records, Moody's Manuals, Fitch Corporation Manuals,* or *MacRae's Bluebook.*

THE BIG MOMENT

This is it! Your big moment has arrived. You're about to see the personnel director, an assistant, or possibly a department manager where there is an opening. You will be ushered or called in and introduced to the interviewer. Your first major challenge will be avoid tripping or falling as you enter the office.

You have only been in the presence of the interviewer a few seconds and you have already made a big impression (whether you tripped or not). How? By your appearance. Of course, you have groomed yourself and dressed properly.

What is proper? Well, not necessarily a pinstriped suit for a man or an evening gown for a woman. Dress appropriately for the job or somewhat better. If you are seeking an office job, a coat and tie is recommended for the male; a smart dress or suit for the female. If you are color blind or have notoriously poor taste, get someone to help you decide what to wear. Clashing and nonharmonious colors can communicate negatively, even subconsciously, and hurt your cause.

If you are seeking a nonoffice job, such as one with a manual skill, a coat and tie is not necessary, although it will not detract from your appearance. But whatever you do, be neat and clean. Experienced employers know that there is a correlation between an unkempt appearance and sloppy work habits because appearance represents a frame of mind. Also, they assume that any thinking person will look his best for an interview. If your best is bad, what will you look like on the job?

Women should not overdo the makeup. Some Christian employers may not like it at all, but that would be rare. In most cases, modesty is the rule in all matters of appearance.

The interviewer will ask you to be seated and will initiate some small talk. Let the interviewer take the initiative in steering the conversation. You may have a lot you need to say but wait for the right moment. Timing is important.

The initial small talk is to break the ice and help you relax. So relax. Be yourself. The interviewer will sense your naturalness and appreciate it. Believe me, pretentiousness is obvious and always counterproductive, communicating not only falseness but insecurity.

It will take the interviewer just a few moments to get down to business. He will probably ask you a lot of questions. Below are some you should be prepared to discuss, though not necessarily in the order given.

ABOUT YOUR FAITH

In a Christian organization, an astute interviewer will somehow ask about your faith, though how it is done may vary with the situation. Regardless, it is important for such an organization to know where your Christian position is. The approach might be something subtle, "Why are you interested in working for a Christian organization?'' It might be more direct, ''How long have you known the Lord?'' The important thing for you at this point is to know where you stand with your faith and that you have a positive stand. Be able to articulate it to some degree.

If you are not sure what you believe, come to grips with it before the interview. It's much more important to you than the job is, but the Lord may be using the situation to cause you to examine certain things.

ABOUT YOUR EXPERIENCE

The interviewer will probably want to know more than what is on your resume. Be honest and answer all questions; still, if there is any area of weakness in your experience, be careful about volunteering it. Point out your strengths and accomplishments.

The employer wants a ''can do'' person. Radiate confidence, not conceit—there's a big difference. Confidence can contain humility, an ''I can do all things through Christ'' attitude. A word of caution: Do not say you can do something you cannot do. ''If you have a horse,'' an old farmer once said, ''don't say you have a cow. If you do, somebody will tell you to milk it some day.''

ABOUT YOUR REFERENCES

You will probably be asked for personal and professional references, the latter only if you have a work record. The interviewer may ask, ''Will any of your references give you anything other than a good report?'' A sharp personnel department will diligently check references, including your former bosses whether or not you included them as references. Surprisingly, some companies are lax on this. If you have a problem in the past and it was not your fault, best mention it now and tell your story. Otherwise, they may find it out without the benefit of your explanation, then jump to a conclusion.

Unless you are Public Enemy Number One, your personal references should be no problem. After all, you picked them and surely you picked people who are *very objective* and will testify that you walk on water! In case you do not know it, it is considered a courtesy to request permission before you use someone as a reference.

ABOUT SALARY

The interviewer may want to know your salary expectations and ask, "What kind of salary do you feel is necessary for you now?"

This is a touchy one. At this point, be a little vague. If you come back too high, you may box yourself out of a job. Even though you might work for less, they may fear you would be unhappy and not stay long. If your answer is too low, you may be volunteering to work for even less than they are willing to pay, giving them an unnecessary bargain.

Counter with something like this, "Well, I do have some responsibilities and would trust that any position would pay a fair salary. Are your salaries competitive?" You might also ask, "What is the salary range for this job?" You and the interviewer can maneuver on this one, and a possible starting range will emerge.

OTHER QUESTIONS YOU MAY BE ASKED

You may be asked a lot of open-ended questions just to see how you react and how you think. They are interested in you, the whole person, not just in whether you can perform certain tasks. Why? Because your whole person comes on board when they hire you. A company buys into a lot more than a task performer when they hire someone. They will have to relate to you eight or more hours a day and need to be able to trust you as a member of their team. They will invest a lot of time and money in you, including fringe benefits, and the government will tax them heavily because of you with FICA and unemployment taxes. They want you to be the *right* person.

To help you prepare, here are some types of questions you may expect:

How did you hear about us?

Why would you like to work for this company?

What did you like best about your previous job?

What did you like least?

What is your primary skill or ability?

What do you think you can do for this company?

What are your long-range goals?

Are you willing to relocate?

What do you know about our company?

What have you learned from some of the jobs you've held?

What is your major weakness? (Be careful here or you will hurt your cause. If you can do it truthfully, turn it around positively. You might say, "Well, I'm too conscientious about my job and tend to work too hard." That will be music to their ears!)

QUESTIONS YOU CAN ASK

You should be given the opportunity to ask questions. If not, try to seize the opportunity. You'll seem a little dull if you don't ask anything. Besides, there are some important things you need to know.

Could you tell me about this position? (If you are applying for a specific job.)

Could you tell me what you have available?

What do you see as the future for this organization?

Does the company encourage growth and promotion from within?

What opportunity is there for increased responsibilities?

What kind of training and development program do you have?

Why is this position open right now? Did someone hold it before?

What kind of fringe benefits do you have? (Medical insurance, vacation, paid holidays?)

How is the company's financial situation? (The interviewer may not know unless it is near disaster, in which case the response would reveal a problem. Some Christian organizations remain at or near financial disaster and keep on going. It could mean possible layoffs or minimal salary increases in the future.)

GENERAL GUIDELINES

Here are a few final and general guidelines, which will help you have a successful interview.

Avoid controversial subjects and remarks. There is little to gain and much to lose. The interviewer may hold an opposing view and naturally would think you have faulty reasoning.

Be positive. Avoid critical remarks as much as possible, even if a former employer may have treated you unfairly. Why? A good interviewer knows there are usually two sides to a story and may suspect your former employer had good reason. A critical remark can boomerang.

Try to focus on the needs of the organization and how you can meet them. If you can find out what the job need is, give emphasis to that part of your skill, training, or experience.

Don't get too touchy about your rights if questions are asked that you are not legally required to answer. This will be an immediate turnoff, and you will be labeled as a potential troublemaker. Such questions may be asked harmlessly and in my experience, will not be used to discriminate against you.

My advice to all interviewees is to answer all questions. What have you got to hide? There is happiness in being comfortable with yourself and what you are and in being transparent with others.

IN CONCLUSION

Your interview is over. You may have a job offer. If you do, shout, "Hallelujah." Feel free to skip the next chapter on follow-up, but be *sure* to read the last three chapters.

If you do not have an immediate job offer, be sure to find out the next step before you leave. Are you supposed to do anything? Is the interviewer going to set up another interview or call you? You might say, "Well, where do things stand now?"

Be sure to express your appreciation and thanks to the interviewer and also to the receptionist or other clerical personnel who may have assisted you.

Chapter 12
HOW TO FOLLOW UP

You have sent in your resume with a nice cover letter. You may have even been interviewed. Days have gone by, maybe weeks. You've heard nothing. Naturally, you are anxious to hear something. You felt so good about everything, and your interview seemed to go well. You just knew you would have a job by now. What do you do?

Here are some reasons why you may not have heard yet:

Some organizations move slowly. They don't want to rush because they want to make the right choice.

They want you, but the budget is tight. The particular slot for you is not in the budget, and hiring will be delayed until they have the money.

The personnel people are swamped and haven't been able to take further necessary steps, such as conducting reference checks.

Your references are out of town or, for some reason, unavailable.

They received your resume by mail but have been too busy to reply.

They like you but want to look at as many applicants as possible before they make a hiring decision.

There is no job opening, and they have been too busy to tell you. This should not happen, but sometimes the sheer volume of recruiting and applications keeps them from paying all the courtesies normally desired.

These are just some of the many reasons you may not have heard. But it does sound as though it is time to do something about it.

WHAT YOU SHOULD DO

FOLLOWING-UP A MAILED RESUME

If you are dealing through the mail, I hope you followed the advice of a previous chapter and preceded the mailing with a telephone call to introduce yourself and to let them know your resume is on its way. Whether you did or not, if you have not heard anything in two weeks, call again. Two weeks allows time for mail delays, intra-organizational mail distribution, and processing.

In your follow-up call, ask for, by name, the person you talked with the first time. Thank them for watching out for your resume and ask if they have seen it yet. If they say no, it may have been lost. This is unlikely, but unless they can find it right away, send another just in case.

If they say it has been received, politely ask for the status of your application, "How does it look right now?" It would be best if you were talking with the personnel director or whoever does the recruiting and screening, but talk with whom you can.

Be friendly, courteous, gentle and *just a little* pushy, not too much. Even though personnel people are busy and really do not care for the interruptions and the bother (they're human too), if you are polite, a little aggressiveness can help. That's because you make an impression, and their sensitivity to your expectations can sometimes, even subconsciously, cause them to want to help you. There is a tendency in all of us to want to respond to people's expectations, and it's especially true for Christians, who are prone to want to be helpful.

Pursue this line until you are satisfied that you are being properly considered.

FOLLOWING UP AN INTERVIEW

Let's assume there was a degree of interest in you, and for that reason, you were given an interview. You haven't heard anything in several days. Here's what to do:

> First, sit down and reflect on your interview. Try to remember what was said to you about a follow-up or a notice about the decision. Make some notes to have available as you follow up.
>
> Telephone the person who interviewed you. If he is unavailable, ask for a return call. If your call is not returned, call back again. But always be courteous and polite. If you are politely persistent, you will probably get through. Ask how it's going with your job possibility.
>
> The answer may be no, which closes the door. If they are still considering and the door is ajar, ask if there is anything you can do to help things along. For example, ask if you can speak directly with the person who will need your services. If they prefer that you not, ask, "Well, you don't mind if I contact him, do you? Could you give me his name and phone number?"
>
> Always be searching for another avenue to explore, such as the one I've just suggested, something to keep your case active and drawing the company's attention,

if not in one department then in another. Most companies have so much paper work, it is easy for them to fall victim to the "out of sight, out of mind" syndrome. The adage "the squeaking wheel gets the grease" is often true in follow-up.

FOLLOWING-UP A REJECTION

No one likes a rejection of any kind. It's one of the worst things that can happen to us, a real stab in the old ego.

Ater you recover from the initial shock, everything gets back into perspective. It's really not all that bad. Besides, you didn't really want to work at that place if the Lord didn't want you there. The question is what should you do now? Should you follow up with this company any more or just forget it?

Before you decide, review the events to date. Ask yourself if you gave it your best. If so, let it go for now. But if three months go by and you are still waiting for the Lord to open a door, inquire again with a personal telephone call or visit. Keep inquiring periodically. It's possible that a vacancy may occur that didn't exist the first time around, and by keeping your name on the front burner, you may get a chance at it.

WRITTEN FOLLOW-UP

Even though I place so much value on the personalized telephone call, make it a practice to follow up a telephone call with a nice, brief letter, beginning like this:

"This is a follow-up to our telephone conversation of (date). I really appreciate your taking the time to talk with me. Your personal interest is sincerely appreciated."

This is a good place to reiterate a major principle: According to the Word of God, He is the one who opens doors that no man can close and closes doors that no man can open. *Never* be discouraged at closed doors because our wonderful heavenly Father always has something better for us. I know it is true because His Word says it; I have seen it happen many times.

Accordingly, do not try to knock the door down with all the force of your personality and cunning. If God closes the door, you do not want to go in. Move on. Greater things are waiting.

Chapter 13 ⎯⎯⎯⎯⎯⎯⎯⎯
HOW TO CHANGE CAREERS

Maybe you remember the old television sitcom in which a harried corporate executive in a high-pressure big-city job gets fed up with the "rat race." To the consternation of his employer and wife, he resigns, sells his home, and moves to an idyllic country location with cows, pigs, and, we find later, bad plumbing, a broken tractor, and rural neighbors who think he is peculiar. Outlandish as it may seem, this is a fantasy held by many people as they reach a certain *season* in life: They desire *change*.

Could this be you? Have you been pursuing a certain career for some time, only to find you are bored? Are you 30, 40, 50 or more years of age, and lately, there seems to be a growing dissatisfaction with what you are doing?

You discover that your heart really isn't in your work. You no longer look forward to going to work in the mornings or whenever. In fact, you dread it. At the office, you find yourself daydreaming about being somewhere else and doing something else. What's going on? A midlife crisis? Is it you and your attitude?

Perhaps God is stirring up a "holy discontent," as some call it, to cause you to move on to another place He has for you.

Some people seem to find a niche early in life and are happy ever after; others are discontented. It's a real problem for many people and needs to be recognized. More than that, it needs to be solved.

As Christians, we must first rely on an all-wise and all-loving Master who oversees every aspect of our lives. Therefore, we can view *all* circumstances as wonderful opportunities that our Father has given for our growth, direction, and blessing. If you find yourself dissatisfied with your work, consider *a change in your situation,* or *a change in how you view your situation.* We will consider both.

The possibility of a career change at any time in life is a very important decision and should not be treated lightly because of the investment in your present career: an investment of time, energy, and dedication, then a harvest of experience, seniority, pay, and prestige. It's possible, of course, that you have made the investment above but have not acquired the dividends that should have come to you, such as fair pay or promotion. That may be the root of your problem. Nevertheless, you are in a career crisis, and it needs to be faced prayerfully, wisely, and systematically.

The classic approach to problem solving involves several steps, which we will work through.

ANALYZING THE SITUATION

A big question is facing you: *Is God leading you to make a significant career change?*

The symptoms you are experiencing also present other possibilities. *Consider them carefully.*

Basically, you're in the right occupation, but your present job has lost its challenge or has become a dead end. Rather than a career change, a transfer within the same company or maybe to another company will give you the challenge and renewed interest you need.

You are in the right occupation, but your dissatisfaction is coming from a demoralizing climate, a company philosophy, or management style that has a negative impact on you. What you really need is a new employer. It just may be that the environment is at fault, and a total career change is not in order.

You don't feel appreciated. No one ever compliments your efforts or recognizes you. This does not necessarily mean you are seeking self-glory. Even the most sacrificial people need approval or at least the knowledge that their superiors are pleased with them. If you know that you're effective in what you're doing, however, don't let ego needs destroy your efforts. Some employers are dreadfully negligent in this area of human relations, too often caught up in their own affairs. A Christian's "meat" is to do the Father's will and, if necessary, you can survive without the accolades of men.

You have succumbed to bad working habits—maybe even laziness—and feel your present responsibilities are a threat to your preferred work style. You want to escape to greater ease and comfort. Be careful, for this can be an unconscious desire. You'd better get your battery recharged and be thankful for what you have.

Your mother-in-law is giving you a hard time, and you transfer your bad feelings to your job. No offense to mothers-in-law, but personal problems can spill over and affect entire lives, even on the job. As you analyze your situation, evaluate your whole life to give yourself the widest possible perspective.

For whatever reason, you have developed a negative attitude. You may have caught it from someone else, and you are probably infecting others. A negative attitude produces negative words that produce negative actions (toward others) and reactions (toward us). Before you know it, you are a sourpuss, and everything about your job is wrong, so wrong that you really do need a change. Unfortunately, unless you deal with the problem now, it will follow you.

Let's assume that none of the above applies to you, which puts you back to the original question.

Is God leading you to make a significant career change?
God sometimes calls people to make radical leaps of faith into the unknown, and He may be calling you. Do not do anything rash that would endanger your present income until you have assurance that God is leading. You may have family responsibilities; you may be locked into a budget bracket based on a child's educational need or a family member's health. Remember, when you take that leap of faith, you are taking them with you.

You may be willing to sacrifice by assuming an austere lifestyle, at least until "things work out" and you reestablish yourself. But does your family feel the same way? God is interested in their needs and emotional well-being, as well as yours. And they look to you as God's provision for them. Strongly consider a loss or a significant reduction of income for a period of time as you make transition from one career to another.

Second, consider the amount of experience, credibility, and expertise you have in your present career, purchased with the price of sacrifice, sweat, and tears. It should not be cast aside whimsically, but only after prayerful deliberation.

Third, ask yourself whether your present career is making use of the basic gifts and talents that God has given you. Or is your career just the result of opportunistic job openings in the past. Did you get where you are by occupational osmosis? *Are you optimizing your gifts in your present career?* This is a key question. A yes answer will cast doubt on the wisdom of a career change; a no answer will tend to confirm it.

A theory of some Christian vocational counselors is that most people are in opportunistic jobs for which they are ill equipped and not called, thereby causing a lack of job satisfaction, fulfillment, and productivity. I believe this is true to some extent but not to the degree that some claim. In God's sovereignty, I believe He can also bring good out of what appear to us as only opportunistic jobs. He provided the opportunities!

CONSIDERING AND SELECTING A SOLUTION

The foregoing appears slanted toward dissuading you from making a career change. The slant is on purpose, not to dissuade, but to insure that you cautiously consider all these factors before you make up your mind. If you have gone through the above steps and after prayerful consideration, you are convinced that a career change is what God wants for you, the questions are now simple: What? Where? And in applying your solution, when?

Parts I, II and III to this book are as applicable to you as they are to someone who has never held a job before. You are on the verge of blazing a new trail for yourself in parts unknown. You need to reevaluate God's calling and will for your life. You need to take a deliberate, serious, and systematic look at yourself, at who and what you are. You need the self-assessment exercise in part II. And at this critical stage in your life, I would strongly recommend professional vocational guidance and testing. It can help you find the *real you* who wants to come out and be expressed. A small investment in professional advice is well worth the expense. These steps will help you establish *what* you are going to do.

Now, you have to discover the *where*. Your task is no different than anyone else's in seeking employment. You need to analyze the job market, decide whether to use a placement organization, and develop a strategy for presenting yourself to a potential employer.

Maybe you plan on being self-employed. Then, you are not seeking a job; you are creating one. This can be an exciting challenge for anyone. America was made by entrepreneurial and industrious people who struck out on their own. Such an adventure has both risks and rewards. Books are written about this, and you would be wise to read one or two. Success will largely depend on good planning, adequate capitalization and controls, plus hard work. For the first year at least, it is best to overestimate your expenses and underestimate your income because it often works out that way. Many new businesses go under because of unrealistic cash flow projections; others who estimate conservatively often find themselves pleasantly surprised.

If you seek employment, decide in what kind of an organization you want to work and where you want to live, if that is important. This is a new life you are making for yourself, so make it as pleasant as possible.

If you have always had a desire to live in a certain place—a state, city, or section of the country—then consider it. Why not? There may be constraints against it, confining you to a certain location; otherwise, broaden your horizons. After all, the world is your Father's orchard, and you are His child.

Sometimes, you just get into a rut and need a change to make the world look a little brighter. Everyone seems to need some kind of change now and then. It is very interesting that the Bible compares us to sheep, and sheep are prone to follow the same path over and over. They graze the same fields, even after the food is inadequate and pollute the same ground until their well-being is threatened. The wise and loving shepherd always leads his sheep into new and better paths and pastures. It is the same with our Good Shepherd. He knows when we have overgrazed our location and are in need of a new life.

The fringe benefits for being a believer are simply incredible. The Lord is our Shepherd . . . He restores our soul . . . He leads us . . . His rod and staff comfort us . . . goodness and mercy follow us all the days of our lives. These promises are for you occupationally, as well as for all areas of your lives.

As you decide on the *what* and the *where,* do it prayerfully. Although I have discussed the systematic approach, do not be so systematic as to restrict the Spirit's leading. In the final analysis, life is subjective, not objective. Give proper emphasis to the desires of your heart and assume that your intent is to please God and be in His will.

MAKING THE CHANGE

You have made your decision. You have decided on a new direction. You have picked a new career; you have done some vocational planning; and you are itching to get on with it. It's time to move ahead. Your heart is already separated from what you are doing, and you want to move as soon as possible. There is one final word of advice about the *when.*

Timing is important. Make events work in your favor, not against you. Manage events and do not let them manage you by acting impulsively or rashly. Stay with your present employment until you have done all your planning. If at all possible, obtain any necessary retraining or get additional education while still employed and drawing an income.

If you work it properly, you can transition from one career right into the other. Patience will always pay off. If you feel that you "just can't take it anymore," it's not true. You can take it until the time is optimal for you. Make a rational, Spirit-led decision.

Many factors affect your timing, such as retraining needs, job search, present employer's vesting or benefit accrual plan, children's school year, spouse's employment, seasonal housing market considerations, anticipated extraordinary expenses, and current indebtedness. There are others. The point is that all possible factors must be considered when selecting an optimal time to make your change.

One last word. Conditions will never be *perfect*. Discernment is important here. Sometimes, all you can do is optimize the conditions as best you can, then take a bold step and trust God to see you through. He will.

Proceed with boldness and confidence. Never look back to question your decision; look forward to new and greater things in the Lord. You have the promise of your loving Creator who says:

'Do not fear, for I am with you;
Do not anxiously look about you, for I am your God.
I will strengthen you, surely I will help you,
Surely I will uphold you with My righteous right hand' (Isa. 41:10).

RECOMMENDED READING

Starting Over, Allen A. Swenson, A and W Publishers, Inc., New York, NY, 1978.

PART V

Now That You Are Hired

Chapter 14

HOW TO MAKE YOUR NEW EMPLOYER GLAD THAT HE HIRED YOU

Congratulations on your new job! It may be your first or your twenty-first. Nevertheless, it is a new start for you. You are about to enter a whole new world that will occupy most of your waking hours and give you a whole new circle of relationships.

In your new position, you want to do well, not only for the sake of doing your best but also to learn and grow, as well as make a favorable impression on your company, especially when future promotions and pay raises are considered. Also, if you leave this company, it's essential that they give you a good reference. Good or bad, your record always follows you.

This is the time to consider what will help you begin work and do well in your new job.

YOUR RELATIONSHIPS

Your relationships take top priority with God. And practically, how you relate to others is of utmost importance to your success. Studies have shown that the largest single reason people get fired from their jobs is not incompetence but failure to get along with others.

You may think this is not important if you are going to work for True Paradise Christian Ministries, since everyone there must be so spiritual and loving. Invariably, however, there will be a *porcupine* personality around, which will rattle your cage. I call them "grace testers" because they test the level of the grace and love in your life.

If you are going to work in a Christian organization, plan to be a positive and edifying influence. One of the best ways you can do this is to watch your tongue. Some of the most spiritual people I know still have trouble with that little, fiery member that the Bible talks about in James 3. Remember, God did not lead you there to be a critic.

In any organization, there are two things that can tempt you to complain and criticize.

The first is something going contrary to your opinion. In some way, however slight, your ego is offended. Then what happens? Something inside called Self (which you thought was crucified) experiences a temporary resurrection. Self's weapon is only about three inches long but so powerful that the Bible compares it to a spark, which can set an entire forest ablaze. Of course, it's the tongue.

The result is often complaining and criticism of others, even to the point of slander. Sometimes this comes out harshly, or it can be cloaked in the most spiritual terms that others may think you are exceedingly wise and saintly for your insightful analysis as to what really should have been done!

The second situation is when we may not personally be affected by something, but someone else is. We catch it, however, because it is contagious.

It is strange yet true: both positive and negative attitudes are contagious. If a fellow employee is beefing about something, there is a tendency in everyone to be a good Joe and agree. But if you do, your own spirit is affected, and you are likely to spread the contagion by passing it along.

Conversely, a good positive word is also contagious. Did you know that little old you, whoever you are, can enter a group and set the tone and attitude of the whole gathering by an uplifting and positive word or a negative one? That's why Scripture says:

> Keep thy heart with all diligence: for out of it are the issues [forces] of life (Prov. 4:23 KJV, definition mine).

It's not easy to avoid saying the wrong things and to say the right things always. But by giving this subject attention in the workplace and elsewhere and with the Spirit's help, you can heed the words of this important Scripture.

> Let no unwholesome word proceed from your mouth, but only such a word as is good for edification according to the need of the moment, that it may give grace to those who hear (Eph. 4:29).

TEMPTATIONS

Those of you who may be working in non-Christian organizations face a special problem. You will often be faced with temptations to do things that grieve the Holy Spirit and hinder your spiritual walk. You will know too that refusing to do certain things will damage your relationship with your peers, even your boss.

Let me advise you from years of experience in secular work. If you maintain your position with love, wisdom, and tact, you probably will *not* offend them but will gain their admiration and respect. You can either come across to them as a self-righteous, finger-pointing fanatic and lose your effectiveness with them, or you can tactfully decline any questionable activities. Let them experience the life of Christ in you in everyday matters, and they will know why you are declining. They may thereby sense the "sweet fragrance of the Spirit" in your life and be attracted by it.

For example, I was the commander of an organization in the United States Air Force when I first committed my life fully to Christ. It was customary for the commander to give a Christmas party, and alcoholic beverages were expected. My wife and I made the decision to give the party without alcohol. There were complaints among some who had heard about our plans; one young officer and his wife were downright angry. We felt the pressure and were both very apprehensive as the day approached. Mary Ann and I prayed beforehand for the Lord to help make it a blessing. The party day dawned.

That evening everyone came, some begrudgingly. But there was a mysterious warmth present, which we had never before experienced at a party. Everyone sang carols about the Savior so heartily and with such feeling, I was dumbfounded. Most didn't even know Him. They all left the party feeling wonderful, and the next day, the couple who had been so angry at us called to say it was the best Christmas party they'd ever attended.

They had savored the sweet fragrance of the Savior. May those in darkness always experience that from our presence in their lives. What a privilege to be able to touch someone's life with, perhaps, an eternal result. Is there anything more important?

YOUR ATTITUDE

The attitude of a Christian in any organization should be that of a servant.

This goes against the world's teaching, which instructs us to gain mastery over others, even through deception and manipulation. If you don't believe this, check some of the latest books on how to get ahead and be successful.

Once upon a time, Someone was starting to put together a worldwide organization. It became obvious very early that His staff was already vying for positions of leadership.

This Leader was very wise. In fact, He was the wisest leader ever. He told them, in effect, "Listen fellows. That's the way the world does it. But that's not the way it works in this organization. Around here, if any of you want to be great, you must become a servant." In case that quotation seems familiar, it's Bramlett's paraphrase of Matthew 20:26–27.

The Lord did not say that it's wrong to be great. What He did say was that the route to *true* greatness is in becoming a servant. The Savior went on to tell us that if we humble ourselves, we will be exalted and vice versa. That's a pretty good promise, one worth believing.

How do you translate this into a hard-nosed job situation? Easy. Make up your mind that your purpose in being there is not just to claim a paycheck on Fridays but genuinely and faithfully to serve the needs of people who may be touched by your work. No matter what or where your work is, you cannot do a job unless it affects others. Whether or not you come in contact with people is irrelevant, what you do still directly affects either the public or those in another department.

Here's another attitude necessary for success: *You need to have a team attitude.* Every group of two or more engaged in a common purpose is a team—your family, your civic organization, your Sunday school, and your department. If one member acts without regard to the others, the team effort is damaged, and the team can even be destroyed.

An independent attitude is usually just another manifestation of that old nemesis Self and can be called what it is—*selfishness*. A team attitude, on the other hand, is a manifestation of *unselfishness*, with the common good as its goal.

Have you ever seen a basketball player with the ball near his goal *not* take a shot to pass off to a teammate who is in a better position to make the shot? That's team spirit and unselfishness. The first player stood to improve his statistics by taking and making the shot and drawing the cheers of the crowd, but points for the team were more important. That kind of basketball player is recognized as great by those who really know the sport, and he is in greater demand by the college and professional scouts.

Since you have these attitudes, your new boss is really starting to feel glad that he hired you. Nonetheless, you need to be concerned with only one other thing.

YOUR PERFORMANCE

Unfortunately, you can be the greatest man or woman in the world with a positive attitude and a servant's heart and still miss the mark.

I hate to mention performance here at the end of the chapter and spoil all the fun, but it's not without importance. Some folks place this too far down their list of priorities and opt for more fellowship and fun. They usually don't last very long.

The *bottom line* is that you were hired because there was an important function to be performed, so important that the company agreed that it was worth it to invest in you. That investment is not only your salary but also the many added costs, such as social security taxes, unemployment taxes, fringe benefits, and training. You not only owe it to the Lord to perform well, you also owe it to the company. In addition, you owe it to yourself, your self-esteem, and your future.

Here are some valuable tips on how to do this and to have your new boss say to himself, *Hey! This new person is super. What wisdom I displayed in hiring him!*

TRAINING

If your new job has a formal training program, enter it and learn as much and as fast as you can. If you are forced to learn on your own, find out what you need to study and start immediately. Read publications applicable to your job; ask appropriate questions; stick around after hours, studying, learning, asking, doing. Be obvious that your goal is excellence and that you want to know everything there is to know about your position and the jobs affecting yours.

I cannot emphasize too much—learn.

It will enhance your performance, your self-confidence, your standing in your company's eye, and your future.

NEVER SAY NEVER

Eagerly take on responsibility and more work. There is a limit to how much you can take, but until you establish yourself as a performer, do as much as you can. Never tell your boss you can't. Find a way; make a way; at least try. Let them know early that you have a *can do* attitude and that they can rely on you to get the job done. You will become invaluable and respected.

Never say or imply, "That's not in my job description." If you are worried about sticking to your job description, you are starting off on the wrong foot, so to speak. Most job descriptions are not very accurate. My advice is to do what's on the job description, not be bound by it. With your sterling performance and budding promise, they will soon be writing a new one for you, much more to your pleasure and suitable for your obvious talents.

OVERKILL

Do your job so well and so thoroughly that it will be much more than was really expected of you. Yes, it will take some extra time and effort but it will be worth it, especially on your first few assignments. Those initial assignments are critical in the impression you make and the pattern you set for yourself.

In the military, they have medals and citations for performance above and beyond the call of duty. Your company may not give you a medal for your work, but they may give you other more practical forms of recognition, perhaps a pay raise.

THE NEED FOR ENTHUSIASM

Here's a big warning, maybe one of the most important in this book:

Never think about your work as that yucky, old place you have to go between periods of time off. If you do, it will invariably show in your face, attitude, and performance.

Instead, *radiate enthusiasm*. Sometimes, you may have to force yourself to do it, but do it. Later, it will be natural and affect your performance significantly. You will do more and be happier doing it; so will everyone else.

Chapter 15

HOW TO ADJUST TO A CHRISTIAN WORKPLACE

Working in a full-time Christian vocation can be the most glorious and rewarding vocational experience of a lifetime; it can also be one of the most difficult experiences. Since becoming a committed Christian, I have suffered two major disappointments: I discovered that other Christians were not yet perfect; I discovered that I was not yet perfect either.

At first, I perceived in other Christians nothing but outward love, joy, peace, and holiness, so I decided that that was how it was for them all the time. All I had to do was "be one of them" and I would reach perfection on earth too. My problems would be over.

The problem was, I never reached perfection. And when I got to know those other *perfect* Christians, I learned that they hadn't reached it either.

In the meantime, we learned to tolerate one another. It dawned on me one time that if loving each other were an automatic result of being born again, then the Bible would not have to remind us to do so.

I say this to warn you that none of your fellow employees at True Paradise Christian Ministries, or wherever you are, is likely to be perfect. You will find yourself in a crucible with others, and sometimes rough edges will grate together. In my Christian work, I have yet to meet anyone who already has his glorified body. All are still in process.

But before you get disappointed, let me tell you the good news. There is a big and wonderful difference in a Christian vocational environment—the Spirit. People in God's work really experience the power of His Spirit. As the apostle Paul said:

> We have this treasure in earthen vessels, *to show that the transcendent power belongs to God and not to us* (2 Cor. 4:7 RSV, italics mine).

That's it! You are just the earthen vessels. All the fruit of your efforts is not really caused by you at all—it is His transcendent power operating through us.

This is that mystery of "Christ in you," which Paul talks about (Col. 1:27). It's an example of his profound proclamation, "It is no longer I who live, but Christ. . . . " (Gal. 2:20). So when great things happen through your work and ministry, who gets the glory? Not you, but He.

Another big difference in a Christian organization is that the Holy Spirit is at work in a special way in departmental matters and relationships. Though our lower nature may sometimes manifest itself, a spirit of reconciliation and forgiveness prevails. With co-workers praying for and with one another, friction is usually short-lived; wounds are quickly healed.

Sometimes, there are exceptions. Certain people may carry hurt or hard feelings. Rare incidents of this give you opportunities to demonstrate longsuffering, love, and grace in a way that only the Lord can do through you. You can "bear one another's burdens and thus fulfill the law of Christ" (Gal. 6:2).

HARD WORK

"Boy, I can't wait to go to work with True Paradise Christian Ministries, Inc. Good ol' Reverend Blessum is so sweet, kind, and spiritual. I'll bet it's a ball working for him. I'll bet he goes around blessing the employees all day.''

Do you think this way? If so, forget it. Reverend Blessum may be putting in sixteen-hour days of hard labor under the pressure of his ministry, running the organization, responding to the public, and trying to raise enough money to pay all the bills, including your salary.

Part of your job will be to help support him and bear his burden. You will be expected to produce, not only just to do your job but also to make improvements and be innovative. No matter what your job or where you are in the organization, you can expect difficult, demanding work. It probably won't be easy.

Did Jesus promise an easy time? No, but He did promise He would be with us. When you undertake the Lord's work, remember, He didn't promise you a rose garden.

Be prepared with the correct mental attitude when you start, and you will have the problem in hand.

SPIRITUAL WARFARE

This is the least desirable subject to discuss but a necessary one. I don't like to give the Devil any credit because he is already a defeated foe; nevertheless, a reality. You can remember and heed the Spirit's warning.

> For our struggle is not against flesh and blood, but against the rulers, against the powers, against the world forces of this darkness, against the spiritual forces of wickedness in the heavenly places (Eph. 6:12).

You know who the winner is; but meanwhile you are in a wrestling match. This is true in your personal life whether or not you are in a full-time Christian vocation, but it is especially true in the special work of the Lord.

If the organization is moving in the Spirit, you *will* be in spiritual warfare. You, your department, your family, and everyone may experience buffeting and attack, especially at your weak spots. Don't be surprised. Satan wants to discourage you and dull your effectiveness. True to his biblical description, he wants to "steal, kill, and destroy" the work of the Lord. The enemy may attack one person with discouragement; another with financial loss or gain; another with sickness; another with greed or lustful temptations.

More importantly, I want to remind you that the enemy's attacks can all be thwarted and defeated very simply. You really need not fear because God has given us the answer. Our solution is found in Ephesians 6.

> *Be strong* in the Lord and the strength of his might . . . (and) *put on* the whole armor of God, that you may be able to *stand* against the wiles of the devil (vv. 10–11 RSV, italics mine).

Therefore, you continually "put on" the Son by letting Him be Lord of your everyday situations, remembering that you are "in Him" and that He is with you.

I love the words of Martin Luther in his soul-stirring hymn "A Mighty Fortress is Our God."

> " . . . Our ancient foe doth seek to work us woe; his craft and power are great; and armed with cruel hate. . . . "

Despite this dire threat, the third verse rings with our sure victory.

> "We tremble not for him; His rage we can endure, For lo! his doom is sure; One little word shall fell him."

Chapter 16

HOW TO BE HAPPY AT WORK

Have you ever noticed a person who is obviously very happy with his work—the smile, the sense of peace? It just seems that some people find their perfect niche, and you cannot imagine anyone doing the job better.

Have you ever seen the opposite—a sourpuss who is obviously very unhappy with his work? You know something is wrong: Maybe he's just having a bad day; maybe he's in the wrong place, using the wrong skills. But more than likely, he just doesn't know how to be happy at work.

I can think of examples of both.

Tina knows how to be happy at work. She's a receptionist and switchboard operator for a large organization. Over the telephone or in person, she radiates joy. She has been offered other positions within the company, some of which would have paid more money and held more potential for growth. Yet, she has always turned them down, feeling that God had her exactly in the right place, where she could be a special blessing to people in the way she knew best.

I can understand that. It would not seem right for Tina not to be there. She fits. She touches hundreds of lives daily, each of which cannot help but feel a little better after her touch. She is what I call one of God's "sunbeams." Her light might shine somewhere else but be under a bushel.

I have known others who were dealing with the public

and had the opposite effect. Paulette seemed to irritate everyone. She dealt with the public all day, and just about everyone was given the feeling that they were imposing on her. Her attitude seemed to say, "Why are you bothering me? Don't you know I'm too busy to help you? Do it yourself." Although she didn't actually say it, that was her nonverbal message.

After a while, people would call her only as a last resort, then with much apprehension. Paulette was actually a very bright, sharp young lady, and I don't believe she meant to be that way. In other ways, she could be very thoughtful and loving. Of course, there is no excuse for rudeness. But with her, it seemed less a case of bad manners and more the wrong attitude about her job. The message she communicated to people was "I'm not really happy about my work. Why are you bothering me?"

What's the cause of happiness or unhappiness with work? First, you must be careful about saying it's always one thing or another; nevertheless, you can observe some important principles. If you apply them, no matter where you are—even in a job that's not right for you—you can be happy.

A NECESSARY TOIL

Aside from the fact that work is necessary to supply you food and shelter, it's also a means of fulfillment, of expressing yourself to other people. And though you do not always think of it this way, it's also a means of serving others. In some form or another, we all manufacture, sell, or administer products or services for other people. People other than Christians often find fulfillment in their work. How much more should God's people be in the niche for which they were created and be happy and fulfilled in it?

It is God's gift to man that everyone should . . . take pleasure in all his toil (Eccl. 3:13 RSV).

HOW TO TAKE PLEASURE IN YOUR TOIL

One of the best ways to enjoy your work is to be in the right job, using the gifts and talents God has given you. This should be your aim. But whether or not you are in a perfect job for you, there are ways in which you can look forward to getting up in the morning and going to work, feeling fulfilled about where you're spending your waking hours. Below are three ways that will really help you.

HAVE A HEALTHY ATTITUDE TOWARD WORK

As human beings, work is our lot. God has ordained it, and all His ways are perfect. He is Love and always looking out after your best interests. Accept work generally, not just as something necessary to buy groceries and pay rent but as a means to do that for which God created you.

RESOLVE TO GIVE IT YOUR BEST SHOT

Whatever your hand finds to do, do it with all your might (Eccl. 9:10 RSV).

Whatever you do, whether in word or deed, do all in the name of the Lord Jesus, giving thanks. . . . (Col. 3:17).

Did you understand these verses? Combining these means that wherever you are and whatever you are doing, you should do it with all your might in the name of the Lord, then give thanks. *This is a true prescription for happiness and success in the workplace.* It also means that, even though you may not be in God's best job for you now, whatever you are doing, you should do it with all your might in the name of the Lord.

RESOLVE TO BE A BLESSING TO OTHERS

Your job may seem isolated and remote. You may be like Joe Lugwrench on the assembly line, who does nothing but install bolt number 47 all day. But have you ever thought about how many people, or things, depend upon bolt number 47 functioning properly. At the very least, Joe's work has an effect on the installers of bolt number 46 behind him and number 48 ahead of him!

The point is you *affect* people. Chances are you affect them much more than you realize. Regardless of your actual job, your attitude and demeanor at work greatly affect those around you. It's a fact that *emotions and attitudes are contagious*. If you act positively, those around you will also tend to act positively; if you are negative, you will soon be surrounded by negative people.

Here is an awesome thought: If you don't like the attitudes of some of those around you, consider that they may be a mirror image of you—a reaction to your own attitudes. On the contrary, if you are blessed with a happy workplace and positive fellow workers, it may be that your light is shining more than you know.

To be happy and to enjoy your work, *make a decision and resolve to be a blessing to everyone you touch, directly and indirectly*. You will then be a true ambassador for Christ.

My prayer is that the Father will richly bless you vocationally, that you will be happy in your work and a source of happiness and blessing to those around you.

Appendixes

Appendix I

REAL-LIFE EMPLOYMENT SITUATIONS

CASE HISTORIES

Do you want to know how some people get into full-time Christian work? The examples below are from situations with which I am familiar and give testimony that there is a power beyond you and me in charge of all this. The Lord is truly the Personnel Director, and the rest of us in the personnel field just help Him out sometimes, if that's possible. Sometimes we even hinder Him, but He still does what He wants to do, as you will see.

These cases are included to help you understand that if God wants you in a particular organization or job, no person can stop you. If He doesn't, no person can help you.

CASE 1

Ella applied for a job one day after her college graduation. After reviewing her qualifications and all of our vacancies, I advised her there was nothing available at the time, but we would surely keep her in mind. I was impressed with her and had a feeling that she was supposed to have a job but I could see absolutely nothing for her. We terminated the interview and parted. As far as she was concerned, she had heard the final and authoritative word from the personnel director himself. I left for a meeting down the hall.

I returned from the meeting thirty minutes later, and guess what? Ella had been hired. How could that be if the director had said no? Well, there was a Higher Director who said yes. After I had left, Ella was talking to my secretary, and during the conversation, previously unknown information about a vacancy became available to my assistant. Ella got the job because God wanted her there. That first job was an entry clerical position, but Ella has since progressed to be the head of a major department and has been a continual blessing to everyone. And she was hired in spite of me.

CASE 2

Speaking of "in spite of me," this is a good example. One day a young man came to volunteer as a telephone counselor, not an employment situation. He seemed a little young, so I asked his age, to which he replied, "Seventeen." I explained that our policy had always required a counselor to be at least eighteen, largely because of the number of calls that require a degree of experience and maturity. I told him I appreciated his offer, but our rule prevented us from using him. I was about to learn a lesson about rules and grace.

I invited him to sit in the counseling center at a vacant position to observe what was going on, assuming it might be interesting to him. I took the phone off the hook, so it would not ring and would give a busy signal to the caller.

After he had been sitting there just a few moments, *the telephone rang.* Puzzled, our young friend picked up the handset and put it to his ear, not knowing what, if anything, to expect.

Believe it or not, the caller was another seventeen-year-old, and our young friend turned out to be the perfect person for the job.

Ever since then, I have had no trouble believing the

impossible or trusting in God's sovereign power. We have the privilege of being co-workers with Him, but it is comforting to know that if our frailty causes us to fail, He will still accomplish His purpose.

CASE 3

At one time, I had to travel to recruit representatives in certain major cities. Usually I knew no one in the cities I visited and relied solely on prayer and one or two referrals as initial contacts. On different occasions in two different cities I had made a contact or two, but absolutely nothing was happening. I had no prospects for the job, important work needed to be done, and my time was rapidly running out. As some say, I was between a rock and a hard place. Have you ever been there? It's no fun.

Actually in both situations, I was forced to my knees on the floor of my hotel room. I remember it vividly. And in both situations, precisely when I was on my knees praying, the telephone rang. Frankly, I was a little bothered that the telephone had interrupted me.

I know this will sound too good to be true, but in one case, the caller was the one chosen for the job; in the other, the caller quickly led me to the right person. The timing was simply incredible.

Would they have called if I had not prayed? I doubt it. I do know for certain that my respect for the power of prayer was dramatically increased, as well as my dependence on God to provide in times of need. From then on, I have been careful to take no chances. The kneeling position is a reliable place to get answers.

CASE 4

In Case 1, I gave you an example of a situation where I perceived no job availability for a person, but God had a different idea. The opposite has also happened to me.

Mike was one of the sharpest fellows I had ever met. He had excellent administrative skills, outstanding experience and education, and was very personable. He had it all. In fact, I couldn't think of a single negative.

Mike had been trying to be employed with the Christian ministry I represented for several years, but the door never opened. As personnel director, I tried my best to get him on staff, but my best was not enough. No one had any negatives about him. It just could not be made to happen because it was not the will of Him who closes doors no man can open.

CASE 5

My middle son was just finishing high school and looking for a job. He would be available in about two weeks. He did not have a trade but was adept at electronics from hobby work. Though not adept enough to be called a technician, he was prepared for a minimum-wage entry position somewhere.

As a personnel director, I was always a "straight arrow" in not allowing relations or acquaintances to affect my hiring decisions, a "company man" through and through. Therefore, I was really reluctant to help my son get a job where I worked. Frankly, I feared the accusation of nepotism or favoritism, even though I could have gotten away with it as others sometimes did. My pride too was probably a factor.

But God had other plans, my pride notwithstanding. Again, the timing was incredible. Just when Steve started looking for a job, the head of the engineering department expressed a desperate need for four young men who would be willing to work for minimum wage, preferably knowing a little about electronics. As only temporary positions with minimum-wage pay, they would be very difficult to fill. His immediate need became my immediate recruiting problem.

Where could I find four such people so quickly? I was trapped.

You've guessed the solution. Steve, out of necessity, was one of the four. It was our Father's plan to bless Steve and our family.

Steve's performance not only led to his acquiring a permanent job and increased responsibilities but also to his meeting a wonderful girl, Ruth, who became my daughter-in-law. I'm so glad that God is managing our lives, not me.

CASE 6

By now, you are probably wondering what I was doing there as personnel director. Sometimes I wondered that too. But occasionally I saw evidence that maybe I was in the right place.

In reviewing the mail one day, I noticed the resume of a pilot. He had felt led to make his services available, assuming that we had a corporate airplane. We didn't, so I sent him a courteous reply to that effect but saved his resume for future reference in case we needed him.

Just a short time later, the president of the company asked me to look for a pilot because the organization had just purchased an airplane. The pilot applicant was soon hired and at the controls. Once again, the timing was amazing. Of course, you know Who is really at the controls.

CASE 7

Andy had recently had an experience with the Lord. In a radical act of commitment, he decided to forsake his high-salaried, executive position and offer his services to the Lord's work by sending us a resume. He did not realize, however, that our large volume of mail often caused a two-week, maybe longer, delay in responses. Even then, there were internal and built-in delays that were unavoidable.

A lot of time had elapsed, and he had not heard anything. His boss knew that he might lose Andy soon because of his commitment and application. But Andy could not keep his boss dangling any longer. He had to make a decision and not having heard from us, assumed that it was not the Lord's will. He was within two or three minutes of walking into his boss's office and reaffirming his commitment to the company.

Just before he walked out of his office, the telephone rang. Guess who was on the other end of the line? Yes, yours truly calling to express our interest in him and wanting to set up a serious interview, just in the nick of time. A few more seconds, and it would have been too late.

How did I know to call at that very moment instead of, say, the next day? I didn't know. That's what is amazing about being led of the Spirit. It's natural. You don't have to strain to be spiritual; He works through you just the way you are.

At that time, we did not know, but God knew, that we would soon be losing a key manager and without Andy, the organization would have had a serious problem. My awareness of God's omniscience and sovereignty is increased whenever I witness it this way.

Can you doubt that He will take care of your life, with no less efficiency and adequate timing? Trust Him.

CASE 8

Linda had been a secretary for several years and had just moved to the city from a small town. She and her husband rented an apartment near one of our office complexes in the suburbs. She decided she wanted a job in a Christian company, if possible, but didn't know the city or where there might be such a thing. She had never even heard of our ministry.

She decided to look in the Yellow Pages for a Christian

organization and saw our name listed. Though she didn't know anything about us, we immediately appealed to her because our office was directly across the street from her apartment. Of course, she didn't know that our personnel office had a desperate need for a secretary.

Linda walked in, applied for the job, was interviewed, checked out, and within hours was hired. In addition, she had a need, and one of our volunteer prayer counselors prayed for her in my office. She was instantly and dramatically touched by the Lord with an answered prayer. Linda was truly called for that job, and she became one of the most efficient secretaries I have ever known.

CASE 9

This is about me, but don't stop reading. You will enjoy this. Once I reached a place in my own search for God's vocational direction where I had to step out in faith, so the Holy Spirit, the rudder of my life, could do some steering. With all the discernment I could muster, I picked out what I thought was the will of the Lord. Then with all the courage I could muster, I sent my resume to the ministry I had selected.

Days, weeks went by. No response. My personal situation was dictating that something happen soon, and I was becoming a little frantic. Had I missed the Lord's guidance? Had I really blown it?

My concern reached a climax one morning. I awakened very early. I went to my usual morning prayer location and decided I was really going to get serious with the Lord. I needed an answer desperately. I prayed fervently for about an hour, pounding heaven's gates, pleading for a break-through. I finally sensed my prayer had been heard. I said my amen, got up, and went about the rest of my morning routine.

I happened to remain home that day. About five hours

after my prayer ended, the telephone rang. It was a dear elderly lady from across town, whom I had met only one time. Constance was one of those rare people who was called into a deep intercessory prayer ministry. For some reason (obviously the Spirit's promptings), she had felt she should pray for me ever since we met. But she did not know about my vocational desires or that I had sent a resume to a certain ministry.

Constance immediately began to reveal a most intriguing story. The preceding day, she had been reading her Bible when suddenly she experienced the sense of the Lord's presence in her room. She did not see anything but heard what she described as an audible voice saying, "Jim's going to (the name of the ministry where I had applied)."

For some reason, she chose not to call that day but the next day to tell me. Frankly, I didn't know what to make of it. I believed in such things, but it was a heavy message. Could it really have been the Lord? And a voice? We chatted a moment; I thanked her, and she hung up.

Would you believe that thirty minutes later the postman brought me a letter from the president of the ministry where I applied, asking me to come over to talk about a job? I noticed the postmark was the same day Constance had received the message.

Needless to say, a job quickly evolved, and I was where God intended. I sometimes hesitate to tell that story because I sense some people's question, "Why doesn't He give me such strong confirmation?" I can't say why it happens. I suspect in my case it may have had something to do with the weakness of my faith and the testings to come. This strong confirmation helped see me through them.

If you have prayed and asked Him to take over your life, you may rest in the confidence that He has everything under control and on schedule. You are His child; you have only to watch as He unveils His steps before you. What an exciting life you have ahead!

Appendix II
DESCRIPTION AND QUALIFICATIONS NEEDED FOR SELECTED OCCUPATIONS

This appendix gives vital information about selected occupations, including

a description of the work,

training and other qualifications needed,

typical earnings (otherwise found in appendix III),

sources of additional information.

There are actually many thousands of different types of occupations, depending on how they are classified. The purpose of this appendix is to give you some representative information on different occupations, covering a wide range of categories. This selection may not include the exact occupation you are considering, but you may find one that is close, giving you an approximate picture of your specific interest. The source of most of this information is the *Occupational Outlook Handbook*, 1986–87 Edition, published by the U.S. Department of Labor, Bureau of Labor Statistics. In selecting the following occupations, possible applicability to Christian organizations was a factor.

Many of the potential salaries for these positions are listed in appendix III.

INDEX OF OCCUPATIONS

ACCOUNTANTS AND AUDITORS

NATURE OF THE WORK

Managers must have up-to-date financial information to make important decisions. Accountants and auditors prepare and analyze financial reports that furnish this kind of information. Three major fields are public, management, and government accounting. Public accountants have their own businesses or work for accounting firms. Management accountants handle the financial records of their company. Government accountants and auditors examine the records of government agencies and audit private businesses and individuals whose dealings are subject to government regulations. Most work in offices and have structured work hours, although in some cases extra-long hours are needed, such as with tax accountants during income-tax season.

TRAINING AND OTHER QUALIFICATIONS NEEDED

Training is available at colleges, universities, accounting and business schools, and correspondence schools. Most firms require at least a bachelor's degree in accounting or a related field. Many require a master's degree, and firms are increasingly requiring a knowledge of computer applications in accounting and auditing. Previous experience in accounting or auditing can help an applicant. Many colleges offer students an opportunity to gain experience through summer or part-time internship programs, conducted by public accounting or business firms.

SOURCES OF ADDITIONAL INFORMATION

American Institute of Certified Public Accountants, 1211 Avenue of the Americas, New York, NY 10036.

National Association of Accountants, 919 Third Avenue, New York, NY 10022.

Institute of Internal Auditors, 249 Maitland Avenue, Altamonte Springs, FL 32701.

For information on educational institutions offering a specialization in accounting, contact the American Assembly of Collegiate Schools of Business, 11500 Olive Boulevard, Suite 142, St. Louis, MO 63141.

ACCOUNTING CLERKS AND BOOKKEEPERS

NATURE OF THE WORK

Every business needs systematic and up-to-date records of accounts and business transactions. Bookkeepers and accounting clerks maintain these records in journals, ledgers, or other accounting forms. They also prepare periodic financial statements, showing all money received and paid out. Duties vary with the size and type of business. Most use calculating machines; many use check-writing and bookkeeping machines. In a small firm, one general bookkeeper may handle all the bookkeeping; in large firms, the work may be very specialized with an accounting clerk, for example, just handling accounts receivable (money owed to the company), or accounts payable (money owed by the company), payroll, or other functions. These would work under the direction of a head bookkeeper or accountant. Working conditions are typical for an office. Workers must sit for long hours, working with numerical information.

TRAINING AND OTHER QUALIFICATIONS NEEDED

High school graduates who have taken business arithmetic, bookkeeping, and principles of accounting meet the minimum requirements for most bookkeeping jobs. Many employers prefer those who have completed courses at business schools or community colleges. Many such programs are available in most cities. The ability to use bookkeeping machines and computers is also an asset. Bookkeepers and accounting clerks need to be good using numbers and doing detailed work for long periods of time. Small mistakes can be very serious, so carefulness and accuracy are very important.

SOURCES OF ADDITIONAL INFORMATION

For schools in your area, check your local Yellow Pages.
Many state employment offices can provide information on job opportunities in your area.

ACTORS AND ACTRESSES

NATURE OF THE WORK

Actors and actresses entertain and communicate with people through their interpretation of dramatic roles. They rely on facial and verbal expression as well as body motions for their creative effort. Acting requires persistence, practice, and hard work, in addition to special talent. Only a few become stars in their profession; more become well known in lesser and supporting roles; still more struggle for a toehold in their profession, with pick-up parts wherever they can. Employment for actors is characteristically unsteady, so many take temporary jobs, often as waiters and waitresses, while waiting on their next part. Beginning actors usually start with bit parts, where they may speak only a few lines. If successful, they progress to larger roles. Some actors move into acting-related jobs, such as drama coaches or directors, or possibly teaching.

TRAINING AND OTHER
QUALIFICATIONS NEEDED

Aspiring actors should take part in high school and college plays as much as possible, in local little theater, or in other drama activities. Some people enter the field with no formal training, but some formal training or acting experience is usually considered necessary. Training in the dramatic arts can be obtained at specialized schools in New York and Los Angeles or in about 620 colleges and universities in the United States.

EARNINGS

Acting jobs surveyed in off-Broadway productions earned as low as $200 per week, whereas Broadway productions paid a minimum of about $700 per week. Motion picture and television actors and actresses earned a minimum daily rate of $361, or $1,256 for a five-day week. But the Actors Equity Association, which represents about 30,000 actors, reported that about 20,000 of their members had no earnings in the year surveyed, and 4,700 of them made less than $2,500. Only 650 earned more than $35,000.

SOURCES OF ADDITIONAL INFORMATION

American Theater Association, 1000 Vermont Avenue NW, Washington, DC 20005.

Theater Communications Group, Inc., 355 Lexington Avenue, New York, NY 10017.

AIR-CONDITIONING, REFRIGERATION, AND HEATING MECHANICS

NATURE OF THE WORK

Almost all homes and buildings have some sort of climate control to allow heat in the winter and cooling in the summer or both. Installing and maintaining these systems is a highly technical specialty. Some mechanics specialize in one of the functions, such as heating or air conditioning; others are competent in all areas. These systems require more than just a single machine and may involve fans, compressors, condensers, evaporators, control devices, ducting, and pipes. Many companies with large buildings hire their own technicians to take care of their systems; others may contract the work to an outside firm. The work can be strenuous and may involve outside exposure in both hot and cold weather. Mechanics sometimes must work in awkward and cramped positions. They are exposed to occasional hazards, such as high voltage and burns.

TRAINING AND OTHER QUALIFICATIONS NEEDED

Most mechanics start as helpers and acquire their skills after several years of experience in assisting and observing. Formal training is available in many high schools and, of course, vocational schools in most areas. Training is not always required to get a job but it helps. A mechanical aptitude is a necessity.

EARNINGS

The average weekly salary for those surveyed and not self-employed was $370.

SOURCES OF ADDITIONAL INFORMATION

Air-Conditioning and Refrigeration Institute, 1815 N. Ft. Myer Drive, Arlington, VA 22209.

For additional information, contact local contractors or the state employment office.

ATTORNEYS

NATURE OF THE WORK

Attorneys, or lawyers, act as both advocates and advisors. As advocates, they represent opposing parties in criminal and civil trials by presenting arguments that support their side in a court of law. As advisors, lawyers counsel their clients as to their legal rights and obligations and suggest particular courses of action in business or personal matters. In common with all is the interpretation of the law and its application in a specific situation, often requiring much research. Many practice independently in their own business; many others are employed by the government or by private companies. There is much specialization, such as in communications law, tax law, international law, etc. Some use their law background in fields such as journalism, management consulting, lobbying, and political office. Most of the work is in offices and courtrooms with frequent travel to attend meetings, gather evidence, and appear before courts and other bodies.

TRAINING AND OTHER QUALIFICATIONS NEEDED

This is a highly regulated occupation with its practice needing state approval, usually by passing its bar. Applicants must take a written examination to pass the bar, although some states drop this requirement for graduates of their own law schools. In most states, a bar applicant must have had three years of college and be a graduate from a law school approved by the American Bar Association or appropriate state authorities.

SOURCES OF ADDITIONAL INFORMATION

Information Services, American Bar Association, 1155 East 60th Street, Chicago, IL 60637.

National Association for Law Placement, Boston University School of Law, 207 Bay State Road, Boston, MA 02215.

BROADCAST TECHNICIANS

NATURE OF THE WORK

Broadcast technicians operate and maintain the electronic equipment used to record and transmit radio and television programs. They work with microphones, sound and videotape recorders, light and sound effects, television cameras, transmitters, and other equipment. In small stations, they perform a variety of duties; one person may perform most or all the technical duties. In large facilities, tasks are more specialized; there are transmitter operators, maintenance technicians, audio-control engineers, video-control engineers, lighting technicians, recording technicians. The terms "operator," "engineer," and "technician" are often used interchangeably; although within a particular company, they may have very distinct definitions pertaining to responsibility. Most work locations are indoors and in very pleasant surroundings. Work, though, sometimes involves long hours and the pressures of broadcast deadlines.

TRAINING AND OTHER QUALIFICATIONS NEEDED

Some of these positions require a license or permit from the Federal Communications Commission, and some with a written examination required. Many schools are available that help train people for these examinations. High school students who hope to pursue this occupation would be helped if they took as many mathematics courses as possible as well as physics and electronics, if available. Technical school, community college, and regular college training is an advantage. The more you can learn, the better you will be.

EARNINGS

Average earnings for technicians surveyed at radio stations were $15,600; at television stations, about $18,200. Earnings are higher at the larger stations in the larger cities, up to twice as much as for the smaller stations in smaller cities.

SOURCES OF ADDITIONAL INFORMATION

For information about permits and licenses, contact the Federal Communications Commission, 1919 M Street NW, Washington, DC 20554.

For information on careers, contact the National Association of Broadcasters, 1771 N Street NW, Washington, DC 20036.

For a list of schools that offer programs or courses in broadcasting, contact the Broadcast Education Association, National Association of Broadcasters, 1771 N Street NW, Washington, DC 20036.

COLLEGE CAREER-PLANNING AND PLACEMENT COUNSELORS

NATURE OF THE WORK

Career-planning and placement counselors help bridge the gap between education and work by assisting students and alumni in all phases of career planning and job search. They encourage students to examine their interests, abilities, values, and goals and assist them in exploring career alternatives. They help arrange internships, field placements, or part-time or summer employment. They must keep abreast of labor-market information, including salaries, training requirements, and job prospects. They help students find jobs by arranging interviews and campus visits by potential employers. They also may advise school administrators about curriculum and course content.

TRAINING AND OTHER QUALIFICATIONS NEEDED

There is no educational program that specifically prepares people for college career-planning and placement work. Applicants are usually sought with a master's degree in counseling, in college-student personnel work, or in behavioral science. Some people enter the field after gaining broad experience in business, government, or education.

EARNINGS

According to a survey, the average salary of school counselors was about $27,600; salaries vary with the size, level, and locality of the school.

SOURCE OF ADDITIONAL INFORMATION

The College Placement Council, Inc., P.O. Box 2263, Bethlehem, PA 18001.

COLLEGE AND UNIVERSITY FACULTY

NATURE OF THE WORK

Faculty members provide instruction in particular fields of study to meet the needs of the students. Many conduct several courses within the same field. Some specialize in undergraduate studies; some in graduate studies; some in both. They use various methods to present their information. Some lecture to both small and extremely large classes; some work primarily in laboratories; some may use closed-circuit television, computers, and other aids. They must keep up with developments in their field by reading current literature, attending professional activities, and conducting research. Publishing books and articles is also considered very important in the profession. Faculty members work with student organizations, school administration, and the community too. While they may work long hours, they usually have flexible schedules and are not continuously in a particular office or location.

TRAINING AND OTHER QUALIFICATIONS NEEDED

A master's degree is a minimum requirement and is satisfactory in some colleges in some fields; competition is so keen for academic positions, however, that a doctoral degree is often necessary for consideration. Doctoral programs usually require three to five years of study beyond a bachelor's degree.

EARNINGS

Earnings vary greatly depending on faculty rank and the type of institution. A survey showed salaries for full-time faculty members with nine-month contracts to average from $19,200 for instructors to $39,900 for full professors, with an average of $31,000.

SOURCE OF ADDITIONAL INFORMATION

American Association of University Professors, One Dupont Circle NW, Suite 500, Washington, DC 20036.

COMMERCIAL AND GRAPHIC ARTISTS AND DESIGNERS

NATURE OF THE WORK

Some professional artists are painters who produce works of art intended to be displayed in homes and galleries. Most, however, are commercial and graphic artists and designers who illustrate and design the flood of magazine, newspaper, and television advertisements, as well as catalogs, brochures, instruction manuals, technical literature, book and record jackets, textiles, and many other items requiring visual appeal. Illustrators paint or draw pictures. Among them are fashion illustrators, medical illustrators, cartoonists, and animators. Many designers merely create and supervise, deciding such things as art, photography, style, and layout. Designers include package designers, book designers, textile designers, and graphic designers. Many in these fields have full-time salaried jobs, though, many are freelance. Although the latter offers a more flexible schedule, it can be as much or more demanding. Both are faced with frequent rush jobs and tight deadlines.

TRAINING AND OTHER QUALIFICATIONS NEEDED

Formal education is not a primary criterion in this field; demonstrated ability is. A potential employer will want to see an applicant's portfolio, that is, samples of your best work. Evidence of talent and flair in these portfolios is the most important factor influencing a hiring decision. While a good portfolio is all that is needed, some believe such a portfolio can only be put together after necessary training and education. Art training can be accomplished in a specialized technical school or in two- and four-year colleges.

EARNINGS

Entry-level paste-up or layout jobs may make as low as minimum wage; experienced art directors may make as much as $30,000 to $40,000. Some starting freelancers may charge less than minimum wage for their work; others make a comfortable living after gaining experience and a reputation. Federal government workers in art-related jobs averaged $22,338.

SOURCES OF ADDITIONAL INFORMATION

The Graphic Artists Guild, 30 East 20th Street, Room 405, New York, NY 10003.

The National Art Education Association, 1916 Association Dr., Reston, VA 22091.

COMPUTER-OPERATING PERSONNEL

NATURE OF THE WORK

Computer-operating personnel perform various operating duties with computers, consisting of entering data and instructions, operating the computer, and retrieving the results. Data and instructions to be put into the computer are called input and results from the computer are called output. Information input is handled by keypunch operators who operate a machine similar to a typewriter that punches holes in cards that are later read by the computer. This may be done by data-entry or data-typist personnel directly into the computer electronically through a special keyboard. Once the information is entered, console operators then manipulate the computer controls to make it do whatever function is required. The output sometimes is already in the necessary form to be used, although in some cases other operators perform this function. Finally, tape librarians classify and catalog all material, programs, listings, and test data. Work is usually in a physically comfortable environment, although some equipment may be noisy. Also, some companies run odd-hour shifts because of workload and to maximize utilization of the equipment.

TRAINING AND OTHER QUALIFICATIONS NEEDED

A college education is not required for this field, but some training is necessary to enter unless an employer will be willing to train you. Sometimes, an employer will take someone who can type and train them in data entry, a closely related function. or a bookkeeping machine operator may be transferred to operate the computer after some on-the-job training. In most cases, however, training should first be obtained from one of the many sources available, such as high school, a private computer school, a community college, or a vocational school.

SOURCE OF ADDITIONAL INFORMATION

American Federation of Information Processing Societies, 1815 North Lynn Street, Arlington, VA 22209.

COMPUTER PROGRAMMERS

NATURE OF THE WORK

Because computers cannot think for themselves, computer programmers must write detailed instructions called programs that list in a logical order the steps the machine must follow to organize data, solve a problem, or do some other task. Programmers usually work from descriptions prepared by systems analysts who have carefully studied the task that the computer system is going to perform. In some companies, particularly smaller ones, there may be no systems analyst and both jobs are done by a programmer-analyst. Programmer work varies with the type of task, whether it is scientific or business related, for example. The programmer codes instructions into the computer, then tests what he has done, and finally prepares instruction sheets for the computer operator who will run the program and operate the computer. Working conditions are usually pleasant. Hours may be regular or, in some cases, could be very demanding, requiring much overtime.

TRAINING AND OTHER QUALIFICATIONS NEEDED

Because employers' needs vary, there are no universal training requirements. Most programmers are college graduates; others have only taken special courses to supplement their experience in other areas, such as accounting and inventory control. Computer programming is taught in vocational schools, community colleges, and other public and private schools, including high schools and home-study courses. Employers look for people who can think logically and are capable of exacting work. The job calls for patience, persistence, and the ability to work with extreme accuracy under pressure. Ingenuity and imagination are important to problem solving.

SOURCES OF ADDITIONAL INFORMATION

American Federation of Information Processing Societies, 1815 North Lynn Street, Arlington, VA 22209.

The Institute for Certification of Computer Professionals, 35 East Wacker Drive, Suite 2828, Chicago, IL 60601.

CONSTRUCTION OCCUPATIONS

NATURE OF THE WORK

Construction craft workers represent the largest group of skilled workers in the nation's labor force. They represent good opportunities for young people who do not want to go to college but want to learn a trade. Once the trade is learned, jobs are available throughout the country. In addition, it is easy to form your own business as an independent contractor in these crafts.

Workers in these fields build, repair, and modernize buildings of all types. Construction work may be divided into three categories: structural, finishing, and mechanical. Structural includes such specialties as bricklaying and carpentry; finishing includes painting and plastering. All of these jobs require physical exertion and good health and strength. The work is often outdoors and sometimes hazardous.

TRAINING AND OTHER QUALIFICATIONS NEEDED

Many acquire these skills as a laborer or helper. Many also learn via a formal apprenticeship program, which is probably the best way because of the structured training program that includes both on-the-job and classroom training. Obviously, those entering these fields should enjoy and be adept at working with their hands.

EARNINGS

The following represents average weekly rates for selected construction occupations:

Electrician	$440
Pipefitter	405
Bricklayer	380
Carpenter	325
Painter	310

SOURCES OF ADDITIONAL INFORMATION

AFL-CIO, Building and Construction Trades Department, 815 16th Street NW, Washington, DC 20006.

Associated General Contractors of America, Inc., 1957 E Street NW, Washington, DC 20006.

National Association of Homebuilders, 15th and M Streets NW, Washington, DC 20005.

Contact the local state employment office, state apprenticeship agency, or office of the Department of Labor.

ENGINEERS

NATURE OF THE WORK

Engineers apply the theories and principles of science and mathematics to practical, technical problems. Often their work is the link between a scientific discovery and its application. They design machinery, equipment, systems, and processes for efficient and economical performance. Many engineers work in testing, production, operations, or maintenance. They can work in administration, management, or technically oriented sales. Engineers specialize in most scientific areas, such as aerospace, agriculture, chemical, electrical, civil, industrial, mechanical, metallurgical, and petroleum. Though some travel or work outdoors, most work inside at a desk the majority of the time. Work time will vary because some will need to devote much overtime on priority projects with no overtime pay.

TRAINING AND OTHER QUALIFICATIONS NEEDED

A bachelor's degree in engineering is usually acceptable for beginning positions, and in some cases, a degree in a natural science or mathematics is also acceptable. Experienced technicians with some engineering education are often able to advance into engineering positions. Some two-year programs and an associate degree in engineering technology may give adequate preparation for practical design and production work in some companies.

SOURCES OF ADDITIONAL INFORMATION

Engineering Manpower Commission of American Association of Engineering Societies, 345 East 47th Street, New York, NY 10017.

National Society of Professional Engineers, 2029 K Street NW, Washington, DC 20006.

LEGAL ASSISTANTS

NATURE OF THE WORK

Legal assistants, sometimes called paralegals or legal technicians, normally work directly under the supervision of a lawyer. The lawyer always takes final responsibility for the legal assistant's work; a legal assistant, however, is allowed to perform all the functions of a lawyer other than accepting clients, setting legal fees, giving legal advice, or presenting a case. The law is presently being tested in at least one state where a paralegal has been operating independently for years, saving people vast sums of money on legal fees and claiming to give service just as good as a lawyer. If the courts continue to allow this, the practice will undoubtedly spread and change the complexion of the entire legal industry and give new opportunities for the paralegal profession. The actual duties of most legal assistants vary greatly, depending whether it is a private practice, corporate, or governmental legal work.

TRAINING AND OTHER QUALIFICATIONS NEEDED

Some employers just require a high school diploma and train their legal assistants on the job; others train experienced legal personnel, such as legal secretaries, for the job. Increasingly, employers are requiring formal legal assistant training. Some of the training available is completed in an intensive several-week period. Most legal assistant training programs can be completed in two years, although there are some four-year programs.

EARNINGS

According to one survey, legal assistants had a salary range of $14,400 to start and as high as $25,000 or more.

SOURCE OF ADDITIONAL INFORMATION

American Bar Association, Standing Committee on Legal Assistants, 1155 East 60th Street, Chicago, IL 60637.

National Association of Legal Assistants, Inc., 3005 East Skelly Drive, Suite 120, Tulsa, OK 74105.

LIBRARIANS

NATURE OF THE WORK

Librarians make information available to people. They serve as a link between the public and the millions of sources of information by selecting and organizing materials and making them accessible. Their work is divided into two basic functions: user services and technical services. Librarians in user services, such as reference and children's librarians, work directly with the users to help them find the information they need. Librarians in technical services, such as acquisitions librarians and catalogers, are primarily concerned with acquiring and preparing materials for use. Libraries can be busy, demanding, and even stressful places to work. While the atmosphere is usually pleasant, the job may require much standing, stooping, bending, and reaching.

TRAINING AND OTHER QUALIFICATIONS NEEDED

In most public, academic, and special libraries, a master's degree in library science is necessary to obtain an entry position. Many schools offer such degrees. This may not be necessary for public school libraries, where state certification requirements vary widely. Most states require that school librarians be certified as teachers, so a library degree is not always necessary. Because school libraries have become learning resource centers, they are staffed by personnel with a variety of educational backgrounds. Many are media professionals because of the increased emphasis on audio-visual and other media resources.

EARNINGS

Salaries vary with type of library, its size and geographical location, and the person's qualifications. In the latest survey available, starting salaries ranged from an average of $17,232 in public libraries to $20,243 in special libraries, the latter average moving up to $27,000 with experience. The median salary for experienced librarians in colleges and universities was $26,000 and in the federal government, it was $31,530.

SOURCES OF ADDITIONAL INFORMATION

American Library Association, 50 East Huron Street, Chicago, IL 60611.

Special Libraries Association, 235 Park Avenue South, New York, NY 10003.

American Society for Information Science, 1010 16th Street NW, Washington, DC 20036.

MARKET-RESEARCH ANALYSTS

NATURE OF THE WORK

Market-research analysts analyze the buying public's wants and needs, thus providing the information upon which major marketing decisions can be made. All kinds of activities—profit, nonprofit, and government—have to make marketing decisions constantly, such as when and how to put a product or service on the market, to solicit the public to contribute to charity, to recruit in the armed forces, just to name a few. Market-research analysts plan, design, and implement surveys as well as analyze their results. They are often concerned about discovering the preferences and buying habits of people. Their job is to find out everything possible about the market. For example, market research will tell a television station the approximate number of people watching at different hours of the day, their sex, ages, how long they watch, as well as other things. Accordingly, advertisers base their decisions on commercials. Market-research analysts usually work in offices, either as a member of a team or alone using calculators, preparing statistical charts, and analyzing data. Long hours are not unusual.

TRAINING AND OTHER QUALIFICATIONS NEEDED

Although a bachelor's degree is usually sufficient for trainees, a graduate education is necessary for many specialized positions in market research and also for later advancement. A major study in marketing is essential, especially in undergraduate work. A sizeable number of market researchers have graduate degrees in business administration and other fields. Study and/or experience in statistics and quantitative-research methods is very important in this field; thus, sociologists, economists, and others who have such a background often qualify for market-research positions.

EARNINGS

A recent survey showed beginning salaries with a bachelor's degree to be about $16,000 annually.

SOURCE OF ADDITIONAL INFORMATION

American Marketing Association, 250 Wacker Street, Chicago, IL 60606.

MUSICIANS

NATURE OF THE WORK

Professional musicians are found in all forms of music, and there are many: classical, gospel, country, rock, jazz, just to name a few. They play all kinds of instruments and in all kinds of situations. Many play engagements in nightclubs, restaurants, parties, concerts, weddings, and other special events. Classical musicians play in symphony, opera, ballet, and theater orchestras. Some play in churches. A few well-known musicians give their own concerts, appear as soloists with symphony orchestras, and make recordings. Musicians often work at night and on weekends, spending much time in practice and rehearsal as well as travel. Many musicians only find part-time employment and must supplement their income with other types of jobs.

TRAINING AND OTHER QUALIFICATIONS NEEDED

Study usually begins at an early age; though talent may be discovered and developed at any age. Intensive training is needed to be a competent musician, even with the greatest natural talent. Training may be with a private tutor or in one of the many conservatories or college music programs. About 500 colleges, universities, and music conservatories offer bachelor's or higher degrees in music.

EARNINGS

Minimum salaries surveyed in major symphony orchestras in 1982 averaged from $331 to $778 per week; in regional orchestras, about $150 to $550 per week; in metropolitan orchestras, about $16 to $58 per concert plus $10 to $60 per rehearsal. Other pay varies as much as the field is varied. Musicians employed by recording companies were paid a minimum of about $190 for a three-hour session.

SOURCES OF ADDITIONAL INFORMATION

American Federation of Musicians (AFL-CIO), 1500 Broadway, New York, NY 10036.

National Association of Schools of Music, 11250 Roger Bacon Drive, Reston, VA 22090. (Ask for brochure entitled *Careers in Music*.)

PERSONNEL SPECIALISTS

NATURE OF THE WORK

Personnel specialists interview, select, and recommend applicants to fill job openings. They keep informed about rules and regulations concerning employment and oversee the implementation of policies governing hiring and advancement. They handle wage and salary administration, training and career development, employee records and benefit administration. In a small organization, one person may be able to handle all the duties; in larger organizations, personnel workers are more specialized and may be limited to a single aspect of personnel work. Personnel offices are usually located to offer easy access to the public and designed to provide a pleasant atmosphere for visitors. They tend to be pleasant places to work with work hours structured to include a standard thirty-five to forty hours a week with exceptions, such as for those who may have to travel extensively to recruit.

TRAINING AND OTHER QUALIFICATIONS NEEDED

A college degree is required for most starting positions in this field. Required college majors may include personnel or industrial relations, although some employers may prefer a general business or liberal-arts education.

SOURCES OF ADDITIONAL INFORMATION

American Society for Personnel Administration, 30 Park Drive, Berea, OH 44017.

American Society for Training and Development, 600 Maryland Avenue SW, Suite 305, Washington, DC 20024.

PHOTOGRAPHERS

NATURE OF THE WORK

Photographers use their cameras and film to portray people, places, and events much as a writer uses words. They specialize in scientific, medical, engineering, news, and other areas. Some develop and print their own photographs; others have this done elsewhere. In addition to knowing how to use their equipment, they must know how to compose their pictures with creativity and to recognize a potentially good photograph. Still photographers may specialize in portrait, fashion, or industrial work. Scientific and biological photographers provide illustrations and documentation for scientific publications and research reports. Photojournalists specialize in capturing newsworthy events for publications, such as newspapers and for television news shows.

TRAINING AND OTHER QUALIFICATIONS NEEDED

There are no set entry requirements for education and training. Employers are looking for people with photographic skill and knowledge, but that can be obtained through practice and experience as well as through formal training, perhaps a combination of both. Training is available in art schools and two- and four-year colleges.

EARNINGS

Beginning photographers surveyed who worked with newspapers averaged between $9,360 and $44,500. Those with four to five years of experience averaged from $14,560 to $46,020. The preceding figures are based on Newspaper Guild union contracts. Photographers in the federal government averaged $22,600.

SOURCE OF ADDITIONAL INFORMATION

Professional Photographers of America, Inc., 1090 Executive Way, Des Plaines, IL 60018.

PROTESTANT MINISTERS

NATURE OF THE WORK

Protestant ministers lead their congregations in worship services and administer the various rites of their churches. They prepare and deliver sermons and give religious instruction. They perform marriages, conduct funerals, counsel, visit the sick and shut-ins, and serve church members in many other ways too. They provide the spiritual leadership for their congregations. Their working hours may be long and irregular because they are on call for any type of emergency that may occur and may work long hours on administrative, educational, or community activity matters.

TRAINING AND OTHER QUALIFICATIONS NEEDED

The primary prerequisite to this work is to be especially called. Other than that, churches and denominations have varying requirements for ordination. Some have no formal educational requirements; others require some amount of study in Bible colleges, seminaries, or regular colleges. Many denominations require a three-year course of professional study in an accredited school or seminary. Required or not, a good general education and the discipline of formal biblical studies and counseling courses will greatly increase the effectiveness of a ministry.

EARNINGS

Salaries of Protestant clergy vary greatly depending on age, experience, denomination, size and wealth of the congregation, and geographic location. Based on limited information, the estimated median annual income is about $18,000. In larger, wealthier denominations, the average is $25,000 or more. Also, fringe benefits such as housing can add as much as 25 percent more.

SOURCES OF ADDITIONAL INFORMATION

Counsel should be sought from a minister of your own church. Information can also be obtained from the ordination body of the appropriate denomination. Each theological school can supply information about admission requirements.

PUBLIC-RELATIONS WORKERS

NATURE OF THE WORK

Public-relations workers help businesses, governments, universities, and other organizations build and maintain a positive public reputation. They apply their skills in many different areas, such as in press, community or consumer relations, political campaigning, interest-group representation, fund raising, or employee recruiting. In addition to telling the company's story, public-relations people also keep the company apprised of public attitudes and concerns. Public-relations (P.R.) personnel put together information that keeps the public aware of their organization's policies, activities, and accomplishments and keeps management aware of the public's attitudes. After preparing the information, they contact various media forms, such as newspapers and broadcast stations, to get the information disseminated.

TRAINING AND OTHER QUALIFICATIONS NEEDED

Although most beginners have a degree in journalism, communications, or public relations, some employers desire a degree related to the firm's business, such as science. A college degree is a definite plus in entering this field. Some form of experience with the news media is a good background for public relations. Many editors, reporters, and workers in closely related fields enter public relations.

EARNINGS

In the federal government, starting salaries for college graduates start at $17,000 and for those with graduate degrees about $21,000. In the private sector, the average is about $25,000 for all public-relations specialists who are not self-employed. Top-level workers earn as much as $51,000. According to a survey, salaries for top public-relations people averaged about $38,500, from about $29,300 in hospitals to $48,800 in public-relations consulting firms.

SOURCES OF ADDITIONAL INFORMATION

Career Information, Public Relations Society of America, Inc., 845 Third Avenue, New York, NY 10022.

PR Reporter, Dudley House, P.O. Box 600, Exeter, NH 03833.

PURCHASING AGENTS/BUYERS

NATURE OF THE WORK

If an organization does not have the right materials, supplies, or equipment when they are needed, the entire production process or work flow is interrupted or halted. Purchasing agents, also called industrial buyers, obtain goods and services of the quality required at the lowest possible cost and see that adequate materials and supplies are always available. They buy supplies when the stock on hand reaches a predetermined point, when a department needs and requests it, or when market conditions are especially favorable. They usually work a standard thirty-five- to forty-hour week, although some overtime may be necessary, as well as travel to suppliers, seminars, or trade shows.

TRAINING AND OTHER QUALIFICATIONS NEEDED

There are no standard educational requirements for entry-level positions, although many large employers require a college degree in business administration or management. A few colleges offer a degree in purchasing. Some technologically oriented companies may require an engineering degree or a degree in one of the physical sciences. Courses in purchasing, accounting, economics, and statistics are helpful. An associate degree is sometimes satisfactory, and some companies promote clerical and technical people into purchasing jobs.

SOURCES OF ADDITIONAL INFORMATION

National Association of Purchasing Management, 11 Park Place, New York, NY 10007.

National Institute of Governmental Purchasing, Inc., 1735 Jefferson Davis Highway, Suite 101, Arlington, VA 22202.

RADIO AND TELEVISION ANNOUNCERS AND NEWSCASTERS

NATURE OF THE WORK

In small radio stations, the duties of the announcer are quite varied and may include presenting music, news, weather, sports, commercials, interviewing guests, and other activities. It may also include operating equipment, selling commercial time, and writing copy for advertisers. In television stations and larger radio stations, duties are probably more geared toward a particular kind of programming. These specialized areas, such as sports and weather, require thorough familiarity with the subjects. Television news broadcasting requires specialized on-camera personnel, such as anchors, television news reporters, and analysts. Announcers often work in well-lighted, air-conditioned, and soundproofed studios; but when broadcasting from the location where the news is being made, the environment may even be hazardous, involving fires, floods, or other emergency situations. The fast pace and deadlines can be stressful, but most find the nature of the work and the ability to be creative most satisfying.

TRAINING AND OTHER QUALIFICATIONS NEEDED

Formal training for this can be obtained from a technical school, not just a college or university. Either will help; major importance, however, will be given by an employer to a taped audition, which will demonstrate an applicant's delivery, voice and, for television, appearance and style. New hires usually start out as production assistants, researchers, or reporters and are given a chance to move into announcing if they show an aptitude for broadcasting. Courses in English, public speaking, voice, drama, electronics, music, or sports can all add to your potential in this field.

EARNINGS

Median annual salaries of full-time announcers surveyed were approximately $14,000. Salaries ranged from below $10,400 to above $53,000. Salaries vary markedly, depending on the size of the station (radio or television), size of the market, listening or viewing area and population, and other factors. Annual salaries for radio announcers in small stations averaged from $12,000 to $33,000; television announcers ranged from $12,800 to $182,000.

SOURCES OF ADDITIONAL INFORMATION

Broadcast Education Association, 1771 N Street NW, Washington, DC 20036.

For information on FCC licensing procedures, write Federal Communications Commission, 1919 M Street NW, Washington, DC 20552.

RECEPTIONISTS

NATURE OF THE WORK

Receptionists greet customers and other visitors, determine their needs, and refer callers to the person who can help them. Other duties vary with the function they are serving. Some, such as in doctors' offices, may have to obtain personal and financial information from visitors, then refer patients to the proper waiting rooms. Some arrange appointments; others may escort or arrange escorts. When not otherwise busy, they may type, file, and do other clerical duties. Often a receptionist will also be a switchboard operator, receiving and routing calls. Hours are usually regular; work locations usually pleasant, well-lighted, and quiet.

TRAINING AND OTHER QUALIFICATIONS NEEDED

A high school diploma is usually required. Personal characteristics are of the utmost importance, especially a neat appearance, a pleasant voice, and an even disposition. Previous training in clerical skills will be a plus in obtaining a job as a receptionist, in addition to aiding future promotion.

EARNINGS

Full-time switchboard operator-receptionists surveyed averaged $13,780, depending on the section of the country. Receptionists with the federal government averaged $13,800.

SOURCES OF ADDITIONAL INFORMATION

Many state employment agencies can provide additional information about job opportunities, salary, and other information in your area.

SECONDARY SCHOOL TEACHERS

NATURE OF THE WORK

The primary function of a secondary school teacher is to instruct students in a specific subject, such as English, foreign languages, mathematics, social studies, or science. Within a teacher's specialized subject area, he may teach a variety of courses. The teacher develops lesson plans, prepares and gives examinations, and arranges class projects and other activities. Teachers use a variety of instructional material, including films, slides, and computer terminals. In addition to regular classes, teachers perform other duties, such as supervising study halls and homerooms, advising student groups, and attending meetings and workshops.

TRAINING AND OTHER QUALIFICATIONS NEEDED

All states require that teachers be certified for public school, although not all require it for teaching in Christian or other private schools. Certification requirements vary, but all states require a bachelor's degree from an approved teacher-training program with a prescribed number of credits in the subject they plan to teach. Some states require a written examination; some have health, citizenship, or character requirements. About half the states require graduate degrees.

EARNINGS

According to the National Education Association, public secondary school teachers average $24,276 a year, with salaries highest in the Mid-Atlantic and in the far western states.

SOURCES OF ADDITIONAL INFORMATION

National Education Association, 1201 16th Street NW, Washington, DC 20036.

National Council for Accreditation of Teacher Education, 1919 Pennsylvania Avenue NW, Washington, DC 20006.

SECRETARIES AND STENOGRAPHERS

NATURE OF THE WORK

Secretaries and stenographers are at the center of communications within an organization. Secretaries perform a variety of administrative duties: scheduling, telephone answering, giving information, organizing and maintaining files, taking dictation, and typing. They route mail, compile reports, prepare correspondence, and have many other duties. Some managers delegate decision making to their executive secretaries, usually within narrowly defined parameters, where precedent often dictates the action taken. Stenographers typically take dictation and transcribe their notes on a typewriter, which can call for specialized knowledge, if working in a technical profession. For example, court reporters are a specialized type of stenographer, who use specialized equipment and technique.

TRAINING AND OTHER QUALIFICATIONS NEEDED

A high school diploma is usually required. Most employers prefer applicants who have had training at a business school or college. Courses vary from a few months to one or two years with a broad range of subjects covered. Your typing speed should be sixty-five words per minute or better. A knowledge of shorthand and a speed of at least ninety words per minute will help get a job, even though the skill is not required everywhere.

SOURCES OF ADDITIONAL INFORMATION

Professional Secretaries International, 2440 Pershing Road, Suite G10, Kansas City, MO 64108.

National Association of Legal Secretaries, 3005 East Skelly Drive, Tulsa, OK 74105.

National Shorthand Reporters Association, 118 Park Street SE, Vienna, VA 22180.

SYSTEMS ANALYSTS

NATURE OF THE WORK

Systems analysts plan efficient methods of processing data and handling the results. They help managers analyze problems by breaking the problems into component parts. They use various techniques, such as cost accounting, sampling, and mathematical model building to analyze a problem and devise a new system. Once accepted, they translate the logical requirements of the system into the capabilities of the computer equipment, or hardware. They also prepare applications for programmers to follow and work with them to debug, or eliminate errors from the system. Some improve existing systems; others do research and devise new systems.

TRAINING AND OTHER QUALIFICATIONS NEEDED

Educational requirements vary greatly. Some employers want degrees in computer science, information science, or data processing. Others prefer such fields as accounting, business management, or even the physical sciences, depending on the job. Since the systems analyst marries the computer with the manager's needs, an employer may emphasize either end of the equation for an educational background. Because of this, an aspiring systems analyst should have courses not only in data processing, information science, and computers but also in general business to provide as much balance as possible. Many enter this field from computer-programming experience because computer knowledge is essential.

SOURCES OF ADDITIONAL INFORMATION

American Federation of Information Processing Societies, 1815 North Lynn Street, Arlington, VA 22209.

Association for Systems Management, 24587 Bagley Road, Cleveland, OH 44138.

Information about the Certificate in Data Processing is available from The Institute for Certification of Computer Professionals, 35 East Wacker Drive, Suite 2828, Chicago, IL 60601.

TELEPHONE AND PBX INSTALLERS AND REPAIRERS

NATURE OF THE WORK

These are craft workers who install, service, and repair telephones and switchboard systems on customers' property. They are sometimes referred to as services and systems technicians. They install new systems and make changes to existing systems by adding, relocating, or removing equipment or facilities. There are various specialties in this field: telephone installers, PBX installers, telephone repairers, and PBX repairers. One person, however, may sometimes be responsible for two or more of these duties and sometimes all of them. These jobs were formerly associated primarily with the telephone utilities; but with the proliferation of private telephone companies, this is no longer the case. Many private businesses own their own telephone equipment and employ technicians to handle the repairs, installations, and relocations.

TRAINING AND OTHER QUALIFICATIONS NEEDED

A high school education is usually required. An applicant should be adept at using hand tools and be able to read blueprints and interpret work orders. A basic knowledge of electricity and electronics will be helpful, plus a practical problem-solving ability.

EARNINGS

Pay scales vary greatly across the country. Generally, it takes four to five years to advance from the beginning to the top of the pay scale. The average hourly rate surveyed was $13.02. Weekly salary ranges were $320 to $474 for beginners to above $550 for the highest (the high average is due to low turnover).

SOURCES OF ADDITIONAL INFORMATION

United States Independent Telephone Association, 1801 K Street NW, Washington, DC 20006.

Telecommunications International Union, P.O. Box 5462, Hamden, CT 06518.

International Brotherhood of Electrical Workers, 1125 15th Street NW, Washington, DC 20005.

TELEPHONE OPERATORS

NATURE OF THE WORK

Telephone operators may be employed by one of the many telephone companies that provide commercial phone service. Or thay may be employed by a private business that receives so many calls that it has to operate its own private branch exchange (PBX), or switchboard. Businesses will typically do this so the public will only have to know one number and not have to call maybe dozens or hundreds of numbers to find the person they want to speak with. The PBX enables all calls to come in on one number to a central location where they are answered by one or more operators who in turn route the calls to individual instruments in different offices. Some handle other duties, such as a police communications operator, who handles incoming emergency calls from citizens then transmits messages to and from units in the field. There are many other specialty telephone-operator jobs. Operators may be required to work odd-hour shifts, but otherwise the work can be pleasant and interesting.

TRAINING AND OTHER QUALIFICATIONS NEEDED

Aspirants to this kind of work should enjoy working with the public and be pleasant, courteous, and patient, not objecting to sitting in a chair for long periods of time. A clear, pleasing voice and good hearing are important, as well as good eye-hand coordination and manual dexterity. A high school diploma is sufficient, and most companies will train you if you have no previous experience.

EARNINGS

Operators with telephone companies surveyed averaged $10.38 per hour. Most of this represents union contract wages. Government operators averaged $12,600 that year, with $9,756 the average for beginners.

SOURCES OF ADDITIONAL INFORMATION

International Brotherhood of Electrical Workers, 1125 15th Street NW, Washington, DC 20005.

Telecommunications International Union, P.O. Box 5462, Hamden, CT 06518.

United States Independent Telephone Association, 1801 K Street NW, Washington, DC 20006.

TELLERS

NATURE OF THE WORK

You usually think of banks as the only places that use tellers; but you may find this term used to apply to those in Christian organizations who receive and process the thousands of pieces of daily mail that contain contributions. In banks, the teller deals directly with the public and processes deposits, withdrawals, and other transactions. Some specialize in certain types of transactions. In banks, of course, a personable nature is very important because of the constant face-to-face contact with the public. In all cases, accuracy is probably the most single important factor, so tellers should be gifted at using numbers and have manual dexterity. The job is usually characterized by pleasant working conditions, repetitive work, sometimes constant public contact, and often standing for long periods of time.

TRAINING AND OTHER QUALIFICATIONS NEEDED

A high school diploma is usually required. Employers look for neatness, maturity, tact, and courtesy. Clerical skills, including the use of a calculator, are important. These skills can often be learned in high school.

EARNINGS

Most tellers surveyed earned between $8,000 and $17,200.

SOURCES OF ADDITIONAL INFORMATION

American Bankers Association, Bank Personnel Division, 1120 Connecticut Avenue NW, Washington, DC 20036.

National Bankers Association, 499 South Capitol Street SW, Suite 520, Washington, DC 20003.

WRITERS AND EDITORS

NATURE OF THE WORK

Writers develop original fiction and nonfiction prose for books, magazines, trade journals, newspapers, technical studies and reports, company newsletters, radio and television broadcasts, and advertisements. Editors supervise writers and select and prepare material for publication or broadcasting. Writers start by selecting or being assigned a topic, then gathering information by research and interviews, organizing the material, and finally putting it in words that will most effectively convey the message to readers. Editors do some writing and almost always do much rewriting. Their main job is to plan the contents of the publication and to supervise its preparation.

TRAINING AND OTHER QUALIFICATIONS NEEDED

A college degree is usually, but not always required. There is no agreement on the best major course of study. Journalism would seem the most obvious, but some employers prefer a general liberal-arts education or, if for technical writing, a more specialized degree. Communications is also a good background. Whatever the educational background, writers and editors need the ability to express themselves with the written word, clearly and logically. Any kind of writing experience is desirable.

EARNINGS

According to a survey, beginning salaries for writers and editorial assistants ranged from $16,400 to $21,000. More experienced writers and researchers ranged from $23,200 to $31,900; experienced editors from $22,000 to $39,000; supervisory editors up to $42,500.

SOURCES OF ADDITIONAL INFORMATION

The Newspaper Fund, Inc., P.O. Box 300, Princeton, NJ 08540.

American Society of Magazine Editors, 575 Lexington Avenue, New York, NY 10022.

Appendix III
SELECTED AVERAGE SALARIES IN THE UNITED STATES

The following information is a compilation of average monthly and annual salaries in the United States for selected occupations.

Job titles followed by Roman numerals represent different levels of experience and responsibility and accompanying differences in salary. For example, an Accountant I is the lowest level; Accountant VI the highest.

The average figure shown is the arithmetic mean of the salaries of the employees surveyed.

Data Source: *National Survey of Professional, Administrative, Technical and Clerical Pay,* March, 1985 and U.S. Department of Labor, Bureau of Labor Statistics, 1984. For subsequent years, slightly adjust for cost of living changes.

AVERAGE SALARIES—UNITED STATES

(Employment and average salaries for selected professional, administrative, technical, and clerical occupations in private industry, United States, except Alaska and Hawaii)

Occupation and Level	Average Monthly Salary	Average Annual Salary
ACCOUNTANTS AND AUDITORS		
Accountants I	$1,715	$20,577
Accountants II	2,112	25,349
Accountants III	2,503	30,307
Accountants IV	3,134	37,607
Accountants V	3,907	46,879
Accountants VI	4,960	59,519
Auditors I	1,761	21,128
Auditors II	2,155	25,854
Auditors III	2,604	31,246
Auditors IV	3,270	39,243
Public Accountants I	1,638	19,657
Public Accountants II	1,844	22,134
Public Accountants III	2,158	25,891
Public Accountants IV	2,618	31,416
Chief Accountants I	3,130	37,557
Chief Accountants II	3,876	46,517
Chief Accountants III	5,039	64,466
Chief Accountants IV	6,228	74,735
ATTORNEYS		
Attorneys I	2,490	29,886
Attorneys II	3,105	37,256
Attorneys III	3,979	47,742
Attorneys IV	4,924	59,087
Attorneys V	6,150	73,805
Attorneys VI	7,641	91,690

Need help choosing a career? Try the
NEW QUICK JOB-HUNTING MAP

The **New Quick Job-Hunting Map** was developed by Richard N. Bolles and appears in his bestselling career guidance book *What Color Is Your Parachute?* The **Job-Hunting Map** is a self-evaluation tool used by many job seekers or career changers to educate, enlighten, and entertain them along their job-hunting journey. Bolles guides the job hunter through a variety of self-exploration and self-assessment exercises designed to identify the job hunter's skills and talents.

The Advanced Version is designed for job hunters with some experience in landing a job or who want to change careers; it covers the self-evaluation process in depth. Sixty-four pages. $6.00 a copy ($8.50 in Canada), includes shipping and handling.

The Beginning Version is shorter, easier to read, and has fewer self-evaluation exercises. It's designed for the job hunter or career changer with limited experience in seeking jobs. Thirty pages. $5.00 a copy ($7.00 in Canada), includes shipping and handling.

To order, fill out the reverse side of this card and send it with your check to:
CPP, P.O. Box 60070, Palo Alto, CA 94306.

Need help choosing a career? Try the
NEW QUICK JOB-HUNTING MAP

The **New Quick Job-Hunting Map** was developed by Richard N. Bolles and appears in his bestselling career guidance book *What Color Is Your Parachute?* The **Job-Hunting Map** is a self-evaluation tool used by many job seekers or career changers to educate, enlighten, and entertain them along their job-hunting journey. Bolles guides the job hunter through a variety of self-exploration and self-assessment exercises designed to identify the job hunter's skills and talents.

The Advanced Version is designed for job hunters with some experience in landing a job or who want to change careers; it covers the self-evaluation process in depth. Sixty-four pages. $6.00 a copy ($8.50 in Canada), includes shipping and handling.

The Beginning Version is shorter, easier to read, and has fewer self-evaluation exercises. It's designed for the job hunter or career changer with limited experience in seeking jobs. Thirty pages. $5.00 a copy ($7.00 in Canada), includes shipping and handling.

To order, fill out the reverse side of this card and send it with your check to:
CPP, P.O. Box 60070, Palo Alto, CA 94306.

ORDER BLANK
CONSULTING PSYCHOLOGISTS PRESS

Name (please print) _____

Street Address _____

City _____ State _____ Zip _____

Quantity	Code No.	Description	Unit Price	Extended Price
	7899	Quick Job-Hunting Map—Beginners	$5.00 ($7.00 in Canada)	
	7898	Quick Job-Hunting Map—Advanced	$6.00 ($8.50 in Canada)	

Send Payment to:
CPP
P.O. BOX 60070
PALO ALTO, CA 94306

Subtotal _____
Sales Tax _____
(for Calif. customers only; 6 or 6½%)
AMOUNT ENCLOSED _____

- -

ORDER BLANK
CONSULTING PSYCHOLOGISTS PRESS

Name (please print) _____

Street Address _____

City _____ State _____ Zip _____

Quantity	Code No.	Description	Unit Price	Extended Price
	7899	Quick Job-Hunting Map—Beginners	$5.00 ($7.00 in Canada)	
	7898	Quick Job-Hunting Map—Advanced	$6.00 ($8.50 in Canada)	

Send Payment to:
CPP
P.O. BOX 60070
PALO ALTO, CA 94306

Subtotal _____
Sales Tax _____
(for Calif. customers only; 6 or 6½%)
AMOUNT ENCLOSED _____

SELECTED AVERAGE SALARIES IN THE UNITED STATES

Occupation and Level	Average Monthly Salary	Average Annual Salary
BUYERS		
Buyers I	1,741	20,896
Buyers II	2,134	25,606
Buyers III	2,648	31,774
Buyers IV	3,276	39,306
PROGRAMMERS/ANALYSTS		
Programmers/Programmer Analysts I ...	1,693	20,318
Programmers/Programmer Analysts II ..	1,974	23,690
Programmers/Programmer Analysts III .	2,364	28,367
Programmers/Programmer Analysts IV .	2,809	33,708
Programmers/Programmer Analysts V ..	3,441	41,288
Systems Analysts I	2,350	28,197
Systems Analysts II	2,789	33,465
Systems Analysts III	3,305	39,663
Systems Analysts IV	3,894	46,729
Systems Analysts V	4,705	56,461
Systems Analysts VI	5,734	68,809
PERSONNEL MANAGEMENT		
Job Analysts I	1,731	20,774
Job Analysts II	1,967	23,602
Job Analysts III	2,492	29,905
Job Analysts IV	3,082	36,983
Directors of Personnel I	3,098	37,173
Directors of Personnel II	3,814	45,764
Directors of Personnel III	4,943	59,317
Directors of Personnel IV	5,8889	70,663
CHEMISTS AND ENGINEERS		
Chemists I	1,886	22,631
Chemists II	2,227	26,722
Chemists III	2,705	32,461
Chemists IV	3,285	39,418
Chemists V	3,976	47,706
Chemists VI	4,851	58,210
Chemists VII	5,726	68,710

Occupation and Level	Average Monthly Salary	Average Annual Salary
Engineers I	2,284	27,405
Engineers II	2,523	30,275
Engineers III	2,862	34,348
Engineers IV	3,416	40,991
Engineers V	4,030	48,336
Engineers VI	4,678	56,136
Engineers VII	5,470	65,641
Engineers VIII	6,350	76,205

TECHNICAL SUPPORT

Engineering Technicians I	1,406	16,876
Engineering Technicians II	1,612	19,339
Engineering Technicians III	1,932	23,179
Engineering Technicians IV	2,272	27,259
Engineering Technicians V	2,615	31,386
Drafters I	1,101	13,208
Drafters II	1,374	16,488
Drafters III	1,667	20,006
Drafters IV	1,996	23,950
Drafters V	2,490	29,870
Computer Operators I	1,139	13,670
Computer Operators II	1,414	16,973
Computer Operators III	1,722	20,664
Computer Operators IV	2,001	24,016
Computer Operators V	2,370	28,440
Photographers I	1,464	15,571
Photographers II	1,835	22,019
Photographers III	2,207	26,489
Photographers IV	2,517	30,210

CLERICAL

Accounting Clerks I	1,032	12,380
Accounting Clerks II	1,227	14,728
Accounting Clerks III	1,444	17,327
Accounting Clerks IV	1,759	21,106
File Clerks I	842	10,101
File Clerks II	986	11,836

SELECTED AVERAGE SALARIES IN THE UNITED STATES

Occupation and Level	Average Monthly Salary	Average Annual Salary
File Clerks III	1,226	14,707
Key Entry Operators I	1,100	13,200
Key Entry Operators II	1,383	16,600
Messengers	974	11,685
Personnel Specialists I	1,169	14,023
Personnel Specialists II	1,365	16,375
Personnel Specialists III	1,572	18,870
Personnel Specialists IV	1,863	22,355
Purchasing Assistants I	1,364	16,363
Purchasing Assistants II	1,761	21,135
Purchasing Assistants III	2,346	28,150
Secretaries I	1,322	15,869
Secretaries II	1,477	17,721
Secretaries III	1,666	19,988
Secretaries IV	1,877	22,520
Secretaries V	2,184	26,210
Stenographers I	1,533	18,391
Stenographers II	1,743	20,914
Typists I	1,052	12,621
Typists II	1,321	15,847

Appendix IV ─────────────

POTENTIAL CHRISTIAN EMPLOYERS

COMPREHENSIVE LISTING

The following is a list of over one thousand ministries, companies, associations, and fellowships, along with addresses and telephone numbers. Most of these are a potential source of employment for the Christian job seeker. A few on the list may not have a paid staff, such as the associations, but they are included to give the reader as much comprehensive information as possible. Such organizations may be able to give helpful referral information.

For most of the information, we are indebted to the National Association of Evangelicals and their directory, the *National Evangel*. Most of the organizations listed are members of or are somehow affiliated with the NAE. From their directory, we have included the Christian Organization Numerical Index (CONI), referred to as the IDAK. The index was specifically designed to be compatible with but also supplemental to the U.S. Department of Commerce Standard Industrial Service Organizations. The CONI Index was developed by IDAK Group, Inc., and is available free of charge to all interested organizations. Contact IDAK Group, Inc., Banfield Plaza Building, 7931 NE Halsey, Portland, OR 97213, telephone (503) 257-0189.

For information on membership or other questions, contact the National Association of Evangelicals, P.O. Box 28, Wheaton, IL 60189.

EVANGELISTIC ORGANIZATIONS
(IDAK: 8671/8679)

Agape Force, Inc., P.O. Box 386, Lindale, TX 75771 214-882-5571

Alton Newton Evangelistic Assoc., Inc., P.O. Box 1051, Lake City, SC 29560

The American Association for Jewish Evangelism, 5860 N. Lincoln Ave., Chicago, IL 60659 312-275-2133

American Board of Mission to the Jews, P.O. Box 2000, Orangeburg, NY 10962 914-359-8535

American Remnant Mission, Inc., P.O. Box 2321, Pleasant Hill, CA 94523 415-676-5886

American Rescue Workers, P.O. Box 22, Williamsport, PA 17701 717-323-8401

Anchor Bay Evangelistic Assoc., P.O. Box 288, Aurora, IL 60507 312-896-1248

Artists in Christian Testimony (ACT), 9090 19th St., Alta Loma, CA 91701

Bill Glass Evangelistic Assoc., P.O. Box 356, Dallas, TX 75221 214-291-7895

Billy Graham Evangelistic Assoc., 1300 Harmon Pl., Minneapolis, MN 55403 612-338-0500

Christ Alongside, P.O. Box 29, Bremerton, WA 98310 206-692-5305

Christ For The Nations, Inc., P.O. Box 24910, Dallas, TX 75224 214-376-1711

Christian Communications of Chicagoland, Inc., WCFC-TV 38, One N. Wacker Dr., Chicago, IL 60606 312-977-3838

Christian Destiny, Inc., P.O. Box 100, Wheaton, IL 60189 312-469-7100

Christian Evangelical Assoc., P.O. Box 538, Port Angeles, WA 98362 206-457-4163

Christians in Action, P.O. Box 7271, Long Beach, CA 90807 213-428-2022

Clyde Dupin Ministries, Inc., P.O. Box 565, Kernersville, NC 27284 919-996-2555

CO-UNI-BUS, 2707 Glenwood Ln., Billings, MT 59102 406-259-7734

Correll Missionary Ministries, Box 11793, Charlotte, NC 28220 704-527-1195

Crista Ministries, Inc., 19303 Fremont Ave., N., Seattle, WA 98133 206-546-7200

Deaf Ministries, Intl., P.O. Box 182, Concord, CA 94522 415-686-3966

Delaware County Evangelistic Assoc., 5101 W. Hessler Rd., Muncie, IN 47302 317-288-6566

The Diakonian Society, P.O. Box 11437, Chicago, IL 60611 312-467-4343

Eastern Europe Bible Mission, P.O. Box 73, Walnut Creek, CA 94597 415-825-4939

Evangelistic Association of New England, 88 Tremont St., Boston, MA 02108 617-523-3579

Frontiers, 1605 Elizabeth St., Pasadena, CA 91104 818-798-0807

Ford Philpot Evangelistic Assoc., P.O. Box 3000, Lexington, KY 40533 606-233-0068

Haven of Rest Ministries, 2410 Hypoerion Ave., Los Angeles, CA 90028 213-664-2103

The Heralds Ministries, Inc., P.O. Box 61, Newbury Park, CA 91320 805-492-2915

High Flight Foundation, P.O. Box 1387, Colorado Springs, CO 80901 303-576-7700

Hope Hospital Chaplain, 1800 W. Charleston Blvd., Las Vegas, NV 89102 702-871-6625

Hospital Chaplains Ministry of America, Inc., 5071 Enfield Ave., Encino, CA 91316 213-345-2998

Inter-Church Ministries, P.O. Box 71654, Los Angeles, CA 90071 213-250-2824

International Evangelism Crusades, 14617 Victory Blvd., Sta. 4, Van Nuys, CA 91411 818-989-5942

International Prison Ministry, P.O. Box 63, Dallas, TX 75221 214-494-2302

James Robison Evangelistic Assoc., P.O. Box 18489, Ft. Worth, TX 76118 817-268-4606

Jesus Dayton, Inc., P.O. Box 403, Dayton, OH 45409 513-298-8420

Jews for Jesus, 60 Haight St., San Francisco, CA 94102 415-864-2600

Jimmy Swaggart Ministries, P.O. Box 2550, Baton Rouge, LA 70821 504-769-8300

John Woodhouse Evangelistic Assoc., P.O. Box 205, Indian Rocks, FL 33535 813-596-2853

Lamb's Players, P.O. Box 26, National City, CA 92050 714-474-3385

Lay Evangelism, Inc., P.O. Box N, Pleasant Hill, OH 45359 513-676-8531

Luis Palau Evangelistic Team, P.O. Box 1173, Portland, OR 97207 503-643-0777

Metro Ministries, Inc., 2721 S. Warren Way, Arcadia, CA 91006 213-448-5538

Mission to the World, PCA, P.O. Box 1744, Decatur, GA 30031 404-294-9479

Needle's Eye Ministry, Inc., P.O. Box 14558, Richmond, VA 23221 804-358-1583

Neighborhood Bible Studies, P.O. Box 222, Dobbs Ferry, NY 10522 914-693-3273

New Covenant Evangelical Ministries, Inc., P.O. Box 26, Buffalo, NY 14223 716-786-3044

New England Fellowship of Evangelicals, P.O. Box 99, Rumney, NH 03266 603-7786-9504

Nursing Home Ministries, Inc., P.O. Box 02519, Portland, OR 97202 503-238-0647

Open Air Campaigners, 1444 Martine Ave., Plainfield, NJ 07060 201-757-8427

Open Door Ministries, Inc.. P.O. Box 426, Somerville, TX 77879 713-596-1213

Overseas Chinese Mission, 154 Hester St., New York, NY 10013 212-226-3438

Paul Clark Ministries, P.O. Box 2112, Shawnee Mission, KS 66201 816-942-7588

Personal Ministries, P.O. Box 167, New Lenox, IL 60451 815-448-1286

Presbyterian Evangelistic Fellowship, Inc., P.O. Box 1890, Decatur, GA 30031 404-244-0740

Prison Fellowship, P.O. Box 17500, Washington, DC 20041 703-471-0695

Prison Mission Association, Inc., P.O. Box 3397, Riverside, CA 92519 714-686-2613

Radio Evangelism, Inc., P.O. Box N, Alameda, CA 94501 415-522-4091

The Railroad Evangelistic Assoc., Inc., R.R. 4, Box 73, Spencer, IN 47460 812-829-4667

Reach Out Evangelistic Assoc., P.O. Box 6651, Orange, CA 92667 714-997-2160

Robert H. Schuller Institute, 12141 Lewis St., Garden Grove, CA 92164 714-971-4133

Roger Houtsman World Outreach, P.O. Box 950, Novato, CA 94948 415-892-0714

San Francisco Careers Class, Inc., P.O. Box 14611, San Francisco, CA 94114 415-564-5683

Saints Alive in Jesus, P.O. Box 1076, Issaquah, WA 98027

Sea-Tac Ministries (The Airport Chaplaincy), Rm. 213, Jackson International Airport, Seattle, WA 98158 206-433-5505

Search Ministries, 1020 Macon St., Sta. 11, Fort Worth, TX 76102 817-335-2063

Siloam Christian Mission, 969 Colorado Blvd., Los Angeles, CA 90041 213-255-2413

Steer, Inc., P.O. Box 1236, Bismarck, ND 58502 701-258-4911

Tele-Visitation, P.O. Box 71654, Los Angeles, CA 90071 213-624-2196

Tom Skinner Associates, Inc., 505 Eighth Ave., New York, NY 10018 545-896-5454

United Gospel Outreach, 7225-27 S. Main St., Los Angeles, CA 90003 213-758-1213

Venture Teams Intl., Box 7430, Station E., Calgary, Alberta T3C 3M2 Canada 403-286-3422

Waikiki Beach Chaplaincy, P.O. Box 15488, Honolulu, HI 96815 808-923-3137

Wales Goebel Ministry, 2908 Pump House Rd., Birmingham, AL 35243 205-967-4888

The Watchmen Assoc., Inc., 705 Forest Park Rd., Great Falls, VA 22066 703-759-3110

Wears Valley Bible Conference Center, Inc., R.R. 7, Sevierville, TN 37862 615-453-2382

World Evangelism, Inc., P.O Box 700, San Diego, CA 92138 619-239-4300

World Literature Crusade, 20232 Sunburst St., Chatsworth, CA 91311 213-341-7870

YOUTH AND CAMPUS-RELATED ASSOCIATIONS
(IDAK: 8672/8673)

Awana Youth Assoc., 3201 Tollview Dr., Rolling Meadows, IL 60008 645-394-5150

BCM Intl., Inc., 237 Fairfield Ave., Upper Darby, PA 19082 215-352-7177

Campus Crusade for Christ Intl., Arrowhead Springs, San Bernardino, CA 92414 714-886-5224

Christian College Coalition, 1776 Massachusetts Ave. NW, Sta. 700, Washington, DC 20036 202-293-6177

Christian College Coordinating Council, P.O. Box 254, Glen Ellyn, IL 60137

Christian Service Brigade, P.O. Box 150, Wheaton, IL 60189 312-665-0630

CO-UNI-BUS, 2707 Glenwood Ln., Billings, MT 59102 406-259-7734

Forest Home, Inc., Christian Conference Center, Forest Falls, CA 92339 714-794-1127

High School Evangelism Fellowship, P.O. Box 780, Tenafly, NJ 07670 201-387-1750

Hume Lake Christ Camps, P.O. Box 1868, Fresno, CA 93718 209-251-6043

International Students, Inc., P.O. Box C, Colorado Springs, CO 80901 303-576-2700

Inter-Varsity Christian Fellowship, 233 Langdon St., Madison, WI 53703 608-257-0263

Maranatha Campus Ministries, Intl., Box 1799, Gainesville, FL 32602 904-375-6000

Mount Hermon Assoc., Inc., Box 413, Mount Hermon, CA 95041 408-335-4466

The Navigators, P.O. Box 6000, Colorado Springs, CO 80934 303-598-1212

New Horizons Youth Ministries, 1000 S. 350 E., Marion, IN 46953 317-668-4009

Open Door Ministries, Inc., P.O. Box 426, Somerville, TX 77879 409-596-1213

PEF-Children's Ministry, Box 1890, Decatur, GA 30031

Pioneer Clubs, P.O. Box 788, Wheaton, IL 60189 312-293-1600

Probe Ministries, Intl., 12011 Coit Rd., Sta. 107, Dallas, TX 75251 214-661-8500

Success With Youth Publications, P.O. Box 2789, LaJolla, CA 92038 619-578-4700

Teen Challenge, Inc., 444 Clinton Ave., Brooklyn, NY 11238 212-789-1414

Teens, Inc., Box 322, 724 W. Washington Ave., South Bend, IN 46624 219-232-8523

Young Life, P.O. Box 520, 720 W. Monument St., Colorado Springs, CO 80901 303-473-4262

Youth Development Inc., P.O. Box 9429, San Diego, CA 92109 714-292-5683

Youth Evangelism Assoc. (YEA), 197 Front St., Marietta, OH 45750

Youth for Christ/USA, P.O. Box 419, Wheaton, IL 60189 312-668-6600

Youth Guidance, Inc., R.R. 2, Duff Rd., Sewickley, PA 15143 412-741-8550

Youth Specialties, Inc., 1224 Greenfield Dr., El Cajon, CA 92021 619-440-2333

Youth With a Mission (YWAM), Box 296, Sunland, CA 91040 818-896-2755

BIBLE/LITERATURE AGENCIES
(IDAK: 2700)

American Bible Society, 1865 Broadway, New York, NY 10023 212-581-7400

American Scripture Gift Mission, 1211 Arch St., Rm. D., Philadelphia, PA 19107 215-561-3232

B.B. Kirkbride Bible Co., Inc., P.O. Box 606, Indianapolis, IN 46206 317-634-3252

Barclay Press, Evang. Fr. Al., P.O. Box 232, Newberg, OR 97132 503-538-7345

Bible Literature Intl., P.O. Box 477, Columbus, OH 43216 614-267-3116

Crista Ministries, Inc., 19303 Fremont N., Seattle WA 98133 206-546-7200

Christian Literature Crusade, Inc., P.O. Box C, Fort Washington, PA 19034 215-542-1242

Christian Publications, C&MA, 3825 Hartzdale Dr., Camp Hill, PA 17011 717-761-7044

Church Bible Studies, 191 Mayhew Way, Walnut Creek, CA 94596 415-937-7286

David C. Cook Foundation, 850 N. Grove, Elgin, IL 60120 312-741-2400

Delair Publishing Co., Inc., 420 Lexington Ave., New York, NY 10170 212-867-2255

Evangelical Church Library Assoc., P.O. Box 353, Glen Ellyn, IL 60138 312-668-0519

Free Bible Literature Society / Operation Campus, P.O Box 201, Hawthorne, NJ 07507 201-427-3500

The Gideons Intl., 2900 Lebanon Rd., Nashville, TN 37214 615-883-8533

Gospel Literature Intl. (GLINT), P.O. Box 6688, Ventura, CA 93003 805-644-3929

Here's Life Publishers, Inc., P.O. Box 1576, San Bernardino, CA 92402 714-886-7981

International Bible Society, 144 Tices Ln., East Brunswick, NJ 08816 201-238-5454

InterVarsity Press, P.O. Box 1400, Downers Grove, IL 60515 312-964-5700

Jews for Jesus, 60 Haight St., San Francisco, CA 94102 415-864-2600

John Milton Society for the Blind, 475 Riverside Dr., Rm. 832, New York, NY 10115 212-870-3335

Living Bible Intl., 1809-C Mill St., Naperville, IL 60540 312-369-0100

Logoi, Inc., 4100 W. Flagler St., Sta. B-3, Miami, FL 33134 305-446-8297

Lutheran Braille Evangelism Assn., 660 E. Montana Ave., St. Paul, MN 55106 615-776-8530

Mott Media, Inc., Publishers, 1000 E. Huron St., Milford, MI 48042 313-685-8773

NavPress, P.O. Box 6000, Colorado Springs, CO 80934 303-598-1212

Operation Campus/Pocket Testament League, P.O. Box 368, Lincoln Park, NJ 07035 201-696-1900

Radio Evangelism, Inc., P.O. Box N, Alameda, CA 94501 415-522-4091

Southern Baptists for Bible Translation, 1800 K St. NW, Sta. 801, Washington, DC 20006 202-785-2400

Success with Youth Publications, Inc., P.O. Box 2789, La Jolla, CA 92038 714-578-4700

Walk Thru the Bible Ministries, Inc., P.O. Box 80587, Atlanta, GA 30366 404-458-9300 or 800-554-9300

William Carey Library, 1704 N. Sierra Bonita Ave., Pasadena, CA 91104 213-798-4067

World Home Bible League, 16801 Van Dam Rd., South Holland, IL 60473 341-331-2094

World Literature Crusade, 20232 Sunburst St., Chatsworth, CA 91311 213-341-7870

Wycliffe Bible Translators, 19891 Beach Blvd., Huntington Beach, CA 92648 714-536-9346

Zondervan Bible Publishers, 1415 Lake Dr. SE, Grand Rapids, MI 49506 616-698-6900

BOOK PUBLISHERS
(IDAK: 2700)

The criteria used in determining the following list were: 1) Publisher must be listed in both the Christian Bookseller's Suppliers Directory and the Literary Market Place, and 2) have, as a part of its market, evangelical books or 3) they must be members of the Evangelical Christian Publishers Association.

Abingdon Press, P.O. Box 801, Nashville, TN 37202 615-749-6451 Toll Free: 1-800-251-93320 (orders)

Accent Books, P.O. Box 15337, Denver, CO 80215 303-988-5300

American Bible Society, 1865 Broadway, New York, NY 10023 212-581-7400

Augsburg Publishing House, Amer. Luth. Ch., P.O. Box 1209, Minneapolis, MN 55440 612-330-3300

Baker Book House Co., P.O. Box 6287, Grand Rapids, MI 49506 616-676-9185

Baptist Publishing House, South. Bapt., 7000 Alabama, El Paso, TX 79914 915-566-9656

B.B. Kirkbride Bible Co., P.O. Box 606, Indianapolis, IN 46206 317-634-3252

Beacon Hill Press of Kansas City, Ch. of the Naz., P.O. Box 527, Kansas City, MO 64141 816-931-1900

Bethany House Publishers, 6820 Auto Club Rd., Minneapolis, MN 55438 612-944-2121

Brethren Press, Ch. of the Breth., 1451 Dundee Ave., Elgin, IL 60120 312-742-5100

Bridge Publishing, Inc. 2500 Hamilton Blvd., South Plainfield, NJ 07080 201-754-0745

Broadman Press, South. Bapt., 127 Ninth Ave., N., Nashville, TN 37234 615-251-2544

Brownlow Publishing Co., Inc., P.O. Box 50545, Fort Worth, TX 76105 817-531-1401

The C.R. Gibson Co., Knight St., Norwalk, CT 06856 203-847-4543

Cambridge University Press, 32 E. 57th St., New York, NY 10022 212-688-8885

CBP Press, Chr. Ch., P.O Box 179, St. Louis, MO 63166 314-371-6900

Christian Education Publishers, P.O. Box 2789, La Jolla, CA 92038 619-578-4700

The Christian Library, 164 Mill St., Westwood, NY 07675 201-664-6460

Christian Publications, Inc., C&MA, 3825 Hartzdale Dr., Camp Hill, PA 17011 717-761-7044

Concordia Publishing House, 3558 S. Jefferson Ave., St. Louis, MO 63118 314-664-7000

Creation-Life Publishers, Inc., P.O. Box 15908, San Diego, CA 92115 619-449-9420

Crusade Bible Publishers, Inc., Athens Dr., Mt. Juliet, TN 37122 615-758-0461

David C. Cook Publishing Co., 850 N. Grove Ave., Elgin, IL 60120 312-741-2400

Decker Press, P.O. Box 3838, Grand Junction, CO 81502 303-241-6193

Doubleday-Galilee, 245 Park Ave., New York, NY 10167 212-953-4483

Fleming H. Revell Co., 184 Central Ave., Old Tappan, NJ 07675 201-768-8060

Fortress Press, 2900 Queen Ln., Philadelphia, PA 19129 215-848-6800

Good News Publishers/Crossway Books, 9825 W. Roosevelt, Rd., Westchester, IL 60153 312-345-7474

Gospel Light Publications, 2300 Knoll Dr., Ventura, CA 93003 805-644-9721

Gospel Publishing House, A/G, 1445 Boonville, Springfield, MO 65802 417-862-2781

Green Leaf Press, P.O. Box 6880, Alhambra, CA 91802 213-281-6809

Group Books, P.O. Box 481, Loveland, CO 80537 303-669-3836

Harold Shaw Publishers, P.O. Box 567, Carol Stream, IL 60189 312-665-6700

Harper & Row Publishers, Inc., 1700 Montgomery St., San Francisco, CA 94111 415-989-9000

Harvest House Publishers, Inc., 1075 Arrowsmith, Eugene, OR 97402 503-343-0123

Herald Press, Menn., 616 Walnut Ave., Scottdale, PA 15683 412-887-8500

Here's Life Publishers, Inc., P.O. Box 1576, San Bernardino, CA 92402 714-886-7981

Holman Bible Publishers, 127 Ninth Ave., N., Nashville, TN 37234 615-251-2510

International Bible Publishing Co., Inc., P.O. Box 814091, Dallas, TX 75381 214-620-9190

InterVarsity Press, P.O. Box 1400, Downers Grove, IL 60515 312-964-5700

John Knox Press, Pres. Ch./U.S.A., 341 Ponce de Leon Ave. NE, Atlanta, GA 30365 404-873-1531

Judson Press, Valley Forge, PA 19482 215-768-2122

Keats Publishing Co., P.O. Box 876, New Canaan, CT 06840 203-966-8721

Kregel Publications, P.O. Box 2607, Grand Rapids, MI 49501 616-451-4775

Loizeaux Brothers, Inc., P.O. Box 277, Neptune, NJ 07753 201-774-8144

Master Book Publishers, 111 S. Marshall Ave., El Cajon, CA 92020 619-442-6671

Meriweather Publishing, Ltd. / Contemporary Drama Music, P.O. Box 7710, Colorado Springs, CO 80933 303-594-4422

Moody Press, 820 N. LaSalle Dr., Chicago, IL 60610 312-973-7800

Morehouse-Barlow Co., 78 Danbury Rd., Wilton, CT 06897 203-762-0721

Mott Media, 1000 E. Huron Street, Milford, MI 48042 313-685-8773

Multnomah Press, 10209 SE Division St., Portland, OR 97266 503-257-0526

National Publishing Co., P.O. Box 8386, Philadelphia, PA 19101 215-732-1863

NavPress, P.O. Box 6000, Colorado Springs, CO 80934 303-598-1212

Omega Publications, P.O. Box 4130, Medford, OR 97501 503-826-9877

OMF Books, 404 S. Church St., Robesonia, PA 19551 215-693-5881

Oxford University Press, 200 Madison Ave., New York NY 10016 212-679-7300

Paraclete Press, P.O. Box 1568, Orleans, MA 02653 617-255-4685

Pentecostal Publishing House, United. Pent. Ch., 8855 Dunn Rd., Hazelwood, MO 63042 314-837-7300

Presbyterian & Reformed Publishing Co., P.O. Box 817, Phillipsburg, NJ 08865 201-454-0505

Roper Press, Inc., 915 Dragon St., Dallas, TX 75207 214-742-6696

Scripture Press Publications, Inc., 1825 College Ave., Wheaton, IL 60187 312-668-6000

Servant Publications, P.O. Box 8516, Ann Arbor, MI 48107 313-761-8983

Standard Publishing Co., 8121 Hamilton Ave., Cincinnati, OH 45231 513-931-4050

Sweet Publishing Co., P.O. Box 18928, Fort Worth, TX 76118 817-585-2667

Thomas Nelson Publishers, P.O. Box 141000, Nashville, TN 37214 615-889-9000

Tyndale House Publishers, 336 Gundersen Dr., Carol Stream, IL 60188 312-668-8300

The Upper Room, P.O. Box 189, Nashville, TN 37203 615-327-2700

Victor Books, P.O. Box 1825, Wheaton, IL 60189 312-668-6000

Vision House, P.O. Box 3875, Ventura, CA 93006 805-644-9721

Warner Press, Inc., P.O. Box 2499, Anderson, IN 46018 317-644-7721

The Westminster Press, 925 Chestnut St., Philadelphia, PA 19107 215-928-2700

Whitaker House, Pittsburgh and Colfax Sts., Springdale, PA 15144 412-274-4440

Wm. B. Eerdmans Publishing Co., 225 Jefferson Ave. SE, Grand Rapids, MI 49503 616-459-4591

Word Publishing, a division of Word, Inc., P.O. Box 1790, Waco, TX 76703 817-772-7650

The Zondervan Corp., 1415 Lake Dr. SE, Grand Rapids, MI 49506 616-698-6900

EVANGELICAL PRESS ASSOCIATION
P.O. Box 4550
Overland Park, KS 66204
913-381-2017
Gary Warner,
Executive Secretary
(IDAK: 2700)

Since its formation in 1949, the Evangelical Press Association has sought to enhance the professional stature and spiritual influence of Christian journalism. Members are asked to subscribe to a seven-point doctrinal statement which is NAE's own statement of faith.

Advance, A/G, 1445 Boonville Ave., Springfield, MO 65802 417-862-2781, Ext. 1462

Advent Christian Witness, Adv., Chr. Gen. Conf., P.O. Box 23152 Charlotte, NC 28212 704-545-6161

Advocate, Chs. of Christ in Chr. Union, P.O. Box 30, Circleville, OH 43113 614-474-8856

Again, P.O. Box 106, Mt. Hermon, CA 94051 408-338-3644

ASCW Scope, P.O. Box 1209, Minneapolis, MN 55440 612-330-3413

The Alliance Teacher, C&MA, 3825 Hartzdale Dr., Camp Hill, PA 17011 717-761-7044

The Alliance Witness, C&MA, Box C, Nyack, NY 10960 914-353-0750

Asbury Theological Seminary, N. Lexington Ave., Wilmore KY 40390 606-858-3581

The Associate Reformed Presbyterian, Assoc. Ref. Pres. Ch., One Cleveland St., Greenville, SC 29601 803-232-8297

Athletes in Action, 2700 Little Mountain Dr., San Bernardino, CA 92405 714-886-7229

The Banner, Chr. Ref., 2850 Kalamazoo Ave. SE, Grand Rapids, MI 49506 616-241-1691

Believer's Guide, P.O. Box 3, Round Rock, TX 78680 512-255-9907

Between Times, 1200 East Fifth St., Anderson, IN 46012 307-664-7721

Beyond, P.O. Box 248, Waxhaw, NC 28173 704-843-2185

Bible-In-Life Friends, 850 N. Grove Ave., Elgin, IL 60120 312-741-2400

Bible-In-Life Pix, 850 N. Grove Ave., Elgin, IL 60120 312-741-2400

Bibles For the World News, P.O. Box 805, Wheaton, IL 60189 312-668-7733

Biblical Research Monthly, 4005 Verdugo Rd., Los Angeles, CA 90065 213-257-8162

Blessings, Rt. 2, Box 279, Bradenton, FL 34202 813-747-6481

Books for Better Living, P.O. Box 879, Evergreen, CO 80439 303-670-3390

Bookstore Journal, P.O. Box 200, Colorado Springs, CO 80901 303-670-3390

Bread, Ch. of the Naz., 6401 The Paseo, Kansas City, MO 64131 816-333-7000

Breakthrough, P.O. Box 1122, Wheaton, IL 60189 312-690-8900

The Brethren Evangelist, Breth. Ch., 524 College Ave., Ashland, OH 44805 419-289-1708

Brethren Missionary Herald, Grace Breth., Box 544, Winona Lake, IN 46590 219-267-7158

Briefing, P.O. Box 1173, Portland, OR 97207 503-643-0777

Broadcaster Magazine, Box 1, La Mirada, CA 90637 213-947-4561

Businessgram, P.O. Box 21, Bowling Green, OH 43402 419-354-1037

Call to Prayer, Box WGM, Marion, IN 46952 317-664-7331

Calvinist Contact, 99 Niagara St., St. Catharines, Ontario, L2R 4L3 Canada 416-682-8311

Campus Life, 495 Gundersen Dr., Carol Stream, IL 60188 312-260-6200

CBMC Contact, 1800 McCallie Ave., Chattanooga, TN 37404 615-698-4444

Charisma, 190 N. Westmonte Dr., Altamonte Springs, FL 32714 305-869-5005

The Chosen People, 100 Hunt Rd., P.O. Box 2000, Orangeburg, NY 10962 914-359-8535

Christ For The Nations, P.O. Box 24910, Dallas, TX 75224 214-376-1711

Christian Advertising Forum, 5007 Carriage Dr. SW, Roanoke, VA 24018 703-989-1330

The Christian Chiropractor, 2224 S. College Ave., Fort Collins, CO 80525 303-482-2210; 493-6363

The Christian Contender, P.O. Box 117, Hockley, TX 77447 713-256-2555

01234567890123

5

The Christian Courier, 915 W. Wisconsin Ave., Sta. 214, Milwaukee, WI 53233 414-271-6400

Christian Education Journal, One Pennsylvania Ave., Glen Ellyn, IL 60137 312-668-6000 Ext. 228

Christian Herald, 40 Overlook Dr., Chappaqua, NY 10514 914-769-9000

Christian Home and School, 3350 E. Paris Ave. SE, P.O. Box 8709, Grand Rapids, MI 49508 616-957-1070

The Christian Leader, Menn. Breth., Box L, Hillsboro, KS 67063 316-947-3966

Christian Life, 396 E. St. Charles Rd., Wheaton, IL 60188 312-653-4200

Christian Living, 850 N. Grove Ave., Elgin, IL 60120 312-741-2400

Christian Medical Society Journal, 124 Garden Ln., Decatur, GA 30030 404-634-4912

Christian Mission, R.R. 10, Box 1, Charlottesville, VA 22901 804-977-5650

The Christian Reader, 336 Gundersen, Wheaton, IL 60187 312-668-8300

Christian School, 1308 Santa Rosa, Wheaton, IL 60187 312-653-4588

Christian Standard, 8121 Hamilton Ave., Cincinnati, OH 45231 513-931-4050

Christian Update, 5431 SE Foster Rd., Portland, OR 97206 503-771-1141

The Christian Writer, P.O. Box 5650, Lakeland, FL 33803 813-644-3548

Christianity Today, 465 Gundersen Dr., Carol Stream, IL 60188 312-260-6200

The Church Advocate, Ch. of God/Findlay, OH, P.O. Box 926, Findlay, OH 45839 419-424-1961

Church of God Evangel, Ch. of God, 1080 Montgomery Ave., Cleveland, TN 37311 615-476-4512

The Church Herald, Ref. Ch., 1324 Lake Dr. SE, Grand Rapids, MI 49506 616-458-5156

Co-Laborer, Free Will Bapt., P.O. Box 1088, Nashville, TN 37202 615-361-1010

Command, P.O. Box 36200, Denver, CO 80236 303-761-1984

Commonlife, P.O. Box 7004, Port Huron, MI 48301 313-985-5305

Compassion Today, P.O. Box 4491, London, Ontario N6A 5G8 Canada 519-473-9220

Compassion Update, 3955 Cragwood Dr., Colorado Springs, CO 80933 303-594-9900

Conservative Baptist, P.O. Box 66, Wheaton, IL 60189 312-653-5350

Contact Magazine, Free Will Bapt., P.O. Box 1088, Nashville, TN 37202 615-361-1010

Contemporary Christian Music, P.O. Box 6300, Laguna Hills, CA 92654 714-951-9106

Conviction, 7704-24th Ave. NW, Seattle, WA 98117 206-782-0588

Cornerstone, 4707 N. Malden, Chicago, IL 60640 312-561-2450

Counselor, P.O. Box 632, Glen Ellyn, IL 60138 312-668-6000

The Covenant Companion, Evan. Cov. Ch., 6101 N. Francisco Ave., Chicago, IL 60625 312-784-3000

Covenanter Witness, Reformed Pres. Ch., 800 Wood St., Pittsburgh, PA 15221 412-241-0436

Creator Magazine, 25 Rolling Hills Dr., Wichita, KS 67212 316-722-8092

Crossroads, 40 Kemble St., Lenox, MA 01240 413-637-1520 Ext. 211

Crusader Magazine, P.O. Box 7244, Grand Rapids, MI 49510 616-241-5616

Crux, 2130 Westbrook Mall, Vancouver, British Columbia V6T 1W6 Canada 604-224-3245

Decision, 1300 Harmon Place, Minneapolis, MN 55403 612-338-0500

Design, Wesleyan Ch., P.O. Box 2000, Marion, IN 46952 317-674-3301

Discipleship Journal, P.O. Box 6000, Colorado Springs, CO 80934 303-598-1212 Ext. 291

Door of Hope, P.O. Box 10460, Glendale, CA 91209 818-956-7500

Doorways, P.O. Box C, Colorado Springs, CO 80906 303-576-2700

El Heraldo De Santidad, 64101 The Paseo, Kansas City, MO 64131 816-333-7000

Emphasis on Faith and Living, Miss. Ch., 3901 S. Wayne Ave., Fort Wayne, IN 46807 219-456-4502

Emphasis on Faith and Living, Miss. Ch., 3901 S. Wayne Ave., Fort Wayne, IN 46807 219-456-4502

End Times Messenger, Apost. Ch. of Pent., No. 4-3026 Taylor St. E., Saskatoon, Saskatchewan S7H 4J2 Canada 306-374-1944

ESA Update, P.O. Box 76560, Washington, DC 20013 703-237-7464

Eternity Magazine, 1716 Spruce St., Philadelphia, PA 19103 215-546-3696

Europe Report, 330 Schmale Rd., Carol Stream, IL 60188 312-462-8050

Evangel, Free Meth. Ch. of N. Am., 901 College Ave., Winona Lake, IN 46590 219-267-7656

The Evangelical Baptist, Fel. of Evang. Bapt. Chs. of Canada, 74 Sheppard Ave., W., Willowdale, Ontario M2N 1M3 Canada 416-223-8696

The Evangelical Beacon, Evang. Free Ch. of Am., 1515 E. 66th St., Minneapolis, MN 55423 612-866-3343

Evangelical Friend, Evang. Fr. Al., P.O. Box 232, Newburg, OR 97132 503-538-9419

Evangelical Missions Quarterly, P.O. Box 794, Wheaton, IL 60189 312-653-2158

Evangelical Newsletter, 1716 Spruce St., Philadelphia, PA 19103 215-546-3696

The Evangelical Recorder, 25 Ballyconner Ct., Willowdale, Ontario M2M 4B3 Canada 416-226-6380

Evangelical Visitor, Breth. in Christ Ch., P.O. Box 166, Nappanee, IN 46550 219-773-3164

Evangelizing Today's Child, P.O. Box 348, Warrenton, MO 63383 314-456-4321

Faith Alive, P.O. Box 8800 Sta. B., Willowdale, Ontario M2K 2R6 Canada

Family Life Today, P.O. Box 93670, Pasadena, CA 91109 213-791-0039

Focus, Ch. of the Naz., 6401 The Paseo, Kansas City, MO 64132 816-333-7000, Ext. 354

Focus on the Family, 41 E. Foothill Blvd., Arcadia, CA 91006 818-445-1579

The Forerunner, P.O. Box 1799, Gainesville, FL 32602 904-375-6000

Freeway, P.O. Box 632, Glen Ellyn, IL 60138 312-668-6000 Ext. 327

Fundamentalist Journal, 2220 Langhorne Rd., Lynchburg, VA 24514 804-528-4112

The Gem, Ch. of God/Findlay, OH, P.O. Box 926 Findlay, OH 45839 419-424-1961

General Baptist Messenger, Gen. Bapt., 100 Stinson Dr., Poplar Bluff, MO 63901 314-785-7746

Good News, 308 E. Main St., Wilmore, KY 40390 606-858-4661

Good News Broadcaster, P.O. Box 82808, Lincoln, NE 68501 402-474-4567

Good News Herald, P.O. Box 249, Hiawatha, IA 52233 319-393-2622

Good News Herald, 1416 Larkin Williams, Fenton, MO 63026 314-343-4359

Gospel Call, 232 N. Lake Ave., #209, Pasadena, CA 91101 213-796-5424

The Gospel Message, 10,000 North Oak, Kansas City, MO 64155 816-734-8500

Gospel Tidings, Evang. Menn. Breth., 5800 S. 14th St. Omaha, NE 68107 402-731-4780

The Grace Chronicle, 2695 Creve Coeur Mill Rd., Maryland Heights, MO 63043 314-291-6647

Grace Tidings, 1515 South 10th St., Omaha, NE 68108 402-342-3377

Group Magazine, P.O. Box 481, Loveland, CO 80539 303-669-3836

Growing Together, 850 N. Grove, Elgin, IL 60120 312-741-2400

Heartbeat, Free Will Bapt., P.O. Box 1088, Nashville, TN 37202 615-361-1010

The Helping Hand, Pent. Ho. Ch. Intl., P.O. Box 12609, Oklahoma City, OK 73157 405-787-7110

Herald of Holiness, Ch. of the Naz., 6401 The Paseo, Kansas City, MO 64131 806-333-7000

Heritage Herald, c/o PTL, Charlotte, NC 28279 704-542-6000 Ext. 2116

High Adventure, A/G, 1445 Boonville Ave., Springfield, MO 65802 417-862-2781

Horizon International Magazine, P.O. Box 28429, San Diego, CA 92128 619-566-3404

ICA News, 5189 Verdugo Way, Camarillo, CA 93010 805-987-8888

Impact, Cons. Bapt., P.O. Box 5, Wheaton, IL 60189 312-665-1200

In Other Words, 19891 Beach Blvd., Huntington Beach, CA 92647 714-536-9346

India Journal, 4221 Richmond NW, Grand Rapids, MI 49504 616-453-8855

Insight, P.O. Box 7244, Grand Rapids, MI 49510 616-241-5616

Interlit, David C. Cook Foundation, Cook Square, Elgin, IL 60120 312-741-2411

International Faith Report, 4500 S. Garnett, Sta. 910, Tulsa, OK 74146 918-665-2773

The International Pentecostal Holiness Advocate, Pent. Ho. Ch. Intl., P.O. Box 12609, Oklahoma City, OK 73157 405-787-7110

Inter-Varsity News, 233 Langdon St., Madison, WI 53703 608-257-0263

In Touch, Wesleyan Ch., P.O. Box 2000, Marion, IN 46952 317-674-3301

It's God's World, P.O. Box 2330, Asheville, NC 28802 704-253-8063

Journal of Christian Camping, P.O. Box 646, Wheaton, IL 60189 312-690-8606

Journal of the American Scientific Affiliation, P.O. Box J, Ipswich, MA 01938 617-356-5656

Jubilee, P.O. Box 17500, Washington, DC 20016 703-759-4521

Kindred Spirit, 3909 Swiss Ave., Dallas, TX 75204 214-824-3094

Latin America Evangelist, P.O. Box 141368 Coral Gables, FL 33114 301-444-6228

Leader Ideabank, 850 N. Grove, Elgin, IL 60120 312-714-2400

Leadership, 465 Gundersen Dr., Carol Stream, IL 60188 312-260-6200

Librarian's World, P.O. Box 353, Glen Ellyn, IL 60138 312-668-0519

Light and Life Magazine, Free Meth. Ch., 901 College Ave., Winona Lake, IN 46590 219-267-7656

Light Today, 144 Tices Ln., East Brunswick, NJ 08816 201-238-5454

Lighted Pathway, Ch. of God/Cleveland, TN, 922 Montgomery Ave., Cleveland, TN 37311 615-476-4512

Live, A/G, 1445 Boonville Ave., Springfield, MO 65802 417-862-2781 Ext. 5483

Living Today, 1825 College Ave., Wheaton, IL 60187 312-668-6000

The Lutheran Standard, Am. Luth. Ch., P.O. Box 1209, Minneapolis MN 55440 612-330-3300

Map International Report, P.O. Box 50, Wheaton, IL 60189 312-653-6010

The Mennonite, Gen. Conf. Menn. Ch., P.O. Box 347, Newton, KS 67114 316-283-5100

Mennonite Brethren Herald, Mnn. Br. Chs., 159 Henderson Hwy., Winnipeg, Manitoba R2L 1L4 Canada 204-667-3560

Message, 8435 NE Glisan St., Portland, OR 97220 503-255-0332

Message of the Cross, 6820 Auto Club Rd., Bloomington, MN 55438 612-944-2121

Message of the Open Bible, Open Bible Ch., 2020 Bell Ave., Des Moines, IA 50315 515-288-6761

Messenger, Pent. Free Will Bapt., P.O. Box 1568, Dunn, NC 28334 919-892-4161

Mike Evans Ministries, P.O. Box 709, Bedford, TX 76021 817-540-2221

Miracle Living Magazine, 14240 N. 43rd Ave., Glendale, AZ 85306 602-978-5511

Mission Frontiers, 1605 E. Elizabeth St., Pasadena, CA 91104 818-797-1111

Missionary Monthly, Chr. Ref., Ref. Chs., 1869 Robinson Rd. SE, Grand Rapids, MI 49506 616-458-0404

The Missionary Tidings, Free Meth. Ch., 901 College Ave., Winona Lake, IN 46590 219-267-4656

Montana Christian, P.O. Box 291, Lewistown, MT 59457 406-538-8352

Moody Alumni, Moody Bible Institute, 820 N. LaSalle Dr., Chicago, IL 60610 312-329-4412

Moody Monthly Magazine, 820 N. LaSalle Dr., Chicago, IL 60645 312-274-1879

Mountain Movers Magazine, A/G, 1445 Boonville Ave., Springfield, MO 65802 417-682-2781 Ext. 1213

Narramore Christian Foundation, 1409 N. Walnut Grove Ave., Rosemead, CA 91770 213-228-7000

Navlog, P.O. Box 6000, Colorado Springs, CO 80934 303-598-1212

New Horizons in the Orthodox Presbyterian Church, Orth. Pres. Ch., 7401 Old York Rd., Philadelphia, PA 19126 215-635-1131

New Wine Magazine, P.O. Box Z, Mobile, AL 36616 205-460-9010

O Arauto Da Santidate, Ch. of the Naz., 6401 The Paseo, Kansas City, MO 64131 816-333-7000 Ext. 263

The Omega Times, 835 Prairie Ave., Downers Grove, IL 60515 312-960-4935

OMS Outreach, P.O. Box A, Greenwood, IN 46142 317-881-6751

Onward Christian Courier, P.O. Box 83, Loretto, MN 55357 612-478-6850

Open Doors Magazine, P.O. Box 2100, Orange, CA 92669 714-997-3920

The Open Letter, Cov. Fell. Pres., 7700 Davis Dr., St. Louis, MO 63105 314-727-1240

The Oracle, Oral Roberts University, 7777 S. Lewis, Tulsa, OK 74171

The Overcomer, Open Bible Stan. Chs., 2020 Bell Ave., Des Moines, IA 50315 515-288-6761

Partners, P.O. Box 15025, San Jose, CA 95115 408-298-0965

Pastoral Renewal, P.O. Box 8617, Ann Arbor, MI 48107 313-761-8505

The PCA Messenger, Pres. Ch. in Am., P.O. Box 39, Decatur, GA 30031 404-292-6102

The Pentecostal Evangel, A/G, 1445 Boonville Ave., Springfield, MO 65802 417-862-2781, Ext. 1455

The Pentecostal Messenger, Pent. Ch. of God, P.O. Box 850, Joplin, MO 64802 417-624-7050

The Pentecostal Minister, Ch. of God/Cleveland, TN, P.O. Box 2430, Cleveland, TN 37320 615-472-3361

The Pentecostal Testimony, Pent. Assem. of God, Canada, 10 Overlea Blvd., Toronto, Ontario M4H 1A5 Canada 416-425-1010

People of Destiny Magazine, P.O. Box 2335, Wheaton, MD 20902 301-946-4486

Perspective, P.O. Box 788, Wheaton, IL 60189 312-293-1600

The Planter, P.O. Box 176, Hackensack, NJ 07602 201-342-6202

Possibilities, 2029 P St. NW, Washington, DC 20036 202-296-3760

Power For Living, P.O. Box 632, Glen Ellyn, IL 60138 312-668-6000

The Prayer Line, P.O. Box 55145, Seattle, WA 98155 206-363-3586

The Preacher's Magazine, Ch. of the Naz., 6401 The Paseo, Kansas City, MO 64131 816-333-7000

The Presbyterian Journal, P.O. Box 2330, Asheville, NC 28802 704-254-4015

Presstime, P.O. Box 9215, Chattanooga, TN 37412 615-624-0337

The Printed Page, P.O. Box 477, Columbus, OH 43216 704-267-3116

The Proclaimer, Azusa Pacific University, Citrus and Alostra, Azusa, CA 91702 818-969-3434

Pulpit Helps, 6815 Shallowford Rd., Chattanooga, TN 37422 615-894-6060

The Quiet Miracle, P.O. Box 477, Columbus, OH 43216 614-267-3116

Quiet Revolution, 1655 St. Charles St., Jackson, MS 39209 601-353-1635

Radiance Magazine, Box Z, Eureka, CA 95501 704-443-6315

The Railroad Evangelist, R.R. 4, Box 73, Spencer, IN 47460 812-829-4667

RBC Discovery Digest, P.O. Box 22, Grand Rapids, MI 49555 616-942-6770

Reflections, 6511 Princess Garden Pkwy., Lanham, MD 20706 301-552-1400

The Reformed Journal, 255 Jefferson St. SE, Grand Rapids, MI 49503 616-459-5691

Religious Broadcasting, CN 1926, Morristown, NJ 07960 201-428-5400

Response, 3307 Third Ave, W., Seattle, WA 98119 206-281-2051

Scope, Bluffton College, P.O. Box 668, Bluffton, OH 45817 419-258-8015, Ext. 241

SCP Journal/Newsletter, P.O. Box 4308, Berkeley, CA 94704 415-540-0300

Sharing the Victory, 8701 Leeds Rd., Kansas City, MO 64129 816-921-0909

SIM Now, 10 Huntingdale Blvd., Scarborough, Ontario M2W 2S5 Canada 416-497-2422

Single i, P.O. Box 11394, Kansas City, MO 64112 816-763-9401

The Small Group Letter, P.O. Box 6000, Colorado Springs, CO 80934 303-598-1212

Son Times, P.O. Box 747, Fargo, ND 58107 701-280-2221

S.O.W., Ch. of God / Cleveland, TN, P.O. Box 2430, Cleveland, TN 37320 615-472-3361

The Sower, 16801 Van Dam Rd., South Holland, IL 60473 312-331-2094

Sparks, P.O. Box 1122, Wheaton, IL 60189 312-690-8900

Spirit of Life, 9962 Ferry Dr., St. Louis, MO 63123 314-849-4202

Spiritual Fitness in Business, 12011 Coit Rd., Sta. 107, Dallas, TX 75251 214-661-8500

Sprint, 850 N. Grove, Elgin, IL 60120 312-741-2400

Standard, Ch. of the Naz., 6401 The Paseo, Kansas City, MO 64131 816-333-7000

Student Action for Christ, Inc., P.O. Box 608, Herrin, IL 62948

Success, P.O. Box 15337, Denver, CO 80215 303-988-5300

Sunday Digest, 840 N. Grove Ave., Elgin, IL 60120 312-741-2400, Ext. 428.

Sunday School Counselor, A/B, 1445 Boonville Ave., Springfield, MO 65802 417-862-2781

Symbiosis, 7729 E. Greenway Rd., Scottsdale, AZ 85260 602-998-3100

Team Horizons, P.O. Box 969, Wheaton, IL 60189 312-653-5300

Teen Power, P.O. Box 632, Glen Ellyn, IL 60138 312-668-6000

The Tie, 6675 Worthington-Galena Rd., Worthington, OH 43085

The Times-Arrow, P.O. Box 819000, Dallas, TX 75381 214-620-1586

Today's Christian Woman, 2029 P. St. NW, Washington, DC 20036 202-296-3762

Today's Remnant, P.O. Box 2321, Pleasant Hill, CA 94523 415-676-5886

Together, PTL Television Network, Charlotte, NC 28279 704-542-6000, Ext. 2343

Touch, P.O. Box 7244, Grand Rapids, MI 49510 616-241-5616

Trails, P.O. Box 788, Wheaton, IL 60189 312-293-1600

The Trim Tab, c/o Fellowship of Christian Airline Personnel, 225 McBride Rd., Fayetteville, GA 30214 404-461-9320

Triumph, 114 Bush Rd., Nashville, TN 37217 615-361-1221

TSF Bulletin, 233 Langdon, Madison, WI 53703 608-257-1103

The Twin Cities Christian, 1619 Portland Ave. S., Minneapolis, MN 55404 612-339-9579

The United Brethren, U. Breth. in Christ, 302 Lake St., Huntington, IN 46750 219-356-2312

United Evangelical, ECC, P.O. Box 186, Myerstown, PA 17067 717-866-7581

United Evangelical Action, P.O. Box 28, Wheaton, IL 60189 312-665-0500

U.S. Press, P.O. Box 3275, Silver Springs, MD 20901 301-434-3220

Valley Christian News, P.O. Box 9854, Phoenix, AZ 85068 602-997-9410

The Vanguard, 8435 NE Glisan, Portland, OR 97220 503-255-0332

Venture, P.O. Box 150, Wheaton, IL 60189 312-665-0630

Victory, P.O. Box 700, San Diego, CA 92138 619-239-4300

Virtue Magazine, P.O. Box 850, Sisters, OR 97759 503-549-8261

Vista, Wesleyan Ch., P.O. Box 2000, Marion, IN 46952 317-674-3301

Vital Christianity, Ch. of God/Anderson, IN, P.O. Box 2499, Anderson, IN 46018 317-644-7721

Voice of Prophecy News, P.O. Box 2525, Newbury Park, CA 91320 805-599-1911

The Wesleyan Advocate, Wesleyan Ch., P.O. Box 2000, Marion, IN 46952 317-674-3301

The Wesleyan World, Wesleyan Ch., P.O. Box 2000, Marion, IN 46952 317-674-3301

Wheaton Alumni, Wheaton College, Wheaton, IL 60187 312-260-5173

Wherever, P.O. Box 969, Wheaton, IL 60189 312-653-5300

Witmarsum, Bluffton College, P.O. Box 1208, Bluffton, OH 45817

The Wittenburg Door, 1224 Greenfield Dr., El Cajon, CA 92021 619-440-2333

Woman's Touch, A/G, 1445 Boonville Ave., Springfield, MO 65802 417-862-2781

"Word and Way," MO Bapt. Conv., 400 E. High, Jefferson City, MO 65101 314-635-7931

The Word of Faith, P.O. Box 50126, Tulsa, OK 74150 918-258-1588

The Workman Quarterly, Ch. of God/Findlay, OH, P.O. Box 926, Findley, OH 45839 419-424-1961

World Concern Magazine, 19303 Freemont Ave. N., Seattle, WA 98133 206-546-7201

World Gospel Crusades Bulletin, P.O. Box 3, Upland, CA 91786 714-982-1564

World Harvest, P.O. Box 12, South Bend, IN 46624 219-291-3292

World Mission, Ch. of the Naz., 6401 The Paseo, Kansas City, MO 64131 816-333-7000

World Vision, 919 W. Huntington Dr., Monrovia, CA 91016 213-797-3966

Worldorama, Pent. Ho. Ch. Intl., P.O. Box 12609, Oklahoma City, OK 73157 405-787-7110

Worldteam Harvest, P.O. Box 143038, Coral Gables, FL 33114 305-446-0861

Worldwide Challenge, Arrowhead Springs, Dept. 65-00, San Bernardino, CA 92414 714-886-5224, Ext. 1242

World-Wide Missions, Box 7125 Pasadena, CA 91109 818-449-4313

Worldwide News, Box 368, Lincoln Park, NJ 07035 201-696-1900

Young Ambassador, P.O. Box 82808, Lincoln, NE 68501 402-474-4567

The Young Missionary, Wesleyan Ch., P.O. Box 2000, Marion, IN 46952 317-674-3301

Youth and Christian Education Leadership, Ch. of God/Cleveland, TN, 922 Montgomery Ave. NE, Cleveland, TN 37311 615-476-4512

Youth Illustrated, 1825 College Ave., Wheaton, IL 60187 312-668-6000

FILM PRODUCERS
AND DISTRIBUTORS
(IDAK: 7813)

Allied Film & Video Services, 3011 Diamond Park Dr., Dallas, TX 75247 214-631-5670

Allied Film Laboratory, Inc., 7375 Woodward Ave., Detroit, MI 48202 313-871-2222

Audio Visual Marketing Services, P.O. Box 231, Pacific Palisades, CA 90272 213-454-2966

Baptist Spanish Publishing House, P.O. Box 4255, El Paso, TX 79904 915-566-9656

Bauman Bible Telecasts, 3436 Lee Hwy., Arlington, VA 22207 703-243-1300

Campus Crusade for Christ, Intl., Arrowhead Springs, San Bernardino, CA 92414 714-886-5224

Canon Media Publishing, Ltd., P.O. Box 1616, Wheaton, IL 60189 312-653-1616

Christian Communication, 709 E. Colorado Blvd., Sta. 150, Pasadena, CA 91101 213-449-4400

Christian Leadership Training, 21300 Mack Ave., Grosse Pointe Woods, MI 48236 313-343-8856

Cinema Associates, Inc., P.O. Box 9237, Seattle, WA 98109 206-622-7378

Cornerstone Pictures, 6331 Glade Ave., Sta. H204, Woodland Hills, CA 91367 213-716-7722

Creative Productions, Inc., 968 E. Davies Ave., Littleton, CO 80122 303-794-6482

Crowning Touch Films, P.O. Box 425, Durand, MI 48429 517-288-4290

David C. Cook Publishing Co., 850 N. Grove Ave., Elgin, IL 60120 312-741-2400

Day Star Productions, 326 S. Wille Ave., Wheeling, IL 60090 312-541-3547

Edward T. McDougal Films, 682 Ardsley Rd., Winnetka, IL 60093 312-446-5432

Episcopal Radio-TV Foundation, Inc., Episc. Ch., 3379 Peachtree Rd., NE, Sta. 999, Atlanta, GA 30326 404-233-5419

Evangelical Films, Inc., 2848 W. Kingsley, Garland, TX 75041 214-278-3531

Faith Films, Ltd., P.O. Box 1096, Coquitlam, British Columbia V3J 6Z4 Canada 604-562-7955

Family Films, 14622 Lanark St., Panorama City, CA 91402 213-997-7500

211

Family Life Distributors, Inc., P.O. Box 20059, El Cajon, CA 92021 714-579-0887

Family Resources, R.R. 1, Box 151G, Aurora, NE 68818 402-694-3969

Films for Christ Assoc., 2432 W. Peoria Ave., #1326, Phoenix, AZ 85029 602-997-7400

Gateway Films, Inc., P.O. Box A, Lansdale, PA 19446 215-584-1893

Genesis Project, 5201 Leesburg Pike, Sta. 201, Falls Church, VA 22041 703-998-0800

Glenray Communications, P.O. Box 40400, Pasadena, CA 91104 818-797-5462

Global Films, P.O. Box 805, Wheaton, IL 60189 312-668-7764

Gospel Films, Inc., P.O. Box 455, 2735 E. Apple, Muskegon, MI 49442 616-773-3361

Harvest Productions, Evangelical Baptist Missions, P.O. Box 2225, Kokomo, IN 46902 219-267-2038

Heartland Productions, Inc., P.O. Box 3752 Urbandale Station, 5907 Meredith Dr., Des Moines, IA 50322 515-278-4688

Heritage Media Productions, P.O. Box 1867, Fresno, CA 93718 209-251-8681

Image Associates of Indiana, Inc., Sta. F, 117 Lincolnway East, Mishawaka, IN 46544 219-259-6758

Image Transform Laboratories, 3611 N. San Fernando Blvd., Burbank, CA 91505 213-841-3812

Inspirational Film Distributors, Inc., 2508 Hayes Ct., Burnsville, MN 55337 612-890-1969

John Schmidt Productions, 2300 E. Brookdale Pl., Fullerton, CA 92631 714-871-1933

JRB Motion Graphics, Ltd., 4117 Stone Way N., Seattle, WA 98103 206-632-0834

Ken Anderson Films, P.O. Box 618, Winona Lake, IN 46590 2199-267-5774

Kuntz Bros. Inc., P.O. Box 141109, Dallas, TX 75214 214-691-4500

Leodas & Arbusto & Assoc., Inc., 333 E. 49th St., New York, NY 10017 212-688-4308

Life Productions, Inc., P.O. Box B, Americus, GA 31709 912-924-9601

Lutheran Television, 2185 Hamton Ave., St. Louis, MO 63139 314-647-4900

3M Co., Building 223-25 E., St. Paul, MN 55144 612-733-0740

Mass Media Ministries, 2116 N. Charles St., Baltimore, MD 21218 301-727-3270

Mastersoft, 4961 Sioux Way, Okemos, MI 48864 517-349-9881

Maritz Communication Co., Laboratory Div., 1395 N. Hwy. Dr., Fenton, MO 63026 314-225-1354

Mark IV Pictures, Inc., P.O. Box 3751 Urbandale Station, Des Moines, IA 50322 515-278-4737

Mel White Productions, 1990 Sierra Madre Villa, Pasadena, CA 91107 213-791-3908

Merit Media Intl., 1314 Circle Way, Laguna Beach, CA 92651 714-494-1944

Missionary Enterprises, P.O. Box 2127, LaHabra, CA 90631 213-697-4617

Moody Institute of Science, 12000 E. Washington Blvd., Whittier, CA 90606 213-698-8256

New Day Productions, 7434 Tower, Fort Worth, TX 76118 817-595-2418

New Liberty Enterprises, Inc., 1805 W. Magnolia, Burbank, CA 91506 213-842-6167

Olive's Film Productions, Inc., P.O. Box 9, Madison, AL 32758 205-837-4166

Omega Films, P.O. Box 1872, Rancho Santa Fe, CA 92067 619-756-5078

Paulist Productions, P.O. Box 1057, Pacific Palisades, CA 90272 213-454-0688

Paulmar, Inc., 3316 Commercial Ave., Northbrook, IL 60062 312-498-1020

PSI Film Laboratory, Inc., 3011 Diamond Park Dr., Dallas, TX 75247 214-631-5670

Quadrus Media Ministry, 610 E. State St., Rockford, IL 61104 815-987-3970

Religious Film Corp., P.O. Box 4029, Westlake Village, CA 91359 805-495-7418

Research Technology Intl., 4700 Chase Ave., Lincolnwood, IL 60646 312-677-3000

RJ Communications, Inc., P.O. Box 65633, West Des Moines, IA 60265 515-223-4814

Robert Fuqua Productions, P.O. Box 38261, Dallas, TX 75238 214-343-6721

Southwest Film Lab, Inc., 3024 Fort Worth Ave., Dallas TX 75211 214-331-8347

Sparrow Productions, 8025 Deering Ave., Canoga Park, CA 91304 213-703-6599

Swartwout Productions, 703 Manzanita Dr., Sedona, AZ 86336 602-282-2270

Victory International Productions, P.O. Box 5277, Garden Grove, CA 92645 213-598-7208

Video Communications, Inc., 6535 E. Skelly Dr., Tulsa, OK 74145 908-622-6460

Vision House Films, 2691 Richter Ave., Sta. 117, Irvine, CA 92714 714-863-9440

White Lion Photograph, 146 Melrose, Pl., San Antonio, TX 78212 512-826-3615

Word Publishing, P.O. Box 1790, Waco, TX 76710 817-772-7650

World Thrust Films, 5930 18th St., NE, St. Petersburg, FL 33703 813-527-5205

World Wide Pictures, Inc., The Billy Graham Film Ministry, 1201 Hennepin Ave., Minneapolis, MN 55403 612-338-3335

NRB-MEMBER RADIO STATIONS
Morristown, NJ 07960
201-575-4000
Ben Armstrong, Executive Director

An affiliate of the National Association of Evangelicals, NRB has more than 840 member radio and television stations and evangelical organizations. Its primary functions are to insure quality religious programming and to encourage continued religious freedom in broadcasting.

Alabama

WDJC (93.7 FM), Box 587021, Birmingham, AL 35259 205-879-3324

WNDA (95.1 FM), 2407 9th Ave., Huntsville, AL 35805 205-534-2433

WMOO (1550 AM), 1204 Dauphin St., Mobile, AL 36604 205-432-0595

Alaska

KICY (850 AM), Box 820, Nome, AK 99762 907-443-2213

KICY (100.3 FM), Box 820, Nome, AK 99762 907-443-2213

KJNP (1170 AM), Box 0, North Pole, AK 99705 907-488-2216

KJNP (100.3 FM), Box 0, North Pole, AK 99705 907-488-2216

Arizona

KNLB (91.1 FM), P.O. Box V, Lake Havasu, AZ 86403

KFLR (1230 AM), P.O. Box 6046, Phoenix, AZ 85005 602-258-6717

KHEP (1280 AM), 3883 N. 38th Ave., Phoenix, AZ 85019 602-278-5555

KHEP (101.5 FM), 3883 N. 38th Ave., Phoenix, AZ 85019 602-278-5555

KFLT (1450 AM), P.O. Box 3025, Tucson, AZ 85702 602-882-8511

KHAC (1110 AM), P.O. Box F, Window Rock, AZ 86515 505-371-5587

Arkansas

KITA (1440 AM), 723 W. 14th St., Little Rock, AR 72202 501-375-1440

KJBU (88.1 FM), Box 3100, Siloam Springs, AR 72761 501-524-3131

KLRC (90.3 FM), John Brown University, Siloam Springs, AR 72761 501-524-3131

KMCK (105.7 FM), Siloam Springs, AR 72761 501-524-3154

KUOA (1290 AM), Box 3145 JBU, Siloam Springs, AR 72761 501-524-3154

California

KBRT (740 AM), 1888 Century Park East, Sta. 208, Los Angeles, CA 90067 213-277-9785

KHIS (800 AM), 521 H St., Bakersfield, CA 93304 802-327-0631

KHIS (96.5 FM), 521 H. St., Bakersfield, CA 93304 802-327-0631

KFIA (710 AM), 5738 Marconi, Carmichael, CA 95608 916-485-7710

KGFT (101.7 FM), 5565 Carpinteria Ave., Sta. 23, Carpinteria, CA 93013 805-684-6611

KRDU (1130 AM), 597 N. Alta Ave., Dinuba, CA 93618 209-591-1130

KECR (93.3 FM), 312 W.Douglas, El Cajon, CA 92112 619-442-4414

KIRV (1510 AM), 3636 N. First, Sta. 142, Fresno, CA 93726 209-225-1050

KCVR (1570 AM), Box 600, Lodi, CA 95241 209-368-0626

KGER (1390 AM), 3759 Atlantic Ave., P.O. Box 7126, Long Beach, CA 90807 213-427-7907

KFRN (1280 AM), 447 E. 1st St., Long Beach, CA 90802 213-435-0103

KFSG (96.3 FM), 1100 Glendale, Los Angeles, CA 90026 213-484-1100

KHOF (99.5 FM), 1615 S. Glendale Ave., Glendale, CA 91205 213-245-7575

KDAR (98.3 FM), 500 Esplanade Dr., Sta. 1510, Oxnard, CA 93030 805-485-7357

KPPC (1240 AM), 3844 E. Foothill Blvd. Arcadia, CA 91006 213-681-2486

KEBR (100.5 FM), 3108 Fulton Ave., Sacramento, CA 95821 916-483-8191

KEAR (106.9 FM), 1234 Mariposa St., San Francisco, CA 94107 415-626-3010

KEST (1450 AM), 1231 Market St., San Francisco, CA 94103 415-626-5585

Colorado

KOPF (910 AM), 34555 W. 83rd Ave., Westminster, CO 80030 303-428-0910

Connecticut

WIHS (104.9 FM), Box 117, Middletown, CT 06457 203-346-3846

Florida

WRMB (89.3 FM), 1151 NW 2nd Ave., Boynton Beach, FL 33436 305-737-9762

WSOR (95.3 FM), 940 Tarpon St., Fort Myers, FL 33901 813-334-1393

WGLY (98.3 FM), 20938 S. Dixie Hwy., Miami, FL 33189 305-253-4393

WOZN (970 AM), 2427 N. Univ. Blvd., Jacksonville, FL 33239 904-743-6970

WLIZ (1380 AM), 1939 7th Ave. N., Lake Worth, FL 33461 305-585-5533
WSST (800 AM), Box 800, 8th Ave. SE, Largo, FL 33541 813-581-7800
WMCU (89.7 FM), 2300 NW 135th St., Miami, FL 33167 305-681-4689
WHYM (610 AM), Box 17446, Pensacola, FL 32505 904-438-1605
WWBC (770 AM), 1150 W. King St., Cocoa, FL 32922 305-632-1510
WGNB (1520 AM), Box 8888, St. Petersburg, FL 33738 813-391-9994
WKES (101.5 FM), Box 8888, St. Petersburg, FL 33738 813-391-9994
WTIS (1110 AM), 311 112th Ave. NE, St. Petersburg, FL 33702 813-576-2234
WAJL (1440 AM), Box 17777, Orlando, FL 32860 305-291-9255

Georgia

WAEB (800 AM), 1430 W. Peachtree St., Atlanta, GA 30309 404-875-7777
WHYD (1270 AM), 1825 Buena Vista Rd., Columbus, GA 31906 404-323-3603
WAVO (1420 AM), Box 111, Decatur, GA 30031 404-292-3800
WDGL (1520 AM), 8470 Hospital Dr., Douglasville, GA 30134 404-942-5186
WSSA (1570 AM), Box 831, Morrow, GA 30260 404-361-8843
WYNX (1550 AM), 2460 Atlanta St. SE., Smyrna, GA 30080 404-436-6171
WRAF (90.9 FM), Toccoa Falls College, Toccoa Falls, GA 30598 404-886-6831

Hawaii

KAIM (870 AM), 3555 Harding Ave., Honolulu, HI 96816 808-732-6602
KAIM (95.5 FM), 3555 Harding Ave., Honolulu, HI 96816 808-732-6602

Illinois

WIBI (91.1 FM), Box 1226, Carlinville, IL 52626 217-854-2504
WMBI (1110 AM), 820 N. LaSalle Dr., Chicago, IL 60610 312-329-4300
WMBI (90.1 FM), 820 N. LaSalle Dr., Chicago, IL 60610 312-329-4300
WCBW (104.9 FM), Box 147, Columbia, IL 66236 618-281-5031; 314-487-1006
WCRM (103.9 FM), Sta. 8, 700 Willow Ln., Dundee, IL 60118 312-428-0104
WDLM (960 AM), Box 149, East Moline, IL 61244 309-234-5111
WVVX (103.1 FM), 210 Skokie Valley Rd., Highland Park, IL 60035 312-831-5250
WVLJ (105.5 FM), Box 72, Monticello, IL 61856 217-762-2588

Indiana

WGRT (107.1 FM), Box 301, Danville, IN 46112 317-745-6401
WBCL (90.3 FM), 1025 W. Rudisill Blvd., Fort Wayne, IN 46807 219-745-0576
WFCV (1090 AM), Sta. 200, 909 Coliseum Blvd., Fort Wayne, IN 46805 219-423-2337
WYCA (92.3 FM), 6336 Calumet Ave., Hammond, IN 46324 219-933-4455; 312-734-4455
WBRI (1500 AM), 4802 E. 62nd St., Indianapolis, IN 46220 317-255-5484
WXIR (98.3 FM), 4802 E. 62nd St., Indianapolis, IN 46220 317-255-5484
WSLM (1220 AM), Box 385, Salem, IN 47167 812-883-5750
WSLM (98.9 FM), Box 385, Salem, IN 47167 812-883-5750
WHME (103.1 FM), 61300 S. Ironwood Rd., South Bend, IN 46614 219-291-8613

Iowa

KFGQ (1260 AM), 924 W. 2nd St., Boone, IA 50036 515-432-2092

KFGQ (99.3 FM), 924 W. 2nd St., Boone, IA 50036 515-432-2092

KWKY (1150 AM), P.O. Box 662, Des Moines, IA 50303 515-981-0981

KYFR (920 AM), 618 1/2 W. Sheridan Ave., Shenandoah, IA 51601 712-246-5151

KNWS (190 AM), 4880 LaPorte Rd., Waterloo, IA 50702 319-296-1975

KNWS (101.9 FM), 4880 LaPorte Rd., Waterloo, IA 50702 319-296-1975

Kansas

KCNW (1380 AM), Box 461, Shawnee Mission, KS 66201 913-492-1380

KFTX (101.7 FM), Box 549, Fort Scott, KS 66701 316-223-6064

KSGL (900 AM), 3337 W. Central, Wichita, KS 67203 316-942-3231

Kentucky

WHKK (100.9 FM), 100 Commonwealth, Erlanger, KY 41018 606-727-2500

WFIA (900 AM), 310 W. Liberty, Louisville, KY 40202 502-583-4811

WXLN (103.9 FM), 310 W. Liberty, Louisville, KY 40202 502-583-4811

WJMM (106.3 FM), 1200 S. Broadway, Lexington, KY 40504 606-254-4065

Louisiana

WLUX (1550 AM), P.O. Box 2550, Baton Rouge, LA 70821 504-769-8300

WBSN (89.1 FM), 3939 Gentilly, New Orleans, LA 70126 504-282-4455; 282-3410

Maine

WLOB (1310 AM), 779 Warren Ave., Portland, MI 04103 207-775-1310

Maryland

WFSI (107.9 FM), 918 Chesapeake Ave., Annapolis, MD 21403 301-269-6500

WAYE (860 AM), 334 N. Charles St., Baltimore, MD 21201 301-727-1177

WRBS (95.1 FM), 3600 Georgetown Rd., Baltimore, MD 21227 301-247-4100

WCTN (950 AM), 7825 Tuckerman Ln., Sta. 211, Potomac, MD 20854 301-299-7026

WOLC (102.5 FM), Box 130, Princess Anne, MD 21853 301-543-9652

WCRH (90.5 FM), Rte. 2, Box 325, Williamsport, MD 21795 301-582-0285

Michigan

WUFN (96.7 FM), 2255 N. Concord Rd., Albion, MI 49224 517-531-4478

WDFP (95.3 FM), Box 17, Battle Creek, MI 49016 616-965-0527

WMUZ (103.5 FM), 12300 Radio Pl., Detroit, MI 48228 313-272-3434

WCSG (91.3 FM), 1001 E. Beltline NE, Grand Rapids, MI 49505 616-942-1500

WFUR (1470 AM), Box 1808, Grand Rapids, MI 49501 616-456-9541

WJBL (1260 AM), 5658 143rd Ave., Holland, MI 49423 616-394-1260

WJBL (94.5 FM), 5658 143rd Ave., Holland, MI 49423 616-394-1260

WMPC (1230 AM), 1800 N. Lapeer Rd., Lapeer, MI 48446 313-664-6211

WUNN (1110 AM), 1571 Tomlinson Rd., Box 288, Mason, MI 48854 517-676-2488

WUGN (99.7 FM), P.O. Box 366, Midland, MI 48640 517-631-7060

WEXL (1340 AM), 317 E. 11 Mile Rd., Royal Oak, MI 48067 313-544-2200

WYFC (1520 AM), Box 1520, 17 N. Huron St., Ypsilanti, MI 48197 313-482-4000

Minnesota

WWJC (850 AM), 1120 E. McCuen St., Duluth, MN 55808 218-626-2738

KUXL (1570 AM), 5730 Duluth St., Golden Valley, MN 55422 612-544-3196

KBHW (99.5 FM), P.O. Box 433, International Falls, MN 56649 218-285-7398

KTIS (900 AM), 3003 N. Snelling, Roseville, MN 55113 612-636-4900

KTIS (98.5 FM), 3003 N. Snelling, Roseville, MN 55113 612-636-4900

KTIG (100.1 FM), P.O. Box 409, Pequot Lakes, MN 56472 218-568-4422

Mississippi

WHJT (93.5 FM), Box 4247, Clinton, MS 39058 601-924-4505

WJFR (96.3 FM), Box 8887, Jackson, MS 39204 601-372-6311

Missouri

KCCV (1510 AM), 10841 E. 28th St., Independence, MO 64052 816-252-5050

KGNM (1270 AM), 2414 S. Leonard Rd., St. Joseph, MO 64503 816-233-2577

KXEN (1010 AM), Box 28, St. Louis, MO 63166 314-436-6550

Montana

KGVW (640 AM), 2050 Amsterdam Rd., Belgrade, MT 59714 406-388-4281

KURL (730 AM), Box 31038, Billings, MT 59107 406-245-3121

KKOZ (97.1 FM), Box 31038, Billings, MT 59107

KGLE (590 AM), Box 931, Glendive, Mt 49330 406-365-3331

KIVE (96.5 FM), Box 931, Glendive, MT 59330 406-363-3331

KARR (1400 AM), Box 2204, Great Falls, MT 59403 406-761-6104

KALS (97.1 FM), P.O. Box 1977, Kalispell, MT 406-257-5257

KROA (97.5 FM), Box 193, Doniphan, MT 68832 402-845-6595

Nebraska

KGBI (100.7 FM), 1515 S. 10th St., Omaha, NB 68108 402-342-6494

KCMI (103.9 FM), Box 401, Scotts-bluff, NB 69361 308-635-0104

Nevada

KILA (95.5 FM), 2201 S. 6th St., Las Vegas, NV 89104 702-731-5452

New Jersey

WKDN (106.9 FM), 2906 Mt. Ephraim Ave., Camden, NJ 08104 609-854-5300

WTMR (800 AM), 2775 Mt. Ephraim Ave., Camden, NJ 08104 609-962-8000

WWDJ (970 AM), P.O. Box 970, Hackensack, NJ 07602 201-343-5097

WFME (94.7 FM), 289 Mt. Pleasant Ave., West Orange, NJ 07052 201-736-3600

WCHR (94.5 FM), Woodside Rd., Yardley, PA 19067 215-493-4252

WAWZ (1380 AM), Box 97, Zare-phath, NJ 08890 201-356-0102

WAWZ (99.1 FM), Box 97, Zarephath, NJ 08890 201-469-0991

New Mexico

KNMI (88.9 FM), Box 1230 Farming-ton, NM 87499 505-325-0255

New York

WMIV (95.1 FM), Sonshine Mountain, Newfield, NY 14867 607-272-8080

WOIV (105.1 FM), 7095 Myers Rd. E.,
Syracuse, NY 13057 315-656-2232

WSIV (1540 AM), 7095 Myers Rd. E.,
Syracuse, NY 13057 315-656-2231

WPOW (1310 AM), 1111 Woodrow
Rd., Staten Island, NY 10312 212-
984-4600

WLIX (540 AM), 128 W. Main St.,
Bay Shore, NY 11706 516-666-2200

WFGB (89.7 FM), P.O. Box 1536, 37
Henry St., Kingston, NY 12401 914-
338-8144

WXRL (1300 AM), 5360 William St.,
Lancaster, NY 14086 716-681-1313

WTHE (1520 AM), 266 Maple Pl.,
Mineola, NY 11501 516-742-1520

WWWG (1460 AM), 1850 S. Winston
Rd., Rochester, NY 14618 716-275-
9212

WMHR (102.9 FM), 4044 Makyes Rd.,
Syracuse, NY 13215 315-469-5051

WHAZ (1330 AM), Box 784, Troy,
NY 12181 518-272-1010

North Carolina

WFGW (1010 AM), Box 158, Black
Mountain, NC 28711 704-669-8477

WMIT (106.9 FM), Box 158, Black
Mountain, NC 28711 704-669-8477

WAME (1480 AM), Box 32068, Charlotte, NC 28232 704-377-5916

WHVN (1240 AM), 5732 N. Tryon St.,
Charlotte, NC 28213 704-596-1310

WGAS (1420 AM), Box 250, Gastonia,
NC 28052 704-865-9427

WXNC (92.5 FM), Box 33, Henderson, NC 27536 804-623-6262

WYFL (92.5 FM), 120 E. Belle St.,
Henderson, NC 27536 804-492-9511

WHPE (95.5 FM), Box 1819, High
Point, NC 27261 919-889-9473

WPJL (1240 AM), 515 Bart St., Box
27946, Raleigh, NC 27611 919-834-
6401

WBFJ (1550 AM), 3066 Irenwest Dr.,
Winston-Salem, NC 27103 919-760-
0550

North Dakota

KFNW (97.9 FM), Box 6008, Fargo,
ND 58108 701-282-5910

KHRT (1320 AM), Box 1210, Monor,
ND 58702 701-852-3849

KFNW (1200 AM), Box 6008, Fargo,
ND 58108 701-282-5910

Ohio

WOHP (1390 AM), 1373 Road 235,
Bellefontaine, OH 43311 513-592-
1045

WJYM (730 AM), 8361 Fremont Pike,
Perrysburg, OH 43551 419-874-7956

WTOF (98.1 FM), 619 Ameritrust
Bldg., Canton, OH 44702 216-452-
4009

WCDR (90.3 FM), Box 601, Cedarville, OH 45314 513-766-5595

WAKW (93.3 FM), 6275 Collegevue
Pl., Cincinnati, OH 45224 513-542-
3442

WCRF (103.3 FM), 9756 Barr Rd.,
Cleveland, OH 44141 216-526-1111

WGOJ (105.5 FM), Box 725, Con-
neaut, OH 44030 216-599-7252

WCVO (104.9 FM), Box 7, New Albany, OH 43054 614-855-9171

WPOS (102.3 FM), 7112 Angola Rd.,
Holland, OH 43528 419-865-5528

WCVJ (90.9 FM), Box 112, Jefferson,
OH 44047 216-294-3555

WTGN (97.7 FM), 1500 Elida Rd.,
Lima, OH 45805 419-227-2525

WTGN (97.7 FM), Box 93.7, Dayton,
OH 45449 513-866-2471

WSUM (1000 AM), Box 33250, North
Royalton, OH 44133 216-237-3300

WGGN (97.7 FM), Box 247, Castalia,
OH 44824 419-684-9496

WEEC (100.7 FM), 2348 Troy Rd.,
Springfield, OH 45504 513-399-7837

WRFD (88 AM), Powell Road and N.
High St., Columbus, OH 43285 614-
885-5342

Oklahoma

KJIL (104.9 FM), 3809 N. MacArthur Blvd., Oklahoma City, OK 73157 405-789-1140

KQCV (800 AM), 1919 N. Broadway, Oklahoma City, OK 73101 405-521-1412

KCFO (98.5 FM), 3737 S. 37 W. Ave., Tulsa, OK 740107 918-445-1186

Oregon

KHPE (107.9 FM), Box 278, Albany, OR 97321 503-926-2233

KWIL (970 AM), Box 278, Albany, OR 97321 503-926-2233

KYTT (98.3 FM), 455 N. Broadway, Coos Bay, OR 97420 503-269-2022

KBMC (94.5 FM), 205 W. 8th, Eugene, OR 97401 503-485-6262

KPDQ (800 AM), 5110 SE Stark St., Portland, OR 97215 503-231-7800

KORE (1050 AM), 2080 Laura St., Springfield, OR 97477 503-747-5673

Pennsylvania

WFMZ (100.7 FM), East Rock Rd., Allentown, PA 18103 215-797-4530

WAVL (910 AM), Box 277, Apollo, PA 15613 412-478-4020

WBYO (107.5 FM), Box 177, Boyertown, PA 19512 215-369-1075

WARO (540 AM), Box 191, Canonsburg, PA 15317 412-745-5400

WPLW (1590 AM), 201 Ewing Rd., Pittsburg, PA 15205 412-922-0550

WDBA (107.3 FM), 28 W. Scribner Ave., Du Bois, PA 15801 814-371-1330

WPDC (1600 AM), Box 1600, Elizabethtown, PA 17022 717-367-5575

WIBF (103.9 FM), 100 York Rd., Jenkintown, PA 19046 215-887-5400

WDAC (94.5 FM), Box 3022, Lancaster, PA 17604 717-284-4123

WZZD (990 AM), 117 Ridge Pike, Lafayette Hill, Philadelphia, PA 17444 215-242-9630

WTLR (89.9 FM), 315 S. Atherton, State College, PA 16801 814-237-9857

WCTL (106.3 FM), Old Lincolnville Rd., RD 3, Union City, PA 16438 814-438-7686

Puerto Rico

WCGB (1060 AM), Apartado 258, Juana Diaz, PR 00665 809-837-2440

WFID (95.7 FM), Evangelical Productions, GOP Box A., San Juan, PR 00936 809-724-2727

WERR (104.1 FM), Box RR, 65 Infantry Station, Rio Piedas, PR 00929 809-751-6318

WIVV (1370 AM), Admin. Offices, GPO Box A, San Juan, PR 00936 809-724-2727

Rhode Island

WARV (1590 AM), 19 Luther Ave., Warwick, RI 02886 401-737-0700

South Carolina

WMHK (89.7 FM), Box 3122, Columbia, SC 29230 803-754-5400

WYFG (91.1 FM), Box 578, Gaffney, SC 29342 803-487-5836

WSOL (1370 AM), Drawer 367, Orangeburg, SC 29116 803-854-2671

WSNW (1150 AM), Box 793, Seneca, SC 29678 803-882-2388

WBFM (98.1 FM), Box 793, Seneca, SC 29678 803-882-2388

South Dakota

KNWC (1270 AM), R.R. 3, Box 23, Sioux Falls, SC 57106 605-339-1270

KNWC (96.5 FM), R.R. 3., Box 23, Sioux Falls, SC 57106 605-339-1270

Tennessee

WPJM (1540 AM), P.O. Box 524, Adamsville, TN 38310 901-632-0908

WMBW (88.9 FM), 1002 American National Band Bldg., Chattanooga, TN 37402 615-266-2795

WMOC (1450 AM), 407 Chestnut St., Sta. 210, Chattanooga, TN 37402 615-756-1450

WITA (1490 AM), 7212 Kingston Pike, Knoxville, TN 37919 615-588-2794

KWAM (990 AM), Box 12107, Memphis, TN 38112 901-323-2679

KWAM (101.1 FM), Box 12107, Memphis, TN 38112 901-323-2679

WNAZ (89.1 FM), 333 Murfreesboro Rd., Nashville, TN 37203 615-248-1689

WWGM (1560 AM), 2003 Blair Blvd., Nashville, TN 37212 615-298-4417

Texas

KJOJ (106.9 FM), 29801 I-45 N., Spring, TX 77381 713-367-0107

KCTA (1030 AM), Box 898, Corpus Christi, TX 78403 512-643-3541

KPBC (1040 AM), 3201 Royalty Row, Irving, TX 75062 214-438-1776

KCBI (89.3 FM), Box 1809, Dallas, TX 75221 214-742-8930

KSBJ (88.1 FM), 200 N. Houston Ave., Humble, TX 77338 713-446-4493

KGOL (107.5 FM), 8500-A Kirby Dr., Houston, TX 77054 713-797-6500

KXVI (1600 AM), 1310 Ave. K, Plano, TX 75074 214-424-2586

Virginia

WABS (7800 AM), 5230 Lee Hwy., Arlington, VA 22207 703-534-2000

WIVE (1430 AM), P.O. Box 272, Ashland, VA 23005 804-798-4711

WYFJ (100.1 FM), P.O. Box 57, Ashland, VA 23005 804-798-3248

WBTX (1470 AM), P.O. Box 337, Broadway, VA 22815 703-896-8933

WFAX (1220 AM), 161-B Hillwood Ave., Falls Church, VA 22046 703-532-1220

WJYJ (90.5 FM), 830 Gunnery Hill Rd., Spotsylvania, VA 22553 703-582-5371

WYFI (99.7 FM), Box 33, Norfolk, VA 23501 804-623-6262

Washington

KBIQ (105.3 FM), 19303 Fremont Ave. N., Seattle, WA 98133 206-546-7350

KGDN (630 AM), 19303 Fremont Ave. N., Seattle, WA 98133 206-546-7350

KLYN (106.5 FM), 1843 Front St., Sta. A, Lynden, WA 98264 206-354-5596

KBLE (1050 AM), 114 Lakeside Ave., Seattle, WA 98122 206-324-2000

KMBI (1330 AM), Box 8024, Spokane, WA 99203 509-448-2555

KMBI (107.9 FM), Box 8024, Spokane, WA 99203 509-448-2555

West Virginia

WEMM (107.9 FM), 703 3rd Ave., Huntington, WV 25701 304-525-5141

WSCW (1410 AM0, 605 D St., South Charleston, WV 25303 304-744-5388

WVRC (1400 AM), 106 Radio St., Spencer, WV 25276 304-927-3760

Wisconsin

WYLO (540 AM), Box 25, Jackson, WI 53037 414-677-3333

WWIB (103.7 FM), Cornell, WI 54732 715-239-6138

WOGO (680 AM), Cornell, WI 54732 715-239-6138

WNWC (102.5 FM), 5606 Medical Circle, Madison, WI 53711 608-271-1025

WVCY (107.7 FM), 2712 W. Vliet St., Milwaukee, WI 53208 414-933-1440

WEMI (100.1 FM), 360 Chute St., Menasha, WI 54952 414-725-9456

WRVM (102.7 FM), Box 212, Suring, WI 54174 414-842-2839

NRB-MEMBER TV STATIONS

Alaska

KJNP-TV (Channel 4), Box O, North Pole, AK 99705 907-488-2216

Arizona

KPAZ-TV (Channel 21), 3551 E. McDowell, Phoenix, AZ 85008 602-273-1477

California

KFCB-TV (Channel 42), P.O. Box 6498, 5101 Port Chicago Hwy., Concord, CA 94524 415-676-8969

KTBN-TV (Channel 40), 2442 Michelle, Tustin, CA 92680 714-832-2950

Delaware

WCVI-TV (Channel 61), Box 11006, Wilmington DE 19850 609-678-4201

Florida

WTGL-TV (Channel 52), P.O. Box 1852, Cocoa, FL 32922 605-631-2730

WIYE-TV (Channel 55), 900 W. North Blvd., Leesburg, Fl 32748 904-787-2287

WHFT-TV (Channel 45), 3324 Pembroke Rd., Pembroke Park, FL 33021 305-962-1700

Illinois

WBLN-TV (Channel 43), 1328 E. Empire, Bloomington, IL 61701 309-662-4373

WCFC-TV (Channel 38), 20 N. Wacker Dr., Chicago, IL 60606 312-977-3838

Indiana

WHMB-TV (Channel 40), 10511 Greenfield Ave., Noblesville, IN 46060 317-773-5050

WHME-TV (Channel 46), 61300 S. Ironwood Rd., South Bend, IN 46614 219-291-8200

Kansas

KYFC-TV (Channel 50), 4715 Rainbow Blvd., Shawnee Mission, KS 66205 913-262-1700

Maryland

WKJL-TV (Channel 24), 1008 Ingleside Ave., Baltimore, MD 21228 301-744-2800

Massachusetts

WXNE-TV (Channel 25), 100 2nd Ave., Needham Heights, MA 02194 617-449-4200

Michigan

WWMA-TV (Channel 17), 3117 Plaza Dr. NE, Grand Rapids, MI 49505 616-364-8722

Minnesota

WFBT-TV (Channel 29), 7325 Aspen Ln., Minneapolis, MN 55428 612-424-2929

Missouri

KYFC-TV (Channel 50), 4715 Rainbow Blvd., Shawnee Mission, MO 66205 913-262-1700

Nebraska

Channel 42 Christian Broadcasting of the Midlands, Box 14550, Omaha, NE 68124 402-339-8842

New York

WTBY-TV (Channel 54), P.O. Box 549, Poughkeepsie, NY 12602 914-454-3030

North Carolina

WLFL-TV (Channel 22), P.O. Box 15366, Durham, NC 27704 919-471-4461

Ohio

WDLI-TV (Channel 17), 6600 Atlantic Blvd. NE, Louisville, OH 44641 216-875-5542

WTLW-TV (Channel 44), 1844 Baty Rd., Lima, OH 45805 419-339-4444

WSFJ-TV (Channel 51), 10027 Jacksontown Rd. SE, Thornville, OH 43706 614-323-0771

WTJC-TV (Channel 26), P.O. Box 26, Dayton, OH 45401 513-323-0026

Oklahoma

KAUT-TV (Channel 43), P.O. Box 14843, Oklahoma City, OK 73113 405-478-4300

KTBO-TV (Channel 14), 7908 NW 23rd St., Oklahoma City, OK 73308

Pennsylvania

WFMZ-TV (Channel 69), East Rock Rd., Allentown, PA 18103 215-797-4530

WPCB-TV (Channel 40), Box 17220, Wall, PA 15148 412-824-3930

South Carolina

WCCT-TV (Channel 57), P.O. Box 5757, West Columbia, SC 29171 803-796-7757

WGGS-TV (Channel 16), P.O. Box 1616, Greenville, SC 29602 803-244-1616

Texas

KXTX-TV (Channel 39), 3900 Harry Hines Blvd., Dallas, TX 75211 214-521-3900

KCIK-TV (Channel 14), 3100 N. Stanton, El Paso, TX 79902 915-533-2911

Virginia

WIVE-TV, P.O. Box 272, Ashland, VA 23005 804-798-4711

WORD-TV (Channel 4), Tate Springs Rd., Lynchburg, VA 24506 804-528-2080

WYAH-TV (Channel 27), 1318 Spratley St., Portsmouth, VA 23704 804-393-2501

NRB-MEMBER CABLE TV STATIONS

California

Redwood Chapel Communications Church, 19300 Redwood Rd., Castro Valley, CA 94546 415-886-6300

Teleprompter, 4500 Campus Dr., Newport Beach, CA 92660 714-540-3698

Illinois

Foursquare Church Channel 6, 321 E. Leafland, Decatur, IL 62521 217-428-9563

Grace Presbyterian Church, 114 W. Forrest Hill Ave., Peoria, IL 61604 309-685-3113

Minnesota

Christian Media Network, P.O. Box 20121, Bloomington, MN 55420 612-884-4540

Puerto Rico

Cable TV San Juan, c/o WIVV-TV, GPO Box A, San Juan, PR 00936 809-724-2727/724-4171

Tennessee

WFBA-TV, 819 Gilbert St., Alcoa, TN 37701 615-982-2782

Texas

Missionary Radio Evangelism, Inc., 3100 N. Stanton, El Paso, TX 79902 915-533-2911

Virginia

Channel 22/Evangel Four Square Church, 612 Bullitt Ave. SE, Roanoke, VA 24013 703-982-3694

WORD-TV CCTV, Lunchburg General-Marshall Lodge, Tate Springs Rd., Call Number 4'8', Lynchburg, VA 24506 804-528-2080

Washington

Clearview TV Cable, Box 1048, Auburn, WA 98002 206-939-1902

RECORD COMPANIES
(IDAK: 7399)

Accent Records, 71906 Hwy. 111, Rancho Mirage, CA 92270 714-346-0075

Airborn, P.O. Box 3064, Flint, MI 48502 313-736-5191

Angelsong Records, P.O. Box 2673, Beverly Hills, CA 90213 818-761-4481

Ark Records, P.O. Box 230073, Tigard, OR 97223 503-620-5680

Beegee Records, Inc., 3101 S. Western Ave., Los Angeles, CA 90018 213-258-8011

Birdwing Records (Sparrow), 8025 Deering, Canoga Park, CA 91304 818-703-6599

Birthright Records, 3101 S. Western Ave., Los Angeles, CA 90018 213-258-8011

Bread n' Honey, P.O. Box 3391, Ventura, CA 93006 805-644-1821

Brentwood Records & Publishing, 8005 Church St., Brentwood, TN 37027 615-373-3950

Calvary Records, 142 8th Ave. N., Nashville, TN 37203 615-244-8800

Canaan Records (Word), 4800 W. Waco Dr., Waco, TX 76710 817-772-7650

Castle Records, P.O. Box 7574, Tulsa, OK 74105

Cherub Records, P.O. Box 9245, Little Rock, AR 72219

Cloudburst Records, P.O. Box 31, Edmonton, KY 42129 502-432-3183

Colonial Regency Records, 2199 Nolensville Rd., Nashville, TN 37072 615-259-2247

Comstock Records, Box 3247, Shawnee, KS 66203 913-631-6060

Creative Sound Productions, 6290 Sunset Blvd., Sta. 900, Hollywood, CA 90028 213-871-1010

223

Creed Records (Nashboro), 1011 Woodland St., Nashville, TN 37206 615-227-5081

Crossroads Productions, 10451 Huron St., Denver, CO 80234 303-452-1018

Dawn Records, 830 Fairview Rd., Asheville, NC 28803 704-274-7402

DaySpring Records (Word), 4800 W. Waco Dr., Waco, TX 76710 817-772-7650

Deka Records, P.O. Box 5712, High Point, NC 27262

Destiny Records, P.O. Box 545, Corona del Mar, CA 92652

Epoch Universal Publications, 10802 N. 23rd Ave., Phoenix, AZ 85029

Fingerprint Music Co., 4421 Bollenbacker Ave., Sacramento, CA 95838 916-920-4567

Fourth Man Records, R.R. 1, 459H, Blue Bell Rd., Newfield, NJ 08344

Fountain of Life Records, P.O. Box 10846, Bradenton, FL 33507 812-756-7781

Fro Records, 170 Linwood Ave., Paterson, NJ 07502 201-595-7557

Globe Mission, Inc., (Perlita Lim Concert Ministry), P.O. Box 1212, Glendoar, CA 91740 818-963-8833

Gold Street, Inc., P.O. Box 124, Kirbyville, TX 75956 409-423-2234

Gold Tag Productions, P.O. Box 774, Rialto, CA 92376 714-820-1841

Good News Records, 8319 Lankershim Blvd., N., Hollywood, CA 91605 213-767-4522

Gospel-R-Records, P.O. Box 6617, Washington, DC 20009 301-459-6580

Greentree Records, 365 Great Circle Rd., Nashville, TN 37228 615-259-9111

John Hall Records, Inc., P.O. Box 18344, 5009 Davis Blvd., Fort Worth, TX 76118 817-281-6605

Happy Day Music Co., (BMI), P.O. Box 602, Kennett, MO 63857 314-888-2995

Hartford Music Co., Powell, MO 65730 417-435-2225

Heartwarming Records (Benson), 365 Great Circle Rd., Nashville, TN 37228 615-259-9111

The Herald Association, Inc., Box 218, Wellman Heights, Johnsonville, SC 29555 803-386-2600

Herald Records, Box 218, Wellman Heights, Johnsonville, SC 29555 803-386-2600

Nita Herndon Enterprises, 1920 N. Beverly St., Porterville, CA 93257 209-781-4093

Holy Spirit Records, 27335 Penn, Inkster, MI 48141 313-274-5905

Home Sweet Home Records, 2020 Sunnyside Dr., Brentwood, TN 37027 615-373-8840

Hosanna Music Productions, 71 N. Laurel, Ventura, CA 93001 805-648-1076

HSE Records, 1709 Church St., Nashville, TN 37203 615-320-1561

Impact Records, 265 Great Circle Rd., Nashville, TN 37228

Jasper Records, 2223 Strawberry Village, Pasadena, TX 77502 713-472-5563

Jewel Records, P.O. Box 1125, Shreveport, LA 71163 318-222-7283

Jim Records, P.O. Box 2550, Baton Rouge, LA 70821

Joe Keene Music Co., (BMI), P.O. Box 602, Kennett, MO 63857 314-888-2995

KSS Records, P.O. Box 602, Kennett, MO 63857 314-888-2995

Kenwood Records, 1011 Woodland St., Nashville, TN 37206 615-227-5081

Klesis Records, P.O. Box 218, Wellman Heights, Johnsonville, SC 29555 803-386-2600

Kilgore Records, Inc., 706 W. Mechanic St., Leesville, LA 71446 318-239-2850

L.P.S. Records, Inc., Heartstone, Silverstone, Fourth Corner Music Publishers, 2140 St. Claire St., Bellingham, WA 98226 206-733-3807

Lamb & Lion Records, 9255 Sunset Blvd., Sta. 419, Los Angeles, CA 90069 213-271-3173

Lexicon Music/Light Records, P.O. Box 2222, Newbury Park, CA 91361 805-499-5881

Life Stream (Calvary), 142 8th Ave., Nashville, TN 37203 615-244-8800

Light Records, P.O. Box 2222, Newbury Park, CA 91320 805-499-5881

Little Pilgrim Records, P.O. Box 189, Station W, Toronto, Ontario M6M 4Z9 Canada 416-746-1991

Lodema Records, 5806 Arroyo Dr., Farmington, NM 78401 505-325-1684

Love Bird Records, 5998 NW Olean Blvd., #7, Port Charlotte, FL 33952 813-629-1110

Love/Peace/Service Records, Inc., 2140 St. Clair St., Bellingham, WA 98226 206-733-3807

MCW Records, P.O. Box 50208, Nashville, TN 37205

Maiden Music, P.O. Box 777, Trevilians, VA 23170 703-967-0077

Mainroads Productions, Inc., 100 Huntley St., Toronto, Ontario M4Y 2L1 Canada 416-961-8001

Majega Records, 240 E. Radcliffe Dr., Claremont, CA 91711 714-624-0677

Manna Music & Manna Records, 2111 Kenmere Ave., Burbank, CA 91504

Maranatha! Music, P.O. Box 1396, Costa Mesa, CA 92628 714-979-8563

Mark Five Records, P.O. Box 218, Wellman Heights, Johnsonville, SC 29555 803-386-2600

Master Disc Records, 711 E. Walnut St., #208, Pasadena, CA 91101 818-796-1600

The Master's Collection, P.O. Box 362, Sta. A, Rexdale, Ontario, M9W 5L3 Canada 416-746-1991

Master Source Productions, 440 N. Mayfield, Chicago, IL 60644 312-921-1446

Music Emporium Record Co., 3100 23rd Ave., Meridian, MS 39301 601-483-5991

Myrrh Records (Word), 4800 W. Waco Dr., Waco, TX 76710 817-772-7650

Nashboro Records, 1011 Woodland St., Nashville, TN 37206 615-227-5081

Net Casting Records, 550 Evans Rd., Springfield, PA 19064 215-543-4490

New Dawn Records, 365 Great Circle Dr., Nashville, TN 37228 615-259-9111

New Dawning Records, Dyer Rt., Cowen, WV 36206 304-226-3424

New Day Records, 2832 Spring Grove Ave., Cincinnati, OH 45225 513-681-8400

New Life Records, E. 122 Montgomery, P.O. Box 5378, Spokane, WA 99205 1-800-541-1565, 509-328-4207

Neworld Media Records, South Blue Hill, ME 04615 207-374-5539

New Pax Records, 365 Great Circle Rd., Nashville, TN 37228 615-259-9111

North American Liturgy Resources, 10802 N. 23rd Ave., Phoenix, AZ 85029 602-943-7229

Olde Towne Records, P.O. Box 2, Arcola, VA 22010 703-327-6367

Paragon Records (Benson), 365 Great Circle Rd., Nashville, TN 37228 615-259-9111

Paul Johnson Music Productions, Inc., P.O. Box 552, Woodland Hills, CA 91365 818-703-6707

Phydeaux Records, P.O. Box 189, Sta. W., Toronto, Ontario, M6M 4Z9 Canada

QCA Records & Custom Pressing, 2832 Spring Grove., Cincinnati, OH 45225 513-681-8400

Rainbow Sound, Inc., 2737 Irving Blvd., Dallas, TX 75207 214-638-7712

Refuge Records, P.O. Box 110570, Nashville, TN 37211 615-776-5051

Rite Record Productions, Inc., 9745 Mangham Dr., Cincinnati, OH 45215 513-733-5533

Roadshow Records, 870 Seventh Ave., New York, NY 10019 212-765-8840

Sand Island Records, Honolulu, HI Mainland P.O. Box 688, Eugene, OR 97440 503-686-0779

Savoy Records, P.O. Box 279, Elizabeth, NJ 07207 201-351-6800

Scratched Records, 4511 Roundup Trail, Austin, TX 78745

Season Records, 97 S. Hamilton Ave., Lindenhurst, NY 11757 516-884-5628

Seed Records, P.O. Box 2112, Shawnee Mission, KS 66201

Serenity Records, 10924 Beverly Hills Dr., Little Rock, AR 72211 501-225-3036

Shalom Records, P.O. Box 60446, Oklahoma City, OK 73106 405-521-0777

Singspiration Records, 365 Great Circle Dr., Nashville, TN 37228 615-259-9111

Skylite Records, 1008 17th Ave. S., Nashville, TN 37212 615-327-4557

Snow Records and Productions, E1103 29th St., Spokane, WA 99203 508-624-9359

Sold Out to Jesus, P.O. Box 786, Micaville, NC 28755 704-682-3528

Solid Rock Records, 22020 Buenaventura, Woodland Hills, CA 91364 213-883-0640

Sonrise Records, Inc, 6290 Sunset Blvd., Sta. 900, Hollywood, CA 90028 213-871-1010

The Sparrow Corp., 8025 Deering Ave., Canoga Park, CA 91304 818-703-6599

Spiritual Renaissance Music, P.O. Box 347, Berkeley, CA 94701 415-672-8398

Stamps Baxter, 365 Great Circle Dr., Nashville, TN 37228 615-259-9111

Star Song Records, 12929 Gulf Frwy., Sta. 201, Houston, TX 77034 713-484-5505

Sugar Records, P.O. Box 1181, Florissant, MO 63031 314-837-4095

Supreme Record Co., P.O. Box 150394, Nashville, TN 37215 615-298-3824

Susquehanna Sound Productions, 48 A St., Northumberland, PA 17857 717-473-9733

Sweetsong Records, P.O. Box 2041, Parkersburg, WV 26102 304-489-2911

Third Firkin Music Co., P.O. Box 7027, Ann Arbor, MI 48107 313-996-9509

Tri-Power Records, P.O. Box 1101, Gresham, OR 97030

Triangle Records, 824 19th Ave. S., Box 23088, Nashville, TN 37202

Verite Records, Inc., Box 22398, Nashville, TN 37202 615-242-8102

Voice Box Records, 5180-B Park Ave., Memphis, TN 38119 901-761-5074

Warning Records, 12341 Lincoln Way, Orrville, OH 44667 216-683-1451

Warrior Records, P.O. Box 43, Billings, MT 406-252-4386

Word Record & Music Group, Canaan/Dayspring/Myrrh/Word, 4800 W. Waco Dr., Waco, TX 76710 817-772-7650

Wordsong Records, 520 Palm Ave., National City, CA 92050

VIDEO PRODUCERS AND DISTRIBUTORS
(IDAK: 7813)

Allied Film & Video Services, 3011 Diamond Park Dr., Dallas, TX 75247 214-869-0100

The Bible Study Hour, 1716 Spruce St., Philadelphia, PA 19103 215-546-3696

Campus Crusade for Christ, Intl., Arrowhead Springs, Dept. 6060, San Bernardino, CA 92414 714-886-5224

Christian Communications Technology, 4708 Amberjack Dr., Virginia Beach, VA 23464 804-490-2869

CLP Video, 111 S. Marshall Ave., El Cajon, CA 92020 619-442-6673

Covenant Video, 3200 W. Foster, Chicago, IL 60625 312-478-4676

Crossroads Christian Communications, 100 Huntley St., Toronto, Ontario M4Y 2L1 Canada 416-961-8001

Crown Ministries, P.O. Box 49, Euclid, MN 56722 218-781-6505

Crown Video Services, P.O. Box 844, Wheaton, IL 60189 312-690-1133

David C. Cook Publishing Co., 850 N. Grove Ave., Elgin, IL 60120 312-641-2400

Episcopal Radio-TV Foundation, Inc., Episcopal Church, 3379 Peachtree Rd. NE, Sta. 999, Atlanta, GA 30326 404-233-5419

Films for Christ Assoc., 2432 W. Peoria Ave., #1327, Phoenix, AZ 85029 602-997-7400

GL Media, 2300 Knoll Dr., Ventura, CA 93003 805-644-9721

Good News Productions, P.O. Box 222, Joplin, MO 64802 417-782-0060

Harvest Communications, Inc., 222 N. Kansas, Wichita, KS 67214 316-262-0732

International Christian Video Assoc., 5159 Cahuenga Blvd., N. Hollywood, CA 91601 818-506-7268

Ligonier Valley Study Center, R.D. 1, Stahlstown, PA 15687 412-593-7005

Lutheran Electronic Media, 3400 North IH 35, Austin, TX 78705

The Master's Collection, P.O. Box 362, Sta. A, Rexdale, Ontario M9W 5L3 Canada 416-746-1991

New Liberty Enterprises, 1805 W. Magnolia Blvd., Burbank, CA 91506 213-842-6167

The Salvation Army, Office of Media Ministries, 500 N. Ervay, Dallas, TX 75206 214-741-1381

Schaeffer V Productions, P.O. Box 909, Los Gatos, CA 95031 408-395-1785

Spring Arbor Distributors, 772 Airport, Ann Arbor, MI 48106 313-483-9770

Tyndale Christian Video, 336 Gundersen Dr., Carol Stream, IL 60188 312-668-8300

Video Communications, Inc., 6535 E. Skelly Dr., Tulsa, OK 74145 918-622-6460

Video Dynamics, P.O. Box 20330, Jackson, MS 39209 901-373-7717

Video Ministries, Inc., P.O. Box 5886, Tacoma, WA 98405 206-584-2324

Video Outreach, Inc., 5159 Cahuenga Blvd., N. Hollywood, CA 91601 818-506-7268

Vision Video, 2030 Wentz Church Rd., Lansdale, PA 19490 215-584-1893

Walk Thru the Bible, P.O. Box 80587, Atlanta, GA 30366 404-458-9300

Word Home Video, 4800 W. Waco Dr., Waco, TX 76710 817-772-7650

ASSOCIATION OF NORTH AMERICAN MISSIONS
P.O. Box 9710
Madison, WI 53715
608-835-5489
Richard D. Matthews
Executive Director
(IDAK: 8685)

Formerly the National Home Missions Fellowship, this voluntary associa-

227

tion of conservative, evangelical, nondenominational home mission agencies awakens Christians to the spiritual needs in the homeland.

American Mission for Opening Churches, Inc., 6419 E. Lake Rd., Olcott, NY 14126 716-778-8568

American Missionary Fellowship, 672 Conestoga Rd., Box 368, Villanova, PA 19085 215-527-4439

Appalachian Bible Fellowship, Inc., Bradley, WV 25818 304-877-6428

Berean Mission, Inc., 3536 Russell Blvd., St. Louis, MO 63104 314-773-0110

Bethel Bible Village, Inc., P.O. Box 500, Hixson, TN 37343 615-842-5757

Bible Memory Assoc., P.O. Box 12000, St. Louis, MO 63112 314-726-1323

The Bible Mission of Southwest Virginia, Inc., P.O. Box 88, Clintwood, VA 24228 703-926-6344

Camp Barakel, P.O. Box 157, Fairview, MI 48621 517-848-2346

Campsite Evangelism, Inc., Box 1826, Harrisburg, PA 17105 717-234-3436

Carver Bible Institute & College, P.O. Box 4335, Atlanta, GA 30302 404-524-0291

Cedine Bible Mission, Inc., R.R. 1, Box 239, Spring City, TN 37381 615-365-9565

Children's Bible Fellowship of New York, Inc., 88 Southern Pkwy., Plainview, NY 11803 516-938-4161

Children's Bible Mission, Inc., 1628 Gary Rd., P.O. Box 44, Lakeland, FL 33802 813-686-8714

Dessie Scott Children's Home, Box 54, Hwy. 15, Pine Ridge, KY 41360 606-668-6445

Drive-In Ministries, P.O. Box 12345, St. Petersburg, FL 33733 813-577-6922

Flagstaff Mission to the Navajos, Inc., P.O. Box AA, Flagstaff, AZ 86002 602-774-2802

Frontier School of the Bible, 705-5th Ave., P.O. Box 217, La Grange, WY 82221 307-834-2411

Helps International Ministries, Inc., Rt. 1, Box 171D, Harlem, GA 30814 404-556-3408

Inner City Impact, 2704 W. North Ave., Chicago, IL 60647 312-384-4200

Kentucky Mountain Mission, Inc., Box 588, Beattyville, KY 41311 606-464-2445

The Mailbox Club, Inc., 404 Eager Rd., Valdosta, GA 31601 912-244-6812

Mexican Gospel Mission, P.O. Box 2404, Phoenix, AZ 85002 602-272-0312

Midwest Messianic Center, 13056 Olive Street Rd., St. Louis, MO 63141 314-878-7667

Missionary TECH Team, 25 FRJ Dr., Longview, TX 75602 214-757-4530

Navajo Gospel Crusade, Inc., 24826 County Rd. L, Cortez, CO 81321 303-565-3290

The North Arkansas Gospel Mission, Hasty, AR 72640 501-429-5845

Open Air Campaigners, 1444 Martin Ave., Plainfield, NJ 07060 201-757-8427

"Open Door" Ministries, Inc., P.O. Box 13619, St. Louis, MO 63137 314-868-2203

Pacific Area Mission, Inc., P.O. Box 729P, Paia, Maui, HI 96779 808-579-9573

RMB Ministries, Inc., 5325 W. "F" Ave., Kalamazoo, MI 49009 616-342-9879

Rocky Mountain Bible Mission, P.O. Box 5111, Missoula, MT 59806 406-721-3380

Rural American Mission Society, Rt. 1, Box 231, Kermit, WV 25674 304-393-3565

Rural Home Missionary Assoc., P.O. Box 300, Morton, IL 61550 309-263-2350

Scripture Memory Mountain Assoc., P.O. Drawer 129, Emmalena, KY 41740 606-251-3231

Source of Light Ministries Intl., Inc., Madison, GA 30650 404-342-0397

Southern Highland Evangel, Inc., R.R. 1, Box 115, Pounding Mill, VA 24637 703-964-2398

Southland Bible Institute, R.R. 6, Box 20, Ashland, KY 41101 606-928-5127

Spanish World Gospel Mission, Inc., P.O. Box 524, Winona Lake, IN 46590 219-267-8821

United Indian Missions, Inc., 2920 N. 3rd St., P.O. Box U, Flagstaff, AZ 86002 602-774-0651

EVANGELICAL FOREIGN MISSIONS ASSOCIATION
1430 K St. NW, Sta. 900
Washington, DC 20005
202-628-7911
Wade T. Coggins,
Executive Director
(IDAK: 8681)

Founded in 1945, EFMA operates as a voluntary association of denominational and nondenominational foreign mission agencies. It is affiliated with the National Association of Evangelicals.

Action International Ministries, P.O. Box 490, Bothell, WA 98011 206-485-1967

Africa Inter-Mennonite Mission, 224 W. High St., Elkhart, IN 46516 219-295-3711

American Advent Mission Society, P.O. Box 23152, Charlotte, NC 28212 704-545-6161

American Leprosy Missions, 1 Broadway, Elmwood Park, NJ 07407 201-794-8650

Assemblies of God, Division of Foreign Missions, 1445 Boonville Ave., Springfield, MO 65802 417-862-2781

Associate Reformed Presbyterian Church World Witness, One Cleveland St., Greenville, SC 29601 803-232-8297

Baptist General Conference World Missions, 2002 S. Arlington Heights Rd., Arlington Heights, IL 60005 312-228-0200

Bethany Fellowship Missions, 6820 Auto Club Rd., Minneapolis, MN 55438 312-944-2121

Bible Literature Intl., P.O. Box 477, Columbus, OH 43216 614-267-3116

Brethren Church Missionary Board, 530 College Ave., Ashland, OH 44805 419-289-1708

Brethren in Christ Missions (Canada), 2519 Stevensville Rd., Stevensville, Ontario L0S 1S0 Canada 416-382-3144

Brethren in Christ Missions (U.S.), P.O. Box 27, Mount Joy, PA 17552 717-653-8067

California Yearly Meeting of Friends, P.O. Box 1607, Whittier, CA 90609 213-947-2883

Calvary Evangelistic Mission (WIVV), P.O. Box A, San Juan, PR 00936 809-724-2727

Campus Crusade for Christ Intl., Arrowhead Springs, San Bernardino, CA 92414 714-886-5224

Christian Church of North America Missions Dept., R.R. 1, Box 141A, Transfer, PA 16154 412-962-3501

Christian Literature Crusade, P.O. Box C, Fort Washington, PA 19034 215-542-1242

Christian & Missionary Alliance, Division of Overseas Ministries, P.O. Box C, Nyack, NY 10960 914-353-0750

Christian Nationals Evangelism Commission, 1470 N. Fourth St., San Jose, CA 95115 408-298-0965

Christian Reformed World Missions, 2850 Kalamazoo Ave. SE, Grand Rapids, MI 49506 616-241-1691

Christian Reformed World Relief Committee, 2850 Kalamazoo Ave. SE, Grand Rapids, MI 49506 616-241-1691

Christ's Mission, Box 176, Hackensack, NJ 07602 201-342-6202

Church of God World Missions, P.O. Box 2430, Cleveland, TN 37320 615-472-3361

Churches of Christ in Christian Union, Foreign Missionary Department, P.O. Box 30, Circleville, OH 43113 614-474-8856

Compassion Intl., P.O. Box 7000, Colorado Springs, CO 80933 303-594-9900

Conservative Baptist Foreign Mission Society, P.O. Box 5, Wheaton, IL 60189 312-665-1200

Conservative Baptist Home Mission Society, P.O. Box 828, Wheaton, IL 60189 312-653-4900

Eastern European Mission, 232 N. Lake Ave., Pasadena, CA 91101 213-796-5425

Evangelical Congregational Church, Division of Missions, 100 W. Park Ave., Myerstown, PA 17067 215-589-5517

Evangelical Free Church, Dept. of Overseas Missions, 1515 E. 66th St., Minneapolis, MN 55423 612-866-3343

Evangelical Friends Mission, P.O. Box 671, Arvada, CO 80001 303-421-8100

Evangelical Mennonite Church, Commission on Overseas Missions, 1420 Kerrway Ct., Fort Wayne, IN 46805 219-423-3649

Evangelical Mennonite Conference, Board of Missions, Box 1268, Steinbach, Manitoba R0A 2A0 Canada 204-326-6401

Evangelical Methodist World Missions, 4125 N. Catalina St., Eloy, AZ 85231 602-466-3804

Evangelistic Faith Missions, P.O. Box 609, Bedford, IN 47421 812-275-7531

Far East Broadcasting Co., P.O. Box 1, La Mirada, CA 90637 213-947-4651

Free Methodist Church, General Missionary Board, Winona Lake, IN 46590 615-361-1010

General Baptist Foreign Mission Society, 100 Stinson Dr., Poplar Bluff, MO 63901 314-785-7746

Grace Mission, 2125 Martindale Ave. SW, Grand Rapids, MI 49509 616-241-5666

International Church of the Foursquare Gospel, 1100 Glendale Blvd., Los Angeles, CA 90026 213-484-1100

International Students, Inc., P.O. Box C, Colorado Springs, CO 80901 303-576-2700

Latin American Mission, Box 341368, Coral Gables, FL 33134 305-444-6228

Link Care Center, 1734 W. Shaw Ave., Fresno, CA 93711 209-439-5920

Literacy & Evangelism, Intl., 1800 S. Jackson Ave., Tulsa, OK 74107 918-585-3826

LOGOI, 4100 W.Flagler St., Miami, FL 33134 305-446-8297

Luis Palau Evangelistic Team, P.O. Box 1173, Portland, OR 97207 503-643-0777

Lutheran Brethren World Missions, P.O. Box 655, Fergus Falls, MN 56537 218-739-3336

Mennonite Brethren Missions/Services (Canada), 200-1695 Henderson Hwy., Winnipeg, Manitoba R2G 1P1 Canada 204-339-1663

Mennonite Brethren Missions/Services (U.S.), 315 S. Lincoln St., Hillsboro, KS 67063 316-947-3151

Mexican Mission Ministries, P.O. Box 636, Pharr, TX 78577 512-787-3543

Mission Aviation Fellowship, Box 202, Redlands, CA 92373 714-794-1151

Missionary Church, Dept. of Overseas Missions, 3901 S. Wayne Ave., Fort Wayne, IN 46807 219-456-4502

Missionary Internship, P.O. Box 457, Farmington, MI 48024 313-474-9110

The Navigators, P.O. Box 6000, Colorado Springs, CO 80934 303-598-1212

Nazarene Division of World Mission, 6401 The Paseo, Kansas City, MO 64131 816-333-7000

North American Baptist Missionary Society, 1 S. 210 Summit Ave., Oakbrook Terrace, IL 60181 312-495-2000

OMS Intl., P.O. Box A, Greenwood, IN 46142 317-881-6751

Open Bible Standard Missions, 2020 Bell Ave., Des Moines, IA 50315 515-288-6761

Overseas Crusades, 25 Corning Ave., Milpitas, CA 95035

Pentecostal Assemblies of Canada, Overseas Missions Dept., 10 Overlea Blvd., Toronto, Ontario M4H 1A5 Canada 416-425-1010

Pentecostal Holiness Church, World Missions Dept., P.O. Box 12609, Oklahoma City, OK 73157 405-787-7110

Presbyterian Church in America, Mission to the World, P.O. Box 1744, Decatur, GA 30031 404-292-8345

Primitive Methodist Intl. Mission Board, 30 Linda Ln., Lebanon, PA 17042 717-273-5951

Reformed Presbyterian Church of North America, Board of Foreign Missions, R.R. L, Box 1-A, Winchester, KS 66097 913-774-4585

Samuel Zwemer Institute, P.O. Box 365, Altsdena, CA 91001 213-794-1121

Trans World Radio, 560 Main St., Chatham, NJ 07928 201-635-5775

United Brethren in Christ, Board of Missions, 302 Lake St., R.R. 1, Huntington, IN 46750 219-356-2312

U.S. Center for World Mission, 1605 E. Elizabeth St., Pasadena, CA 91104 213-797-1111

United World Mission, P.O. Box 8000, St. Petersburg, FL 33738 813-391-0195

Wesleyan Church, General Department of World Missions, P.O. Box 2000, Marion, IN 46952 317-674-3301

World Concern, Box 33000, Seattle, WA 98133 206-546-7201

World Gospel Crusades, P.O. Box 3, Upland, CA 91786 714-982-1564

World Gospel Mission, P.O. Box WGM, Marion, IN 46952 317-664-7331

World Mission Prayer League, 232 Clifton Ave., Minneapolis, MN 55403 612-871-6843

World Missionary Service & Evangelism, P.O. Box 123, Wilmore, KY 40390 606-858-3171

World Opportunities, Intl., 1415 Cahuenga, Blvd, Hollywood, CA 90028 213-466-7187

World Salt Foundation, P.O. Box 557037, Miami, FL 33155 305-221-6751

World Vision, 919 W. Huntington Dr., Monrovia, CA 91016 213-357-1111

Worldwide Evangelization Crusade, P.O. Box A, Fort Washington, PA 19034 215-646-2323

Youth for Christ Intl., P.O. Box 419, Wheaton, IL 60189 312-668-6600

INTERDENOMINATIONAL FOREIGN MISSION ASSOCIATION
P.O. Box 395
Wheaton, IL 60189
312-682-9270
Edwin L. (Jack) Frizen, Jr.
Executive Director
(IDAK: 8681)

Since 1917 IFMA has served as an independent association of conservative, evangelical, nondenominational mission agencies.

Africa Evangelical Fellowship (Canada), 470 McNicoll Ave., Willowdale, Ontario M2H 2E1 416-491-0881

Africa Evangelical Fellowship (U.S.), P.O. Box 1679, Bloomfield, NJ 07003 201-748-9281

Africa Inland Mission (Canada), 1641 Victoria Park Ave., Scarborough, Ontario M1R 1P8 416-751-6077

Africa Inland Mission (U.S.), P.O. Box 178, Pearl River, NY 10965 914-735-4014

Arctic Missions (Canada), R.R. 5, Tibbles Rd., Quesnel, British Columbia V2J 3H9

Arctic Missions (U.S.), P.O. Box 512, Gresham, OR 97030 503-668-5571

BCM Intl., 237 Fairfield Ave, Upper Darby, PA 19082 215-352-7177

Berean Mission, (Canada), 132 Crescent Rd, Toronto, Ontario M4W 1T9

Berean Mission, (U.S.), 536 Russell Blvd., St. Louis, MO 63104 314-773-0110

Bible Christian Union (Canada), 845 Upper James St., Sta. 206, Hamilton, Ontario L9C 3A3 416-389-0335

Bible Christian Union (U.S.), P.O. Box 718, Lebanon, PA 17042 717-273-9791

Bible Club Movement of Canada, 798 Main St. E., Hamilton, Ontario L8M 1L4 416-549-9810

BMMF Intl. (Canada), 4028 Sheppard Ave. E., Agincourt, Ontario M2S 1S6 416-293-9832

BMMF Intl. (U.S.), P.O. Box 418, Upper Darby, PA 19082 215-352-0581

CAM Intl. (Canada), 39 Margate, Hamilton, Ontario L8T 1M7 416-389-2584

CAM Intl. (U.S.), 8625 La Prada Dr., Dallas, TX 75228 214-327-8206

Christian Nationals Evangelism Commission, (Canada), P.O. Box 215 Islington, Ontario M9A 4X2 416-236-2705

Christian Nationals Evangelism Commission, (U.S.), 1470 N. Fourth St., San Jose, CA 95112 408-298-0965

The Evangelical Alliance Mission (Canada), P.O. Box 980, Regina, Saskatchewan S4P 3B2 306-525-5444

The Evangelical Alliance Mission (U.S.), P.O. Box 969, Wheaton, IL 60189 312-653-5300

Evangelical Literature Overseas, P.O. Box 725, Wheaton, IL 60189 312-668-4747

Far East Broadcasting Associates of Canada, P.O. Box 2233, Vancouver, British Columbia V6B 9Z9 604-278-2848

Far East Broadcasting Company (U.S.), P.O. Box 1, La Mirada, CA 90637 213-947-4651

Global Outreach Mission (Canada), Box 1210, St. Catharines, Ontario, L2R 7A7 416-684-1401

Global Outreach Mission (U.S.), P.O. Box 711, Buffalo, NY 14240 716-842-2220

Gospel Missionary Union of Canada, 2121 Henderson Hwy., Winnipeg, Manitoba R2G 1P8 204-338-7831

Gospel Missionary Union (U.S.), 1000 N. Oak, Kansas City, MO 64155 816-734-8500

Gospel Recordings of Canada, 2 Audley St., Toronto, Ontario M8Y 2X2 416-251-1861

Gospel Recordings (U.S.), 122 Glendale Blvd., Los Angeles, CA 90026 213-250-0207

Greater Europe Mission (Canada), P.O. Box 984, Oshawa, Ontario L1H 7N2 416-728-8222

Greater Europe Mission (U.S.), P.O. Box 668, Wheaton, IL 60189 312-462-8050

Helps International Ministries, Rt. 1, Box 171 D, Harlem, GA 30814 404-556-9361

Home of Onesiphorus, 2507 Cumberland Dr., Valparaiso, IN 46383 219-464-9035

International Christian Fellowship (Canada), P.O. Box 3077, Station F, Scarborough, Ontario M1W 3P5 416-499-1596

International Christian Fellowship (U.S.), 213 Naperville St., Wheaton, IL 60187 312-668-8569

International Christian Organization (Intercristo), P.O. Box 33487, Seattle, WA 98133 206-546-7330

International Missions (Canada), P.O. Box 101, St. Catharines, Ontario L2R 6R4 416-935-9714

International Missions (U.S.), P.O. Box 323, Wayne, NJ 07470 201-696-4804

Inland Missionary Society, P.O. Box 8971, Greensboro, NC 27410

Janz Team (Canada), 2121 Henderson Hwy., Winnipeg, Manitoba R2G 1P8 204-334-0055

Janz Team Ministries (U.S.), Box 711, Buffalo, NY 14240 204-334-0055

Jews for Jesus, 60 Haight St., San Francisco, CA 94102 415-864-2600

Language Institute for Evangelism, P.O. Box 200, San Dimas, CA 91773 213-289-5031

Latin America Mission, 3251 Sheppard Ave. E., Scarborough, Ontario M1T 3K1 416-491-5779

Liebenzell Mission (Canada), R.R. 1, Moffat, Ontario L0P 1J0 519-822-9748

Liebenzell Mission of the U.S.A., 26 Heath Ln., Schooley's Mountain, NJ 07870 201-852-3044

Mission Aviation Fellowship (Canada), P.O. Box 368, Guelph, Ontario N1H 6K5 519-821-3914

Mission Aviation Fellowship (U.S.), P.O. Box 202, Redlands, CA 92373 714-794-1151

Missionary Internship, P.O. Box 457, Farmington, MI 48024 313-474-9110

Missionary Tech Team, 25 FRJ Dr., Longview, TX 75601

Missions Outreach (Canada), P.O. Box 100, Caronport, Saskatchewan S0H 0S0

Missions Outreach Inc., (U.S.), P.O. Box 73, Bethany, MO 64424 816-425-2277

North Africa Mission (Canada), 205 Yonge St., Rm. 12, Toronto, Ontario M5B 1N2 416-368-7954

North Africa Mission (U.S.), P.O. Box 95, Upper Darby, PA 19082 215-352-2003

North America Indian Mission (Canada), P.O. Box 1027 Delta, British Columbia V4M 3T2 604-943-6125

North America Indian Mission (U.S.), P.O. Box 151, Point Roberts, WA 98281

Northern Canada Evangelical Mission, P.O. Box 2244, Prince Albert, Saskatchewan, S6V 6Z1 306-764-3388

Open Air Campaigners, 1444 Maritime Ave., Plainfield, NJ 07060 201-757-8427

Overseas Christian Servicemen's Centers, P.O. Box 10308, Denver, CO 80210 303-762-1400

Overseas Missionary Fellowship (Canada), 1058 Avenue Rd., Toronto, Ontario M5N 2C6 416-485-0427

Overseas Missionary Fellowship (U.S.), 404 S. Church St., Robesonia, PA 19551 215-693-5881

Pocket Testament League (Canada), P.O. Box 3020, Station F, Scarborough, Ontario M1W 2K0

Pocket Testament League (U.S.), P.O. Box 368, Lincoln Park, NJ 07035 201-696-1900

Portable Recording Ministries, Inc., 760 Waverly Rd., Holland, MI 49423 616-396-5291

Prakash Assoc., U.S.A., 2024 Freedom Blvd., Freedom, CA 95019 408-722-2244

Ramabai Mukti Mission (Canada), 306-543 Granville St., Vancouver, British Columbia V6C 1X8 604-685-5028

Ramabai Mukti Mission (U.S.), P.O. Box 4912, Clinton, NJ 08809 201-735-8770

RBMU Intl. (Canada), 3251 Sheppard Ave. E., Scarborough, Ontario M1T 3K1 416-494-9904

RBMU Intl. (U.S.), 8102 Elberon Ave., Philadelphia, PA 19111 312-665-6503

*Samuel Zwemer Institute, P.O. Box 365, Altadena, CA 91001 213-794-1121

SEND Intl. (Canada), 1111 Finch Ave., W-309, Downsview, Ontario M3J 2E6 416-225-8735

SEND Intl. (U.S.), P.O. Box 513, Farmington, MI 48024 313-477-4210

SIM Canada, 10 Huntingdale Blvd., Scarborough, Ontario M1W 2S5 416-497-2424

Slavic Gospel Assoc. (Canada), P.O. Box 2, Station K, Toronto, Ontario M4P 2G1 416-223-5097

Slavic Gospel Assoc. (U.S.), P.O. Box 1122, Wheaton, IL 60189 312-690-8900

South America Mission (Canada), P.O. Box 1599, Guelph, Ontario N1H 6R7 305-965-1833

South America Mission (U.S.), P.O. Box 6560, Lake Worth, FL 33466 305-965-1833

South American Crusades, P.O. Box 2530, Boca Raton, FL 33432 305-487-6080

Sudan Interior Mission, Cedar Grove, NJ 07009 201-857-1100

Trans World Radio (Canada), P.O. Box 310, London, Ontario N6A 4W1

Trans World Radio (U.S.), P.O. Box 98, Chatham, NJ 07928 201-635-5775

U.S. Center for World Mission, 1605 E. Elizabeth St., Pasadena, CA 91104 213-797-1111

UFM Intl. (Canada), 132 Crescent Rd., Toronto, Ontario M4W 1T9 416-967-3324

UFM Intl. (U.S.), P.O. Box 306, Bala-Cynwyd, PA 19004 215-667-7660

United World Mission, P.O. Box 8000, St. Petersburg, FL 33738 813-391-0195

Venture Teams Intl. P.O. Box 7430, Station E., Calgary, Alberta T3C 3M2 Canada 403-286-3422

World Evangelical Outreach, P.O. Box 527, Sterling, VA 22170 703-450-4770

World Literature Crusade, P.O. Box 1313, Studio City, CA 91604 213-341-7870

World Missions Fellowship (Canada), 9335-94th St., Edmonton, Alberta T6C 3V6 403-466-5091

World Missions Fellowship (U.S.), P.O. Box 1048, Grants Pass, OR 97526 403-466-5091

World Radio Missionary Fellowship (Canada), 3251 Sheppard Ave. E., Scarborough, Ontario M1T 3K1 416-494-5500

World Radio Missionary Fellowship (U.S.), P.O. Box 3000, Opa-Locka, FL 33055 305-624-4252

Worldteam (Canada), P.O. Box 333, Brantford, Ontario N3R 5N3 519-753-6984

Worldteam (U.S.), P.O. Box 143038, Coral Gables, FL 33114 305-446-0861

CHRISTIAN
CONCILIATION SERVICE
Christian Legal Society (CLS)
P.O. Box 2069
Oak Park, IL 60303
312-848-7735
(IDAK: 8100)

CLS is a national fellowship of lawyers, judges, and law students committed to integrating their legal practice with a commitment to the lordship of Christ. As part of this mission, the society has sought ways of ministering with and to the Christian community.

The Christian Conciliation Service (CCS)/Christian Justice Center (CJC) is one form of this ministry. It provides a way of utilizing the gifts and skills of Christians in law in accordance with a biblical challenge to resolve disputes within the body of Christ where reconciliation, forgiveness, peace, and hope may be lifted up.

Arizona

CCS of Central Arizona, Keith Krispen, 9251 N. 36th Dr., P.O. Box 35178, Phoenix, AZ 85069 605-841-1550

CCS of Southern Arizona, Jim Eva, 2229 Cerrado Bala, P.O. Box 31476, Tucson, AZ 85751 602-881-1720

California

CCS of Los Angeles, Richard Hauser, 15303 Ventura Blvd., Sta. 700, Sherman Oaks, CA 91403 213-906-9866

CCS of San Diego, Wally Numbers, 3430 Camino del Rio, North, Sta. 300, San Diego, CA 92108 619-563-6580

CCS of San Joaquin Valley, Russell Templeton, 255 N. Fulton, Sta. 102, P.O. Box 1348, Fresno, CA 93715 209-266-5086

CCS of Santa Clara County, Forest Steenfort, 4631 Houndshaven Way, San Jose, CA 95111 408-287-6001

Colorado

CCS of Denver, Ron Bard, 7244 E. Maplewood Pl., Englewood, CO 80111 303-793-0279

CCS of Colorado Springs, Terry Jackson, 228 N. Cascade Ave., Colorado Springs, CO 80903 303-633-1777

Florida

CCS of Central Florida, Robert Baker, 850 Courtland . St., Orlando, FL 32804 305-644-6691

Illinois

CCS of DuPage County, John Steven Cole, 273 Claremont St., Elmhurst, IL 60126 312-834-4740

CJC of Cook County, Dan Berrum, P.O. Box 484, Chicago, IL 60690 312-957-0413

Indiana

CJC of Greater Indianapolis, Steven Carlock, 2000 N. Meridian, P.O. Box 44198, Indianapolis, IN 46204 317-924-3098

Michigan

CCS of Central Michigan, Kein Bowling, 535 N. Capitol Ave., Lansing, MI 48933 517-485-2270

CCS of Southeast Michigan, Ron Mock, 19500 Middlebelt, Sta. 106W, Livonia, MI 48152 313-478-5881

Northern Michigan CCS, Peter Vallenga, 1218 A. Tebo School Rd., P.O.

Box 458, Boyne City, MI 49712 616-582-6940

Minnesota

CCS of Minnesota, Bill Bontrager, 520 NW Midland Blvd., Minneapolis, MN 55401 612-339-5036

Missouri/Kansas

Heart of America CJC, Kenneth Peery, 1221 Baltimore Ave., Sta. 500, Kansas City, MO 64105 816-421-1555

Montana

CCS of Montana, Kenneth Sande, 804 N. 29th St., Sta. 200, Billings, MT 59101 406-256-1583

New Mexico

CJC of New Mexico, Laury Eck, 315 Arno NE, Albuquerque, NM 87102 505-243-6887

North Carolina

CCS of Forsyth County, Robert Price, P.O. Box 2306, Winston-Salem, NC 27102 919-744-0600
Triangle CCS, Richard Leary, 915 Lamond Ave., P.O. Box 2271, Durham, NC 27702 919-683-1183

Ohio

CCS of Akron, Michael Kura, 680 E. Market St., Sta. 304, Akron, OH 44304 216-253-9332
CCS of Cincinnati, Mary Walter-Feltner, Clifton United Methodist Church, Clifton & Senator Pl., P.O. Box 19167, Cincinnati, OH 45219 513-861-4673

Pennsylvania

CCS of Western Pennsylvania, Jack Rook, 238 S. Main St., P.O. Box 1805, Butler, PA 16003 412-285-5102

Texas

CCS of Greater Houston, Walter Carpenter, One Park Ten Place, Sta. 200, P.O. Box 218945, Houston, TX 77218 713-578-8787

Virginia/Washington DC

CCS of Metropolitan Washington, Mather Archer, 3621 Colony Rd., P.O. Box 396, Fairfax, VA 22030 703-385-4709

Washington

CCS of Puget Sound, Paul Meyer, 316 Maynard Ave., South Seattle, WA 98104 206-825-9887

FAMILY MINISTRIES
(IDAK: 8321/8361)

The following, by no means complete, is a list of family-oriented ministries, including such areas as counseling, enrichment, and programming. The specialized focus of many ministries is identified in parentheses for the user's convenience. While arranged according to states, this listing contains ministries that not only have area but national focus.

Arizona

Calvary Rehabilitation Center (alcohol & drug counseling), 329 N. Third Ave., Phoenix, AZ 85003

Christian Family Care Agency, 1101 E. Missouri, Phoenix, AZ 85014 602-234-1935

Crisis Pregnancy Center, 1403 N. Jones Blvd., Tucson, AZ 85716 602-326-2263

California

The American Institute of Family Relations, 4942 Vineland Ave., North Hollywood, CA 91601 818-763-7285

Christian Marriage Enrichment, 1913 E. 17th St., Sta. 118, Santa Ana, CA 92701

Focus on the Family, P.O. Box 500, Arcadia, CA 91006 818-445-1579

Forest Home, Inc., Christian Conference Center, Forest Falls, CA 92339 714-794-1127

Hume Lake Christian Camps, P.O. Box 1868, Fresno, CA 93718 209-251-6043

Institute in Family Ministries, First Christian Church, 2659 First St., Napa, CA 94558 707-253-7222

Mount Hermon Assoc., Inc., Box 413, Mount Hermon, CA 95041 408-335-4466

Florida

Christian Service Center for Orange County, 47 E. Robinson, Orlando, FL 32801

Shepherd Care Ministries, Inc., (counseling & training program for unwed mothers), 5935 Taft St., Sta. B, Hollywood, FL 33021 305-981-2060

Georgia

Atlanta Counseling Center, 2055 Mt. Paran Rd., Atlanta, GA 30327 404-266-0695

Bethesda Savannah Children's Center, 428 Bull St., Savannah, GA 31401

Family Life Ministries, Mt. Paran Church of God, 2055 Mt. Paran Rd., Atlanta, GA 30327 404-251-0720

Mission Possible (counseling), 380-14th St. NW, Atlanta, GA 30318 404-874-2241

Missions Acres (care for abused & neglected children), 221 Griffin Mountain Trail, Conyers, GA 30208

Illinois

Christian Camping Intl., P.O. Box 646, Wheaton, IL 60189 312-462-0300

Family Concern, Inc., P.O. Box 419, Wheaton, IL 60189 312-668-3220

Institute of Basic Youth Conflicts, P.O. Box 1, Oak Brook, IL 60521 312-323-9800

New Life for Girls (residential help for troubled girls), 5422 N. Winthrop, Chicago, IL 60640 312-878-8978

Indiana

New Horizons Youth Ministries, 1000 S. 350 E., Marion, IN 46953 317-668-4009

Kansas

Friends Marriage Encounter, Evang. Fr. Al., 2018 Maple, Wichita, KS 67213 316-267-0391

The Life Line Children's Home (center for emotionally disturbed youth), 4322 Mission Rd., Kansas City, KS 66103 913-262-3050

The Menninger Foundation (training in marriage and family counseling), Box 829, Topeka, KS 66601

Louisiana

Protestant Home for Babies, 1233 Eighth St., New Orleans, LA 70115

Michigan

Bethany Christian Services (for unwed mothers), 901 Eastern Ave. NE, Grand Rapids, MI 49503 616-459-6273

Missouri

Sabbatical Ranch for Boys, E.S.R., Box 70A, Warsaw, MO 65355 816-438-6398

New Hampshire

His Mansion (center for troubled youth), P.O. Box G. Hillsboro, NH 03244 603-464-5555

North Carolina

Association of Couples for Marriage Enrichment, 403 S. Hawthorne Rd., Winston-Salem, NC 27103

Church of God Home for Children, P.O. Box 64, Kannapolis, NC 28081 704-782-8825

North Dakota

Eckert Youth Home, P.O. Box 223, Williston, ND 58801 701-572-7262

South American Missionary Evangelism (special focus on aiding abandoned children from Columbia & Brazil), P.O. Box 2344, Bismarck, ND 58502 710-222-3960

Ohio

Emerge Ministries (counseling), 1815 W. Market St., Akron, OH 44308 216-867-5603

Christian Counseling Center, 544 S. Westwood, Toledo, OH 43609

Oklahoma

Deaconess Home (care for unwed mothers), 5401 N. Portland Ave., Oklahoma City, OK 73112 405-946-5581

Oregon

Give Us This Day, Inc. (counseling/referral/adoption for black children), Community Service Center, Newberg, OR 97132

PLAN (Plan Loving Adoptions Now), P.O. Box 667, McMinnville, OR 97128

Pennsylvania

Family Life Ministries, R.R. 4, Mountain Rd., Dillsburg, PA 17019

New Life for Girls (residential program for troubled girls), R.R. 3, Dover, PA 17315

Youth Challenge International Bible Institute, R.R. 2, Box 33, Sunbury, PA 17801 717-286-6442

South Carolina

Church of God Home for Children, P.O. Box 430, Mauldin, SC 29662 803-963-5051

Tennessee

Choose Life, Inc., 4400 St. Elmo Ave., Chattanooga, TN 37409 615-821-1424

Church of God/Cleveland, TN Family Life Commission, Keith at 25th St. NW, P.O. Box 2430, Cleveland, TN 37320 615-472-3361

Cornerstone Counseling Services, 3535 Keith St. NW, Cleveland, TN 37311 615-476-5216

Teen Challenge of Cleveland, 100 Church St. NE, Cleveland, TN 37311 615-476-6627

Texas

Christian Home of Abilene, 3425 S. First, Abilene, TX 79605

Minerth Meier Counseling Center, Collins St., Richards, TX 77873

Texas Baptist Children's Home, Drawer 7, Round Rock, TX 78664

Pleasant Hills Children's Home, R.R. 2, Box 110, Fairfield, TX 75840 214-389-2641

Pro Family Forum (publications, books & cassettes), P.O. Box 8907, Fort Worth, TX 76112 817-531-3605

Washington

Regular Baptist Child Placement Agency, Box 16353, Seattle, WA 98116

Wisconsin

Sunburst Youth Homes, Neillsville, WI 54476

FELLOWSHIP/SERVICE ORGANIZATIONS
(IDAK: 8900)

The American Church of the Good Samaritan, Inc., 8323 Sand Lake Rd., Orlando, FL 32811 305-422-3722

Association of Fundamental Ministers & Churches, P.O. Box 7923, 8605 E. 55th St., Kansas City, MO 64129 816-358-7789

B'Rith Christian Union, P.O. Box 11437, Chicago, IL 60611 312-267-1440

Christian Holiness Association, P.O. Box 68289, Portland, OR 97268 503-654-6707

Conservative Lutheran Assoc., P.O. Box 7186, Tacoma, WA 98407 206-383-5653

The Evangelical Church Alliance, P.O. Box 9, Bradley, IL 60915 815-937-0720

Evangelical Curriculum Commission, 922 Montgomery Ave. NE, Cleveland, TN 37311 615-476-4512

Fellowship of Artists for Cultural Evangelism, 1605 E. Elizabeth St., Pasadena, CA 91104 818-794-7970

Fellowship of Christian Athletes, 8701 Leeds Rd., Kansas City, MO 64120 816-921-0909

Friends Disaster Service, 241 Keenan Rd., Peninsula, OH 44264 216-650-4975

Full Gospel Church Assoc., Inc., P.O. Box 265, Amarillo, TX 79105 806-372-1965

Kingsway Cathedral, 901 19th St., Des Moines, IA 50314 513-283-2049

League of Christian Laymen (R.C.A.), Inc., P.O. Box 317, Stout, IA 50673

Maranatha Bible Fellowship, P.O. Box 95, Unicoi, TN 37692 615-743-7793

National Association of Christian Singles, 915 W. Wisconsin, Sta. 214, Milwaukee, WI 53233

New England Fellowship of Evangelicals, P.O. Box 99, Rumney, NH 03266 603-786-9504

Overseas Christian Servicemen's Centers, Inc., P.O. Box 10308, Denver, CO 80210 606-762-1400

Pentecostal Fellowship of North America, 1445 Boonville Ave., Springfield, MO 65802

Presbyterian Evangelistic Fellowship, Inc., P.O. Box 1890, Decatur, GA 30031 404-244-0740

Tennessee District Women's Ministries, P.O. Box 4087, Madison, TN 37115 615-859-1444

HANDICAP MINISTRIES
(IDAK: 8361)

Cascade Chrisian Home (for mildly retarded adults), P.O. Box 485, Lynden, WA 98264

Christian Church Foundation for the Handicapped, P.O. Box 9869, Knoxville, TN 37920 615-577-2638

Christian Horizons, Inc., Box 334, Williamston, MI 48895 517-655-3463

Christian League for the Handicapped, Box 948, Walworth, WI 53184 414-275-6131

The Christian Overcomers, Inc., 264A Third Ave., Westwood, NJ 07675 201-358-0500

Elim Christian School (special education ministry/reformed tradition), 13020 S. Central, Palos Heights, IL 60463

Handi Vangelism, 237 Fairfield Ave., Upper Darby, PA 19082 215-352-7177

Joni & Friends, P.O. Box 3225, Woodland Hills, CA 91365

Missionary Vision for Special Ministries, 640 W. Briar Pl., Chicago, IL 60657 312-327-0489

The Network-Christian Ministries with Disabled People, 5521 Garvin Ave., Richmond, CA 94805 415-232-9114

Shepherds, Inc., (agency for the mentally retarded/Regular Baptist), Box 400, 1805 15th Ave., Union Grove, WI 53182 414-878-2451

PROFESSIONAL ASSOCIATIONS
(IDAK: 8621/8900)

American Scientific Affiliation, P.O. Box J. Ipswich, MA 01938 616-356-5656

Associated Church Builders, Inc., P.O. Box 187, Palatine, IL 60067 312-358-1551

Association of Christian Librarians, P.O. Box 4, Cedarville, OH 45314

Christian Booksellers Assoc., P.O. Box 200, Colorado Springs, CO 80901 303-576-7880

Christian Business Men's Committee of USA, 1800 McCallie Ave., Chattanooga, TN 37404 615-698-4444

Christian Dental Society, 5235 Sky Trail, Littleton, CO 80123 303-794-2290

Christian Educators Association Inc., 1410 W. Colorado Blvd., Pasadena, CA 91105 213-684-1881

Christian Film Distributors Association, Inc., P.O. Box 584, Englewood, CO 80151 303-237-9020

Christian Legal Society, P.O. Box 2069, Oak Park, IL 60303 312-848-7735

Christian Medical Society, 1616 Gateway Blvd., P.O. Box 689, Richardson, TX 75080 214-783-8384

Christian Military Fellowship, P.O. Box 36440, Denver, CO 80236 303-761-1959

Christian Ministries Management Assoc., P.O. Box 4651, Diamond Bar, CA 91765 714-861-8861

Creation Research Society, 2717 Cranbrook, Ann Arbor, MI 48104 313-971-5915

Day Companies Foundation, 2751 Buford Hwy. NE, Atlanta, GA 60624 404-325-4000

Evangelical Council for Financial Accountability, 1825 Eye St. NW, Sta. 400, Washington, DC 20006 202-429-2017

Evangelical Press Assoc., P.O. Box 4550, Overland Park, KS 66204 913-381-2017

Fellowship of Christian Airline Personnel, 225 McBride Rd., Fayetteville, GA 30214 404-461-9320

Lawyers Christian Fellowship, 3931 E. Main St., Columbus, OH 43213 614-231-6614

National Association of Christians in Social Work, Box 90, St. Davids, PA 19087 215-687-5777

National Association of Directors of Christian Education, 810 South Seventh St., Minneapolis, MN 55423

National Association of Nouthetic Counselors, 950 University Dr., c/o

Granada Pastoral Counseling Center, Coral Gables, FL 33134 305-667-4850

Nurses' Christian Fellowship, 233 Langdon, Madison, WI 50703 608-257-1103

Worldwide Dental Health Service (The Missionary Dentist), P.O. Box 7002, Seattle, WA 98133 206-546-1200

RETIREMENT FACILITIES
(IDAK: 8361)

The Alliance Home, C&MA, 770 Hanover St., Carlisle, PA 17013 717-249-1363

The Alliance Home of DeLand, C&MA, 600 S. Florida Ave., De-Land, FL 32720 904-734-3486

Assemblies of God Retirement Center, A/G, 233 Norton Rd., Springfield, MO 65803

Baptist Rest Home, Bapt. Gen. Conf., 1802 17th Ave., Seattle, WA 98122 206-324-1632

Brethren Care, Inc., of Ashland, OH, 2000 Center St., Ashland, OH 44805 419-289-1585

The Brethren's Home of Indiana, Inc., Rt. 1, Box 97, Flora, IN 46929 219-967-4571

Buhler Sunshine Home, Menn. Breth. Chs., 412 W. C St., Buhler, KS 76522 316-543-2251

Carmen Home, Pent. Ho. Ch. Intl., P.O. Box 158, Carmen, OK 73726 405-987-2577

Casa De Verdugo (Verdugo Home, Inc.), Bapt. Gen Cong., 155 N. Girard St., Hemet, CA 92343 714-658-2274

Christian Homes, Inc., Evang. Free Ch. of Am., Holdrege, NE 68949 308-995-4493

Clawson Manor, New Life, Inc., Free Meth. Ch. of N. Am., 244 W. 14th Mile Rd., Clawson, MI 48017 313-435-5650

Colonial Oaks Retirement Center, Wesleyan Ch., 4725 Colonial Oaks Dr., Marion, IN 46953 317-674-9791

Dallas Nursing Home, Menn. Breth. Chs., 348 W. Ellendale, Dallas, OR 97338 503-623-3291

ECC Retirement Village, ECC, S. Railroad St., Myerstown, PA 17067 717-866-6541

Elim Park Baptist Home, Inc., Bapt. Gen. Conf., 140 Cook Hill Rd., Cheshire, CT 06410 203-272-3547

Elim Home, Evang. Free Ch. of Am., 730 2nd St. SE, Milada, MN 56353 612-983-2185

Elim Home, Evang. Free Ch. of Am., 101 S. 7th Ave., Princeton, MN 55371 612-389-1171

Elim Home, Evang. Free Ch. of Am., Box 638, Watertown, MN 55388 612-955-2691

Elim Homes, Evang. Free Ch. of Am., S. Hwy. 81, Fargo, ND 58101 701-237-4392

Evangelical Free Church Home, Evang. Free Ch. of Am., 112 W. 4th St., Boone, IA 50036 515-432-1393

Fairhaven Christian Home, Inc., Evang. Free Ch. of Am., 3470 N. Alpine Rd., Rockford, IL 61111 815-877-1441

Fairview Baptist Home, Bapt. Gen. Cong., 7 S. 241 Fairview Ave., Downers Grove, IL 60515 312-852-4350

Fairview Fellowship Home, Menn. Breth. Chs., 605 E. State Rd., Fairview, OK 73737 405-227-3784

Friendsview Manor, Evang. Fr. Al., 1301 E. Fulton, Newberg, OR 97132 503-538-3144

Garden Valley Retirement Village, Inc., Menn. Breth. Chs., 1505 E. Spruce, Garden City, KS 76846 316-275-9651

Golden Years Home, Pent. Ho. Ch. Intl., P.O. Box 39, Falcon, NC 28342 919-892-6048

Grandview Christian Home, Bapt. Gen. Conf., Cambridge, MN 55008 612-689-1474

Heritage Village (The Gerry Homes), Free Meth. Ch. of N. Am., Gerry, NY 14740 716-985-4612

Hilty Memorial Home, Miss. Ch., P.O. Box 265, Pandora, OH 45877 419-384-3218

Home for the Aged, Menn. Breth. Chs., 207 S. Dewey St., Box 98, Corn, OK 73024 405-343-2295

Hubbard Hill Estates Retirement Community, Miss. Ch., 28070 C.R. 24 West, Elkhart, IN 46517 219-295-6260

Inland Christian Home, Chr. Ref., 1940 S. Mountain Ave., Ontario, CA 91761 714-983-0084

Kah Tai Care Center, Evang. Free Ch. of Am., Lawrence & Kearney Sts., Port Townsend, WA 98368 206-385-3555

Kern Crest Manor, Menn. Breth. Chs., 250 E. Tulare St., Shafter, CA 93263 805-746-6521

Lincoln Glen Manor, Menn. Breth. Chs., 2671 Plummer Ave., San Jose, CA 95125 408-265-3222

Locust Grove Rest Home, Rt. #3, Box 136, Harpers Ferry, WV 25425 304-535-6355

Maranatha Village, A/G, 233 E. Norton, Springfield, MO 65803 417-833-0013

Messiah Village, Breth. in Christ Ch., 100 Mt. Allen Dr., Mechanicsburg, PA 17055 717-697-4666

Michigan Christian Home Association, Bapt., 1845 Boston SE, Grand Rapids, MI 49506 616-245-9179

New Carlisle Adult Care Home, Miss. Ch., 1994 Addison-New Carlisle Rd., New Carlisle, OH 45344 513-845-2150

Ohio Missionary Home, Miss. Ch., 1885 Dayton-Lakeview Rd., New Carlisle, OH 45344 513-845-8219

Oregon Baptist Retirement Home, Bapt. Gen. Conf., 2545 NE Flanders St., Portland, OR 97232 503-232-5055

Palm Haven, Menn. Breth. Chs., 2104 13th St., Reedley, CA 93654 209-638-2417

Parkside Homes, Inc., Menn. Breth. Chs., 200 Willow Rd., Hillsboro, KS 67063 316-947-5700

Piney Mountain Home, U. Breth. in Christ, Rt. 2, Fayetteville, PA 17222 717-351-2721

Pleasant View Home, Menn. Breth. Chs., 108 N. Walnut, Inman KS 67543 316-585-6411

Pleasant View Manor, Menn. Breth. Chs., 856 S. Reed Ave., Reedley, CA 93654 209-638-4518

Reformed Presbyterian Home for the Aged, Ref. Prs. Ch., 2344 Perrysville Ave., Pittsburgh, PA 15214 412-321-4319

Rest Haven Christian Services, Chr. Ref., Ref. Ch., 13259 S. Central Ave., Palos Heights, IL 60463 312-597-1000

Salem Home, Menn. Breth. Chs., 701 S. Main, Hillsboro, KS 67063 316-947-2272

Shell Point Village, C&MA, Fort Myers, FL 33908 813-481-2141

Sunny Ridge Manor, Evang. Fr. Al., 2609 Sunnybrook Dr., Nampa, ID 83651 208-467-7298

Sunset Manor, Inc., Woodstock Homes, Free Meth. Ch. of N. Am., 920 N. Seminary Ave., Box 508, Woodstock, IL 60098 815-338-1749

Town and Country Manor, C&MA, 555 E. Memory Ln., Santa Ana, CA 92706 714-547-7581

Upland Manor, Breth. in Christ Ch., 1125 W. Arrow Hwy., Upland, CA 91786 714-985-1215

Warm Beach Health Care Center and Manor, Free Meth. Ch. of N. Am., 20420 Marine Dr. NW, Stanwood, WA 98292 206-652-7585

Wesley Manor, Free Meth. Ch. of N. Am., 815 Kennedy St., 113A, New Westminster, British Columbia V3M 1R8 Canada 604-521-3172

Wesleyan Arms Retirement Center, Wesleyan Ch., 1901-N. Centennial St., High Point, NC 27260 919-884-2222

Wesleyan Village, Wesleyan Ch., Wesleyan Bible Conference Assoc., Brooksville, FL 33512 904-799-1644

Woodstock Christian Care, Inc., Free Meth. Ch. of N. Am., P.O. Box 508, Woodstock, IL 60098 815-338-1090

SPECIALIZED MINISTRIES

American Family Foundation, P.O. Box 336, Weston, MA 02193 617-893-0930

Association of Church Missions Committees, P.O. Box ACMC, Wheaton, IL 60189 312-260-1660

Bethany Fellowship, Inc., Missionary Training Center, 6820 Auto Club Rd., Minneapolis, MN 55438 612-944-2121

Biblical Counseling Foundation, 915 S. Wakefield, Arlington, VA 22204 703-243-8444

Biblical Dynamics, Inc., (Christian Counseling), 1454 S. 25th St., Terre Haute, IN 47803 812-238-9455

Billy Graham Center, Wheaton College, Wheaton, IL 60187 312-260-5157

CBN University, Virginia Beach, VA 23463 804-424-7000

Christian Answers & Information, P.O. Box 3295, Chico, CA 95927 916-893-0567

Christian Apologetics: Research & Information Service (CARIS), P.O. Box 2067, Costa Mesa, CA 92626 714-957-0249

Christian Camping Intl., P.O. Box 646, Wheaton, IL 60189 714-957-0249

Christian Counseling & Education Foundation, 1790 E. Willow Grove Ave., Laverock, PA 19118 215-884-7676

Christian Counseling Center, Inc., P.O. Box 14558, Richmond, VA 23221 804-358-1343

Christian Ministries Management Assoc., P.O. Box 4651 Diamond Bar, CA 91765 714-861-8861

Christian Psychological Associates, Inc., 4100 War Memorial Dr., Peoria, IL 61614 319-685-7342

Christian Research Institute, P.O. Box 500, San Juan Capiṣtrano, CA 92693 714-855-9926

Christian Resource Associates, P.O. Box 2100, Orange, CA 92626 714-997-3920

Christian Stewardship Council, P.O. Box 527, Glen Ellyn, IL 60138

Church Bible Studies, 191 Mayhew Way, Walnut Creek, CA 94596 415-937-7286

Church Growth Studies, Intl., P.O. Box 2409, South Bend, IN 46680 219-291-4776

Churches Alive! Intl., P.O. Box 3800, San Bernardino, CA 92413 714-886-5361

Correll Missionary Ministries, Box 11793, Charlotte, NC 28220 704-527-1195

Crista Ministries, Inc., 19303 Fremont N., Seattle, WA 98133 206-546-7200

Day Companies Foundation, 2751 Buford Hwy. NE, Atlanta, GA 30324 404-325-4000

Encounter Ministries, Inc., Encounter, Wheaton, IL 60189 312-690-7676

Evangelical Missions Information Service (EMIS), P.O. Box 794, Wheaton, IL 60189 312-653-2158

Evangelical Teacher Training Assoc. (ETTA), P.O. Box 327, Wheaton, IL 60189 312-668-6400

Evangelicals for Social Action, 712 G St. SE, Washington, DC 20003 202-543-5330

Fellowship of Artist for Cultural Evangelism (FACE), 1605 E. Elizabeth St., Pasadena, CA 91104 213-794-7970

Forest Home, Inc., Christian Conference Center, Forest Falls, CA 92339 714-794-1127

Good News, Forum for Spiritual Christianity, 308 E. Main St., P.O. Box 265, Wilmore, KY 40390 606-858-4661

Grace Fellowship, 1455 Ammons St., Denver, CO 80215 303-232-8870

Haggai Institute, Box 13, Atlanta, GA 30370 404-325-2580

Harvesting in Spanish, 90 S. Wadsworth, Sta. 105-458, Denver, CO 80226 303-232-1470

Hume Lake Christian Camps, P.O. Box 1868, Fresno, CA 93718 209-251-6043

Institute for American Church Growth, 709 E. Colorado Blvd., Sta. 150, Pasadena, CA 91101 213-449-4400

Institute for Biblical Preaching, P.O. Box 364, Wheaton, IL 60189 312-690-7676

Institute for Christian Studies (a Christian graduate school), 229 College St., Toronto, Ontario M5T 1R4 613-979-2331

Institute for the Study of American Religion, P.O. Box 1311, Evanston, IL 60201 312-271-3419

Institute of Contemporary Christianity, P.O. Box A, Oakland, NJ 07436 201-337-0005

Institute of Singles Dynamics, Box 11394, Kansas City, MO 64112 816-763-9401

Interaction, Inc., P.O. Box 177, West Brattleboro, VT 05301 802-254-2844

Intercristo, 19303 Fremont Ave., North Seattle, WA 98133 206-546-7330

International Society of Christian Endeavor, P.O. Box 1110, Columbus, OH 43216 614-258-9545

Lamb's Players, P.O. Box 26, National City, CA 92050 619-474-3385

Lay Evangelism, Inc., P.O. Box N, Pleasant Hill, OH 45359 513-676-8531

Leadership Dynamics, Intl., 61 Perimeter Park, Sta. 180, Atlanta, GA 30341 404-458-4644

Ligonier Valley Study Center, Stahlstown, PA 15687 412-593-7005

MARC (Missions Advanced Research Center), 919 W. Huntington Dr., Monrovia, CA 91016 818-574-9005

Melodyland Drug Prevention Center & Hotline, P.O. Box 999, Anaheim, CA 92806 714-778-1000

Mesa Christi, Inc., 22364 Festividad Dr., Saugus, CA 91350 805-254-1796

Ministerial Training Faith Homes, 2820 Eshcol Ave., Zion, IL 60099 312-746-1991

Ministering in Missions, Box 336, Fort Collins, CO 80522 303-493-6491

Ministries, Inc., P.O. Box 4038, Montgomery, AL 36104

Missionary World Service & Evangelism, Inc., P.O. Box 123, 408 Talbott Dr., Wilmore, KY 40390 606-858-3171

Mobile Missionary Assistance Program, 1736 N. Sierra Bonita, Pasadena, CA 91105 213-791-8663

Mount Hermon Assoc., Inc., Box 413, Mount Hermon, CA 95041 408-335-4466

Narramore Christian Foundation, Box 5000, 1409 N. Walnut Grove Ave., Rosemead, CA 91770 818-288-7000

National Training Institute, 1000 S. Interregional Hwy., Round Rock, TX 78664 1-800-531-6789

Nehemiah Ministries, Inc., P.O. Box 448, Damascus, MO 20872 301-253-5433

Overseas Chinese Mission, 154 Hester St., New York, NY 10013 212-226-3438

Pastoral Renewal, P.O. Box 8617, Ann Arbor, MI 48107 313-761-8505

The Salvation Army, National Headquarters, 50 West 23rd St., New York, NY 10010 212-255-9400

Sea-Tac Ministries, Airport Chaplaincy, Rm. 213, Jackson International Airport, Seattle, WA 98158 206-433-5505

Shepherd's Fold Ministries, Intl., 100 W. Ferry St., Sta. 4, Berrien Springs, MI 49103 616-471-4340

Specialized Christian Services, 1525 Cherry Rd., Springfield, IL 62704 217-546-7338

Spiritual Counterfeits Project, Inc., P.O. Box 4308, Berkeley, CA 94704 415-540-0300

Spiritual Overseers Service, Intl., 4362 Vale, Irvine, CA 92715 714-551-5571

U.S. Center for World Mission, 1605 E. Elizabeth St., Pasadena, CA 91104 818-797-1111

United Evangelistic Consulting Assoc., 742 W. 103rd St., Chicago, IL 60628 312-239-7084

Walk Thru the Bible Ministries, Inc., 61 Perimeter Park NE, P.O. Box 80587, Atlanta, GA 30366 404-458-9300

Wears Valley Conference Center, Inc., R.R. 7, Sevierville, TN 37862 615-453-2382

Weber Specialty Photo, 2052 Bennington Circle, Fort Collins, CO 80526 303-493-6491

William Gast & Associates, 5230 Burgess Rd., Colorado Springs, CO 80908 303-495-2770

World Vision/Leadership Development Department, 919 W. Huntington Dr., Monrovia, CA 91016 213-357-7979

Worldwide Prayer & Missionary Union, 6821 N. Ottawa, Chicago, IL 60631 312-763-2553

Youth Challenge International Bible Institute, R.R. 2, Box 33, Sunbury, PA 17801 717-286-6442

Youth Leadership, Inc. (Graduate Training), 122 W. Franklin Ave., Minneapolis, MN 55404 612-870-3632

TELEVISION NETWORKS

The Christian Broadcasting Network, CBN Center, Virginia Beach, VA 23463 804-424-7777

The PTL Television Network, Charlotte, NC 704-542-6000

The Trinity Broadcasting Network, Tustin, CA 714-832-2950